LEGAL RIGHTS OF CHILDREN:
Status, Progress and Proposals

A SYMPOSIUM
Edited by the Staff of
columbia human rights
law review

LEGAL RIGHTS

OF CHILDREN:

Status, Progress

and Proposals

Introduction by RENA K. UVILLER

R. E. BURDICK, Inc., Publishers
Fair Lawn, New Jersey 07410

International Standard Book Number: 0-913638-04-8
Library of Congress Catalogue Card Number: 73—80007

Original text published as pages 303-500 of the
COLUMBIA HUMAN RIGHTS LAW REVIEW, Volume 4, Number 2,
Copyright © 1972 by *Columbia Human Rights Law Review,*
which is published in association with the
Columbia University Institute of Human Rights.

Augmented text of the hardbound book edition
Copyright © 1973 by R. E. Burdick, Inc.,
12-01 12th Street, Fair Lawn, New Jersey 07410

Published simultaneously in Canada
by the Book Center, Inc.,
1140 Beaulac Street, St.-Laurent 382, Quebec.

Printed in the United States of America.

CONTENTS

LEGAL RIGHTS OF CHILDREN:
Status, Progress and Proposals

Staff, *Columbia Human Rights Law Review,* editors

ISBN 0-913638-04-8   LC 73-80007

ERRATA

Jacket front: STEPHEN WIZNER [as on pages 101 ff.].
                   VIRGINIA S. CARSON [as on pages 163 ff.].

Contents: Rena K. Uviller [as on page 12].

Preface (page 13):   Lois G. Forer, Judge, Court of Common Pleas of Philadel-
                       phia [as in footnote, page 49].

Pages 38, 40, 42, 44, 46 (top line):   JONATHAN WEISS AND OSCAR CHASE
                                       [as on page 37].

Page 39 repeats page 40.   The correct page 39 is reproduced on the opposite
                           Errata page.

Page 197: 10/APPELLATE REVIEW FOR JUVENILES:
          A "Right" to a Transcript
          [as on *Contents* page].

APOLOGIA

To our readers and our authors, the publisher, above all, and the compositor and
editors who were variously involved with these errata extend their collective
apologies. These errors — and any others that might be called to our attention —
will be corrected in the next printing of this book. The moral: Do not rush a
book into print; treat it lovingly.

R. E. burdick, inc.

12-01 12th Street
Fair Lawn, N.J. 07410

INTRODUCTION

WE ARE A NATION enthralled by youth culture and self-congratulatory in our attention to the young. Yet while American adults are obsessed about the ephemeral fashions and moods attractive in youths, we are curiously indifferent to their agonies (and who can deny them?), especially of the very young. Adults remember only the carefreeness of childhood but have forgotten its powerlessness. The young are impatient for the power of maturity and do not understand its inherent responsibilities.

One of those responsibilities, surely, is to devise a just body of laws for the young in which their peculiar needs are clearly cognizable and yet are not exploited. Presently, a persuasive argument can be made that the American legal system uses the dependency inherent in childhood as a weapon against children; it fails, for the most part, to address itself to that dependency in any constructive way. This failure is only partly explained by our hostile indifference to the poor generally, and to their children who need the nurturing concern of society most of all.

Our failure toward children is equally, I think, a symptom of a kind of conceptual schizophrenia which afflicts us when devising laws governing youth. We seem unable to discern either the ways in which children require protection or when they must be autonomous. Only one thing seems certain: the dilemma is not resolved simply by identifying a particular chronological age for legal independence.

With the best of intentions we have lately, albeit reluctantly, invested even young children with some small measure of resistance to one of the most ill-defined and potentially most tyrannical of state powers—*parens patriae*. For the most part, however, we have given children the right to resist authority in the context of juvenile delinquency proceedings, by which I mean proceedings to determine violations of law and the sanctions therefor. I don't minimize the importance of this long overdue infusion of procedural rights into such proceedings. Yet by the time a child has been charged with a criminal offense he has generally long been a victim of our indifference. Well before that signpost of failure, the child desperately required both the means to oppose the despotic potential of *parens patriae* and the tools to insist upon its exercise for his nurture and development.

We seem unable to conceive of *parens patriae* as a state obligation to help children thrive, and not just as a rubric for unbridled and tyrannical state power over the young. This conceptual difficulty is part of that same confusion and uncertainty we have in determining who and what children are and what they require in a legal context. This volume of articles does not resolve the uncertainty. That is an awesome task indeed. What it does do, excellently, is to focus upon those areas of the law in which our confusion is manifest and to begin to consider what the state's response ought to be to the paradox of a child's interwoven needs for protection and autonomy.

Hundreds of thousands of very young children, from infancy to early childhood, languish in this nation's bleak institutions or make the dreary trek from foster home to foster home. This most invisible and truly powerless of all our benighted minorities is governed by laws which are wholly amorphous and ill-defined. As a necessary consequence, the destinies of these children are disposed of by juvenile courts as well as public and private agencies with a capricious arbitrariness which would never be tolerated if imposed upon any other segment of the population. Oscar Chase and Jonathan Weiss have dealt here with a small but significant aspect of the law governing such children in New York. They have described the plight of a child whose unwitting mother has voluntarily placed him in state care because, temporarily, she cannot care for him.

Ordinarily one would expect that because the placement was voluntary she might regain the child upon request, since independent laws governing involuntary removal of children upon a factual showing of parental neglect exist in New York. We learn, however, that the New York statute which governs the destiny of children "voluntarily" placed and which is typical of such statutes in other states, is a study in arbitrariness. For the state welfare agency may withhold the child without any evidentiary hearing unless it is of the opinion that by returning the child to its parent "the interest of such child will be promoted thereby and that such parent is fit, competent and able to duly maintain, support and educate such child"—this, without any notice to the mother at time of "voluntary" placement that she may be parting with the child forever.

While such statutes undoubtedly express the state's concern for the helpless and dependent infant *vis à vis* an unfit mother, what assurances does the child have that he is not being separated indefinitely from a caring parent who is only "unfit" by the subjective evaluation of a bureaucracy? It is small comfort that New York law (only as of last year) requires that every two years a court of law review cases of all children "voluntarily" placed and "involuntarily" retained. Obviously, a three-year-old child cannot make an assessment of his best interest. Nor perhaps can a ten-year old who desperately wishes to return to an abusive and violent parent. But may the state respond to this immaturity and helplessness with a caprice which the child, whose destiny is at stake, is powerless to resist?

As lawyers, we begin with the modest expectation that the judicial proceedings (if indeed there be any) by which the monumental authority of *parens patriae* is exercised satisfy at least the most fundamental tenets of due process of law. It is thus with incredulity we learn in the case note to *Ella B.* that the New York State Court of Appeals has only recently insisted upon the assignment of counsel for indigent parents charged with neglect and who stand to lose the custody of their children. How much more incredible it is to learn that in a great number of states, the very children who are the subjects of these proceedings have no independent legal representative.

Our inability to reconcile a child's need to withstand oppressive authority with his need for guidance and care is very clearly focused in Stephen Wizner's piece on the role of counsel in delinquency proceedings. Imagine a ten-year-old who has committed a serious act of arson. He confides his culpability to the lawyer to whose services he is entitled by virtue of the Supreme Court's landmark decision in *In re Gault.* His lawyer, however, knows that the authorities have insufficient evidence against him. If the child chooses to remain silent (*Gault* has also accorded him that right) there will be a dismissal and the state will be powerless to interfere in the child's life. The child feels helpless and leaves the matter to his lawyer's judgment. Although we hold dear the privilege against self-incrimination how, we may well ask, can we forego the reclamation of a ten-year-old child by permitting his lawyer to vindicate that right?

Yet we must pause again when we consider that "reclamation" means confinement in institutions of the sort described by Alan Berns' account of his experiences as a social worker in a Boston juvenile detention facility. Indeed, the facility Berns describes is a virtual Andover Academy in comparison to the Dickensonian institutions revealed in Senator Birch Bayh's piece, aptly entitled "Juveniles v. Justice." The Senator describes an Illinois institution (Illinois was the home of the juvenile court reform movement) where two young boys were punished for homosexual acts by being bound spread-eagle on their beds for seventy-seven hours.

Wizner perceives the rule of counsel in juvenile proceedings to be that of a vigorous advocate, who is "scrupulously deferential" to the wishes of his young client. This view (which is an accurate one, I believe) recognizes the child's need for autonomy *vis à vis* the state. It implicitly acknowledges his capacity to take issue with governmental paternalism, irrespective of his age. On the other hand, a child's capacity to waive his right to counsel is beginning to receive increasing judicial and legislative attention. No matter how diligent the juvenile court judge may be in advising the child of the right to counsel and of the significance and importance of the right, it has been argued (again, correctly in my opinion) that the child has no capacity to waive the right; that the absolute bar which prevents children from negotiating away their rights in, say, an inheritance or commercial transaction must *a fortiori* apply to a critical right when his liberty is at issue. How do we reconcile the child's capacity to determine his counsel's course and at the same time deem him incapable of waiving his right to counsel altogether?

The tension is focused again in the chapter on the applicability of the Fourth Amendment exclusionary rule to juvenile proceedings. Should evidence of heroin possession by a twelve-year-old be suppressed because it was secured by a flagrantly illegal police search? The author persuasively argues for the exclusionary rule. He analyzes the very few Supreme Court decisions we have relating to delinquency proceedings in order to anticipate the Court's resolution when the Fourth Amendment issue eventually comes before it. The piece describes the Supreme Court's efforts in three cases to formulate a doctrine which will at once enable children to resist oppression and yet not insulate them entirely from the state's best efforts. If the legal theories of the different Justices in *Gault*, *Winship* and *McKeiver* seem tortured they are only a reflection of the genuineness of the dilemma. The only thread that is discernible is the Court's refusal to apply the Fourteenth Amendment's Equal Protection Clause to children. Whatever the Due Process Clause may mean for juveniles, the Court seems wholly disinclined to view the posture of a child before authority to be identical with that of an adult.

Reluctance to consider child and adult as one before the law is rationalized by the need to protect the immature from themselves. But we must remain mindful of the disservice we do children with this rationalization. Thus, a child is considered incompetent to consent to medical procedures on his own behalf. This reflects our conviction that parental or other adult participation in such vital decisions protects a youth from his own immature judgment and the unscrupulousness of others. But by this logic young girls in most states must suffer both the physical and psychological devastation of unwanted childbirth because adults are uncaring or unwilling to provide the necessary consent for abortion and/or birth control.

Instinctively we recognize that very young children who continually run away from home or who seem unable ever to attend school require some sort of special attention. It is anathema to our sense of paternalism to abandon them to their own fate. But how does our concern presently manifest itself? We have never addressed ourselves to the individual and varied needs of the thousands of children in this country who wander the streets or who cannot learn. We have made no serious effort to nurture them toward maturity. That is too complex and costly. Rather, we have developed a single label to cover a multitude of problems. Children, from those who suffer with such diverse handicaps as organic brain damage and related learning disabilities to those whose abusive parents cause them to run away, are conveniently categorized by the law as "incorrigible" or "morally depraved." Thus labeled they are simply put out of sight for a few years where their only tutelage is in the institutional mentality, if not in bitterness and crime. But by keeping them invisible for a few years our conscience is salved. Such is the stuff of *parens patriae.*

Lest the picture seem unbearably bleak, a few concerned people are beginning to think constructively. Judge Lois Forer and William Statsky, as well as Senator Bayh, have perceived the state's duty to children as something more than wielding the parental rod. The model law for children proposed by Judge Forer envisions a forum in which children and their representatives can affirmatively litigate a child's rights to proper care and education—presumably not only against their parents and other private parties but against the state as well. Whether the proposal is practicable or not, at least it envisions the child as something other than a passive object worth attention only after his difficulties have made him a public nuisance.

William Statsky describes a novel pilot project in Bronx County, New York with which this writer has been personally involved. The Youth Diversion Project is designed to involve the immediate local community in the problems of its own children. Youngsters who may have school or family problems or who have committed relatively non-serious law violations do not go to court. Rather, community residents who serve on rotating local forums try to mediate the child's differences with his family and teachers. Insofar as the problems are traced to larger state derelictions, forum participation hopefully educates the local community and energizes it for political action.

These are modest beginnings. The Supreme Court in *In re Gault* deplored the fact that children have suffered the worst of both worlds. They have had neither the right to resist the excesses of officialdom nor the power to demand their due. *Gault* gave them some right to resist. Now perhaps, we will begin to insist.

22 East 40th Street
New York, New York 10016
March 28, 1973

Rena K. Uviller, Director
Juvenile Rights Project
American Civil Liberties Union

PREFACE

IN 1967 THE SUPREME COURT made its landmark decision in *In re Gault* requiring juvenile courts to provide children with many of the constitutional rights that adult criminal defendants already enjoyed. The continuing controversy over the quality of juvenile justice has called into question the integrity of the judicial process and the nature and importance of fundamental constitutional rights. This book presents an especially broad range of legal and social science articles that confront the major issues in the juvenile justice debate. The Board of Editors of the *Columbia Human Rights Law Review* is most pleased that these articles, recently published in periodical form, will now be more effectively presented and widely disseminated in this hardcover edition.

Our symposium opens with a personal description of juvenile detention by Alan Berns, a social worker at the Institute for Youth Development and Juvenile Justice in Boston, Massachusetts. In simple language Mr. Berns describes the dilemma that pre-trial juvenile detention poses for both the children involved and their social workers. Senator Birch Bayh, Chairman of the Subcommittee to Investigate Juvenile Delinquency of the Senate Committee on the Judiciary, describes the problems of juvenile crime. The Senator's approach to reducing juvenile crime is comprehensive and includes community-based rehabilitation programs and a centralization of all federal juvenile justice efforts in a new executive agency. Senator Bayh's article has been augmented and updated for inclusion in this hardcover edition. Jonathan Weiss and Oscar Chase, two distinguished children's attorneys, attack the constitutionality of section 383 of the New York Social Services Law. This statute requires that a parent who has voluntarily relinquished custody of a child to the state must get a court order before the child can be returned. Judge Lois G. Forer, a Family Court Judge in Philadelphia and a frequent contributor to the juvenile rights debate, proposes a comprehensive and innovative Youth Court Act which would invest children with more effective rights and remedies including the right to institute a civil cause of action. Stephen Wizner in his article, "The Child and the State: Adversaries in the Juvenile Justice System," emphasizes that children embroiled in the juvenile court are in fact adversaries. Mr. Wizner concludes that lawyers who represent juveniles have generally not comprehended this reality. William P. Statsky describes the development of a unique program he headed in the Bronx, New York which trained laymen from that community to act as judges in certain juvenile court proceedings.

Our first article by a staff member of the *Human Rights Law Review*, "The Fourth Amendment Exclusionary Rule and Juvenile Justice" by William O. Flannery, considers whether the protections of the Fourth Amendment right to be free from unreasonable search and seizures ought to be applied to juveniles. Virginia S. Carson has written a case note analysis of *In the Matter of Ella B*. This opinion by New York State's highest court affirmed the right of an indigent parent to be represented by court-appointed counsel in a child neglect proceeding. "Juvenile Police Record-Keeping" by Edward R. Spalty reviews the extent and the dangers of present police record-keeping practices. The author proposes comprehensive statutory and administrative reforms to insure the protection of the juvenile. Jonathan I. Mark, in "Appellate Review for Juveniles: A 'Right' to a Transcript," considers the importance of a transcript for meaningful appellate review of juvenile hearings. Our book closes with a review by James Woller of Sanford N. Katz's controversial and important monograph, *When Parents Fail: The Law's Response to Family Breakdown*.

Although every anthology is the collective product of many authors and editors, I want to take this opportunity to emphasize that this book owes much of its quality and grace to the extraordinary efforts of Charles D. Bock, the Revisions Editor of the *Columbia Human Rights Law Review*.

New York, New York
March 1973

Robert R. Belair
Editor-in-Chief
Columbia Human Rights Law Review

1 | # JUVENILE DETENTION:
An Eyewitness Account

ALAN BERNS*

The author of this piece has spent the last year and a half working with juvenile delinquents as a social worker in Boston. He spent the first part of that time in a clinic intended to provide social services to paroled boys and their families; and describes that involvement as "typically that of a middle class (white) social worker providing social services to lower class (black) clients." Since that time, his agency has shifted its focus to services during pre-trial detention. Working out of a floor of a maximum security prison he deals with juveniles from the time immediately after arrest until court disposition.

We present this account, by a person who is not law-trained, as first-hand insight into the treatment of juvenile offenders; and to express what he feels to be "the need for an ombudsman meeting the social, physical, emotional needs of boys in detention status."

Okay, so Johnny gets busted, what happens next? He usually will have an arraignment[1] for the following morning. Or if arrested on a Saturday, he is arraigned Monday morning. In the smaller towns serving us, much is settled without the boy coming to the detention center. With closer personal ties and stronger community resources, boys from smaller/wealthier communities are infrequently detained. This is especially true if the charges are not serious (e.g., a joy ride in a stolen car). Invariably the boys from larger, more impersonal towns and cities are detained no matter what the charge. Thus our admissions are disproportionately urban, poor, and black.

In both suburban and urban courts, arraignments are only the first step. Very little is disposed of. If a parent is present, the boy may get released on personal recognizance or to the custody of his parents. If no one is there, bail is set and he is returned to us until his next court appearance.

---

* B.A. Boston University; M.S.W. University of Michigan; Social Worker, Institute for Youth Development and Juvenile Justice, Boston, Mass.
1. Much will depend upon in which court the arraignment will take place.

It is also at the arraignment that lawyers are assigned. It is usually the case that the urban kids get public defenders. Suburban kids either have private counsel or have a bar association lawyer appointed. There are other discrepancies in the treatment of urban and suburban juveniles. The suburban courts have more time, have fewer cases, and depend less on public provision of legal and social services. The urban courts, on the other hand, have less time, have more cases, and depend more on already overburdened state services.

If only half of the kids' stories are accurate, there is much physical abuse prior to admission at the detention center. Issues of mistreatment and abridgements of rights are rarely raised before the court and then only by the private attorneys. The public defenders can focus only on the case itself and find little time to deal with some of these prior abuses. It is my guess, again, that most of these abuses occur in urban neighborhoods—it is circular. The urban kids who are most frequently abused get the overburdened public defenders who rarely have time to deal with the abuses in court. The rarer abuses in suburbia are confronted because the child probably has a private or bar association attorney; and also, perhaps, because such abuses are more unusual.

So, Johnny returns after his arraignment with maybe a one or two week continuance. This is where I first meet him and begin to deal with a number of social and legal binds. I have been told that a bail call is a legal right. Theoretically that call is to be made prior to his detention. But more often than not, most kids I see have received that "later, kid" routine. Unfortunately, one of the policies of our floor is that the detainees are not allowed to use the phone. We have but two and on a limited budget cannot really afford too many long distance calls. Some kids get arrested in Boston but live in Oshkosh and want to call there. Therefore, a boy who missed his chance to make a bail call before detention has lost it. This is true, unless a social worker makes the call for him. Although this involves compromising agency policy, I do it.

If the boy cannot make the bail set for him, he is also entitled to a bail reduction hearing. But that too is complicated. First, his lawyer must process certain papers. If he has an overburdened public defender the processing may take more than the legally prescribed time limits. Again it is the private attorneys who handle bail hearings more quickly. Another aspect of bail concerns the boy and the nature of his case. What if the charges are serious and I feel he is a "danger" to himself and others? The high bail may then have a legitimate basis. Well, I still go along with the idea that he has a right to bail and to the bail reduction hearing[2] if necessary. If the

---

2. It has been my experience that bail is rarely reduced. And, in a fit of pique, I would suggest that the black kids make more wasted trips to bail reduction hearings than the white kids. If Johnny does get bailed either before a hearing or after, I will not see him again unless he runs into more trouble.

charges are so serious and the kid is a "menace to society," the judge won't reduce bail anyhow. Often in spite of the high bail, his parents wish to bail him. In this case I suggest that if they have to choose between bailing their son and hiring a private attorney, then they should choose the latter. With serious charges it is better for the boy to stay in detention than to risk an appearance in court without an adequate defense.

So, we are left with the kids whose parents cannot or will not bail them. They remain with us on the average of two weeks. Most of our activity during that time is directed to technical rather than therapeutic problems. This is due in part to the newness of our program and its philosophy; but also to the high turnover of kids, and bureaucratic red tape, which nearly prevents meaningful therapeutic relationships from developing.

In Massachusetts there are a number of less secure, more open, detention facilities than ours. Some kids go directly to them from arraignment. Others come to us and then we must decide if they are appropriate referrals to lesser security institutions. These facilities have been developed under the innovative leadership of Dr. Jerome Miller of the Department of Youth Services. Whether the child is in the lesser security facilities or not the courts still have legal custody over him.

Because the court retains legal custody, I cannot transfer a kid who doesn't belong in the maximum security facility on my own initiative. I would exercise this initiative if I had it, where I felt the kid was not a potential runaway, would not get along on the floor, or is likely to get abused (physically, sexually) on the floor. Instead I must present these reasons in a request for a court letter authorizing the transfer. A probation officer of the court usually handles this in an administrative manner. No lawyer is involved. Such a transaction takes time and in the end the request may be refused. The court, simply put, may not want Johnny to have the chance to run. So without a hearing Johnny may get turned down. Then, too, the smaller facilities may have no vacant beds and Johnny may have to wait. The waiting game is hard for a boy. And it is hard for me to justify to them. I simply bother people into hurrying. Kids like answers of yes or no. Contrary to popular mystique, they can handle it. Sure they get mad and yell but they are tough and resilient. What they dislike is the vague and unknown quality of what is happening to them. At the least I try to give them answers and refuse to hand out deceitful "I don't knows". If the answer is especially hard to accept I am available to help them deal with it. That, in fact, is one clear area where I can be what I am supposed to be. In those times of stress for a boy he can use me effectively as someone he can talk to.

If Johnny does not get either bail or transfer, then only one other possibility exists that will take him out of our hands prior to trial. He can escape. Escapes occur regularly and I think are a rather natural phenomenon given the setting. Jail is not a nice place and it may be quite healthy for a kid to attempt or make an escape. The police are notified but rarely look for the boy.

They usually will wait until he commits a new offense—then they start the whole process over and throw in a default warrant to boot.[3]

It is also possible Johnny will show up in court anyhow. This is especially true if he is innocent or if he has support lined up for his appearance. Though the judge may frown upon his escape, there is no charge that can be added unless he did something more than simply escape. There is an underlying bind here. If a kid is confident he can make it until the trial, if he cannot get bailed or transferred, and since escaping cannot be charged against him, what arguments can be used to convince a boy not to run? My argument to him usually suggests that his confidence is false. If he could make it on the street he would not be with us at all. He cannot go home, has no money, and is nearly channelled straight towards some offense, if only to survive.

Beyond the legal and bureaucratic problems most of my daily events center on immediate detainee needs: Can I have a cigarette; can you spare a nickel; can I have a cup of coffee; can I make a phone call; can I go to arts and crafts, the gym, or the game room? All of these have to be answered; seemingly every five minutes. What privileges do exist must be dispensed carefully and wisely. For example, the question of which five kids are allowed to work as K.P.'s becomes a major struggle. Who has the pleasure (?) of cleaning the administrative office is another problem. These tasks are clamored after (despite the fact that they are unpaid), as are the minimal recreational activities that are provided. Fights and disputes must be settled equitably. We have banned lock up/isolation and are still searching for some other means to "punish." One alternative we use is to restrict the boy to the floor and not allow him to use the gym.

It is important for me to be able to say no. Not only can I not deliver all the things a boy may ask, I am also concerned with what good I can do for the other 25 if I am constantly tied up doing favors for the five verbally aggressive ones. Cigarettes, for example, are prized. But I don't smoke and avoid the hassles they present. As a reward for tasks accomplished I may give cigarettes in payment or buy some candy or a Big Mac for the kid. But to protect myself from the "why-was-he-allowed-but-not-me" accusations, I either do it secretively or make sure I am rewarding a rather unique task to which no other kid can lay claim.

Another way of humanizing the experience is to make special provisions for visits and interviews. While only parents can visit, I attempt to have them come as often as they can. In addition, if there is a possibility the boy might be placed by the court into a foster home, halfway house, drug program, or private school, I attempt to contact these people and urge them to interview

---

3. It is to be noted that urban kids can lose themselves easier and are less likely to be searched for than the suburban kid.

the boy prior to his trial. This helps cut down on extended and unnecessary continuances. Visits and interviews also tend to minimize the isolation that a boy feels. When people come in from the outside, the boy knows he has not been forgotten. This is especially true in the case of lawyers interviewing their clients. The less that is unknown, the easier it is for the boy. Unfortunately not many lawyers visit.[4]

Once Johnny goes for his trial, my work with him is over (unless there are continuances). Ideally, we plan to develop an outreach program to serve kids in their community after detention. We feel that in a sense, any treatment we give behind locked doors in the detention center is isolated and dislocated. By turning to the community, where kids develop their problems, we can hope to pinpoint where problems begin and determine what needs must be met.

Before concluding I would like to mention two more areas of concern to me. The first involves the line staff (i.e., the guards). These men work on three eight-hour shifts and are responsible for security. They have no weapons and often feel quite threatened by the size and numbers of boys. The jobs do not pay much and consequently the turnover rate is high. Their anxieties and frustrations must be given as much attention as the detainees'. They are, in my opinion, a key to life on the floor. They can effectively and easily sabotage the best intended plans or programs. Or they can make things run smoothly by internalizing the non-penal philosophy we are attempting to foster. What is needed is an orientation manual and group sessions for the line staff, but neither is provided as of this moment. In order for humane detention programs to work detention guards must be committed to insuring their success. Guards can't feel such a commitment if they are isolated from activities on the floor or alienated from the social work staff. A wedge between the line and social work staffs can be used by the kids to play one group off against the other. It has happened and will continue to happen until the critical importance of the line staff's role is justifiably recognized.

A second point I would like to raise concerns the unfortunate "mix" of detainees on our floor. Combined with the great majority of kids, charged with "typical" juvenile offenses and "status" offenders[5], are juveniles that have been "bound over" to adult court.[6]

Juveniles that are bound over to adult courts stay in detention longer. This is true for at least two reasons. One is that cases thought serious enough to be bound over to adult court are often those in which high bail is set. Another reason is the fact that (adult) Superior Courts have more backlog

4. Of course, private lawyers do have time to visit. As mentioned, this doesn't help urban kids (served by public defenders) too much.
5. Typical status offenders are "stubborn children" and "runaways".
6. In Massachusetts anyone over 14 can be tried as an adult.

problems than do juvenile courts. Grand juries (which must indict) do not meet all the year round, and some counties do not have year round Superior Court sessions. Suffolk County (which includes Boston), for example, has no Superior Court session in the summer. So, if the bound over detainee cannot make bail and misses either the grand jury or Superior Court sessions, the wait may be long indeed.

Since the kids who get bound over tend to be bigger, more aggressive and more vocal their presence on the floor makes a great demand on social workers' time. This means less opportunity for social workers to provide rehabilitative treatment to smaller kids, who are often better suited to being helped. Therefore, the fact that bound-over boys stay longer is disruptive of the humane treatment program we are trying to administer.

In the meantime, all these kids are thrown together. We separate them by age into wings. But one learns from the other and passes it on. Judges never come to see what the place is like that they are sending kids to. These kids are ignored, isolated, abused, and forgotten. You hear little public outcry or publicity. If our ideas and plans reach fruition, detention might be a reasonable and rational place to spend some time. For the time being I am putting bandaids on re-opened scars. These kids will grow up and that is when we will all take notice: "crime in the streets"; "junkies"; "overdoses"; and on and on. Until we pay attention to their needs as kids, we will never be able to meet their needs as adults.

2 | JUVENILES v. JUSTICE

BIRCH BAYH*

Evaluations of our juvenile justice system are usually couched in abstractions, but the significance of all our investigations is best summarized in the life of one individual. Larry Smith is symbolic of the failure of our efforts to prevent and control juvenile delinquency. He is thirty years old and was recently committed to the Lorton Correctional Complex, the medium security facility receiving adult offenders from the District of Columbia. When he reached Lorton, he arrived at the last step in what had been a continuous succession of failures. When he entered the adult system he officially became a mature criminal—considered by society to be responsible for his actions, not easily rehabilitated, and definitely not to be trusted. Larry arrived at his new status as the product of the system we have devised to control and prevent juvenile delinquency.

Smith has spent most of the last eighteen years inside our correctional system. At the age of twelve he was committed to the Industrial Home School for Colored Boys (now Junior Village), which housed neglected children from the District of Columbia. His most memorable experience there was fighting off sexual attacks of older boys. Since that time he has been successively incarcerated in Cedar Knoll (the facility for juvenile delinquents from the District of Columbia), the now defunct National Training School for Boys, three Federal prisons, the Federal drug hospital for the psychiatrically disturbed, the Lorton Youth Center, and now the Lorton Correctional Complex. He will spend at least the next five years in prison, and when released will probably continue what has been a lifelong career of crime.

Larry Smith's life dramatizes the rather impersonal term, "recidivism." He represents the all too common pattern in which one institution's failures become another institution's problems. Our juvenile justice system is too often a revolving door which for many ultimately leads to the adult criminal justice system and a lifetime of criminal behavior.

---

* U.S. Senator, D-Ind.

I. Morrisania—A Community-Based Comprehensive Response

In the Bronx in New York City, there is developing a prototype which I believe is the hope of the children who will, or already have, embarked on the road that Larry Smith has taken. The Morrisania Youth and Community Service Center[1] is a community-based multiservice organization established by people in the community to serve the needs of the residents. It provides many different services from nearly a dozen storefront offices scattered throughout the community. Certain programs focus on the young. Morrisania operates a day-care center for pre-school youngsters, a tutoring service for all children through high school, and an indoor and outdoor recreational program for the many residents who find the South Bronx devoid of worthwhile activities. Additionally, there are programs for those who have more serious troubles. A drug counseling and rehabilitation program is designed for the hard drug users, and a legal services project helps juveniles who might otherwise not be effectively represented in court. Other programs concentrate on general needs of the community, young and old alike. There are employment services and housing services to help ameliorate conditions in this ghetto community. In short, Morrisania Youth and Community Service Center is a self-help program operated by community residents to serve the total needs of community residents.

Young people become involved with Morrisania in many ways. They may join the recreation program which features basketball and boxing in the winter, baseball in the spring and summer, and football in the autumn. They may seek help for a drug problem or be aided by the legal services program which acts as advocate for defendants in juvenile court. Alternatively, they can be involved without actually approaching Morrisania themselves. Their father might seek a job in the employment office, or their mother might use the day care facilities for a younger brother or sister. Regardless of how the young person becomes involved, the response of the organization is basically uniform. It attempts to serve the varied needs of the individual by coordinating the services of many different programs. Thus, a young person may be represented by the Morrisania legal services for joyriding in a car. He may be adjudicated a delinquent and placed on probation that requires participation in the tutorial program to improve his performance in school and in the recreational program to relieve his many hours of boredom.

While the needs of individual clients are the primary concerns, the needs of entire families are also served where possible. Thus, Morrisania

---

1. Morrisania, founded by William Satterfield, is a many-faceted community center providing programs for the very young and the very old. It concentrates, however, upon the needs of the young.

may help a young drug addict by treating his father's addiction as well as his own. Similarly, a teenage mother may be encouraged to put her pre-school daughter in the day care facility so that she can find a job. In this way, a number of approaches can be brought to bear on the individual problem, which is perceived as a single entity but actually has a number of underlying causes.

Multi-service community centers are today's hope for preventing juvenile delinquency in the future. The fundamental justification for treating juvenile delinquents differently than adult offenders is that they are considered to be more easily rehabilitated and not yet wedded to a life of crime. In a real sense, therefore, all juvenile programs should be prevention programs. Whether the young person has broken the law or not, the strategy of an effective program must be to prevent the juvenile from becoming a mature and hardened criminal. Such a program must provide services as varied as the clients it serves. Like Morrisania, a good juvenile program must treat clients as individuals, determine their needs as individuals, and attempt to meet those needs. By attacking the underlying problems that produced delinquent behavior or could lead to delinquency in the future, young people can be prevented from following the path taken by Larry Smith.

II. THE NEED FOR A NEW APPROACH

As Chairman of the Subcommittee to Investigate Juvenile Delinquency of the Senate Committee on the Judiciary, I have been concerned with our failure to prevent juvenile delinquents from becoming adult criminals. During the past year, the Subcommittee has studied, in depth, the problems of prevention, treatment and rehabilitation. The dimensions of the juvenile delinquency problem have been explored, and a series of legislative responses have been proposed to clarify and strengthen the Federal government's role and to encourage the states to adopt new approaches for dealing with juveniles.[2] As the culmination of these efforts, I have introduced in the Senate a bill which proposes a comprehensive national strategy to aid our youth.[3]

---

2. *Cf. Hearings on the Role of the Federal Government in the Area of Juvenile Delinquency Before the Subcommittee to Investigate Juvenile Delinquency of the Senate Committee on the Judiciary* [hereinafter referred to as *Subcomm.*], 92d Cong., 1st Sess., March 31 and April 1 (1971); *Hearings on Juvenile Confinement Institutions and Correctional Systems Before the* Subcomm., 92d Cong., 1st Sess., May 26 (1971); *Hearings on S. 674 Before the* Subcomm., 92d Cong., 1st Sess., July 15 and 16 (1971); *Hearings on S. 2507 Before the* Subcomm., 92d Cong., 1st Sess., Sept. 13, 14, Oct. 5, 27, and Nov. 1 (1971).

3. *Hearings on S. 2829 Before the* Subcomm., 92d Cong., 2d Sess., Jan. 13 and 14 (1972).

A new strategy is absolutely essential. The uncoordinated efforts of the Federal government and the lack of imagination and resources at the State level have allowed the problem of juvenile delinquency to reach crisis proportions. Today, children between the ages of ten and seventeen account for 45.3 percent of all arrests for serious offenses even though they comprise only sixteen percent of the population.[4]

Crime by young offenders grew spectacularly in the 1960's. During the period 1960 to 1971, violent crime by persons under eighteen increased 193 percent.[5] Over the same period property crimes such as burglary, larceny, and auto theft by those under eighteen increased by 99 percent.[6] The sad truth is that persons under twenty-five account for 59 percent[7] of all crimes of violence and for 80 percent[8] of all property crimes each year. It has been estimated that juvenile delinquency costs the nation billions of dollars each year, but this economic loss is dwarfed by the immeasurable human cost of young lives wasted in criminal activity and victimized citizens who fear for their physical safety.

Our present approach to the problems of juvenile delinquency usually fails to treat young people as individuals with specific needs and problems. Most young people receive no individual care at all until they commit a serious offense or come to the attention of the state by refusing, or being unable, to live at home. Tragically, at that moment of extreme need, the system can provide only one response. Young persons who have committed serious crimes as well as young persons who can no longer live at home are generally incarcerated in large, rundown, understaffed institutions which encourage criminal behavior more often than they correct. While this seems to be a cynical judgment, it is hardly an exaggeration.

Approximately 1,000,000 juveniles will enter the juvenile justice system this year. Fifty percent will be informally handled by the juvenile courts' intake staff.[9] This amounts to no more than a warning. Forty percent will be formally adjudicated and placed on probation or other supervisory release.[10] However, because probation officers often have case loads of 100 or more, no meaningful solution to individual problems can be developed. Finally, ten percent or approximately 100,000 young people, will be incarcerated this year in a juvenile institution.[11] During previous years many

---

4. Source: FEDERAL BUREAU OF INVESTIGATION, CRIME IN THE UNITED STATES, UNIFORM CRIME REPORTS—1970, at 124 (1971).

5. *Id.* at 118.

6. *Id.*

7. *Id.* at 124.

8. *Id.*

9. Congressional briefing to *Subcomm.* by R. Geminiani, Commissioner of Youth Development and Delinquency Prevention Administration, Department of Health, Education, and Welfare (January, 1971).

10. *Id.*

11. *Id.*

of those young people in the latter class were members of either of the two larger classes formerly described. They needed help from the beginning, but received nothing but threats until now.

The cost of this system is enormous—nearly one billion dollars a year —and it is increasing at a rate of $50 million a year.[12] By far the most expensive and wasteful part of this system are the institutions in which juveniles are incarcerated on a long term basis. The average cost per youth is $5700—far higher than the average cost of halfway houses or group homes ($1500 per youth) or probation services ($500 per youth).[13] Yet it is in these larger institutions that most young people are placed, and where the most damage is done. This is made clear by the startling fact that recidivism among juveniles is far more severe than among adult offenders. While recidivism among adults has been variously estimated from 40 percent to 70 percent, recidivism among juveniles has been estimated at 74 percent to 85 percent.[14]

III. THE FAILURE OF CONVENTIONAL JUVENILE INSTITUTIONS

Our juvenile correctional institutions fail to rehabilitate because, even if there were sufficient resources and interest to develop an effective program of rehabilitation, the physical conditions are so bad that rehabilitation cannot take place. Typical of our nation's reform schools is the Indiana Training School. Opened in 1867, few physical improvements have been added in the last thirty-five years. While the normal capacity of the institution is 550, the average population in 1970 was 643.[15] Thus, a cottage designed for 20 boys holds a minimum of 35 boys and often more than 40 boys. Overcrowding increases tensions among the inmates and reduces contact between the staff and the boys. Even without overcrowding, experts agree that institutions as large as the Indiana Training School cannot effectively rehabilitate.

Deficiencies in the physical plant and overcrowding are only two of the problems faced by the Indiana Training School. Inadequacies in staffing are also freely admitted. While salaries for cottage supervisors have risen substantially in the last two years, from $380 to $500 a month, this is still conceded to be insufficient compensation. Moreover, the ratio of staff to boys is extremely poor. In many cottage living units the ratio of super-

---

12. *Id.*

13. *Id.* (But estimates vary).

14. Source: U.S. DEPARTMENT OF HEALTH, EDUCATION, AND WELFARE, SOCIAL AND REHABILITATION SERVICE, STATISTICS ON PUBLIC INSTITUTIONS FOR DELINQUENT CHILDREN—1970 (1971).

15. *Hearings on Juvenile Confinement Institutions and Correctional Systems Before the* Subcomm., 92d Cong., 1st Sess., at 112 *et seq.* (1971).

visors and counselors to boys is 1 to 35. Psychologists are in a ratio of 1 to 144 with the total inmate population. Academic and vocational teachers enjoy a better ratio of 1 to 15, but recreational workers face a staggering 1 to 216 ratio. Summarizing the staff problems, Superintendent Alfred Bennett said:

> Faced with such conditions, theirs [the staff] is virtually an impossible task. Those staff members who deal with the counseling functions within the institution feel frustrated by the large number of boys on their caseloads, the extremely short stay of most boys due to continuing overcrowded conditions, and the burden of paperwork requirements that are placed on them from many sources. Those staff members whose duties are [to] teach academic or vocational skills feel a constant pressure to include too many boys into too few programs. Because of the short stay of most boys, these staff members feel that they are "baby sitting" with their students and trainees. Institutional psychologists are unable to furnish psychological services to the large number of boys referred to them. They receive individual referrals at a rate that has caused a backlog too great to evaluate every boy in need of their services. As a result, some boys who need specialized psychological help may never receive it. The analysis may be summed up by saying that pay raises would be one way of improving general staff qualifications in each and every staff category.[16]

As well as providing few services, most institutions do not differentiate between offenders. As a result, murderers, rapists, petty thieves and drug abusers are all incarcerated in the same institution, often in the same cottage. Younger offenders, less sophisticated in crime, learn from older, more experienced offenders. It is not unusual for a young person, incarcerated for possession of marihuana, to leave the institution, nine months or a year later, conversant in the skills of "hot wiring" an automobile ignition. This "learning process" which is indigenous to all large institutions has caused them to be labeled "colleges of crime."

Even more destructive is the common practice of incarcerating "juvenile status offenders" with those who have committed criminal-type offenses. The most common juvenile status offenses include ungovernability, truancy, running away, and sexual promiscuity in girls. The distinguishing characteristic of these offenses is that if they were committed by an adult there would be no legal consequences. While the effects of these offenses on society are not as serious as criminal offenses, the child who commits them often suffers serious legal consequences. It

16. *Id.* at 114.

is commonly acknowledged that half of the children currently in juvenile institutions are incarcerated for juvenile status offenses.

A. The Crime of Running Away

As an example, half of the girls at the Illinois Training School for Girls are runaways.[17] Extensive hearings by the Subcommittee revealed that as many as a million children a year leave home without parental permission.[18] These children, the majority of them girls, are often fourteen or fifteen years old. After leaving home, often without much money, and usually with no clear idea of where they are going, these children become easy marks for the pusher, the pimp, and the street thug. Moreover, running away is against the law. Runaways are subject to arrest, detention in a juvenile hall or local jail, and even incarceration in juvenile institutions.

Though the problem of runaways is severe, it has received virtually no attention from the government. The Federal government partially supports a handful of runaway programs in various cities,[19] but State governments support none at all. Nevertheless, locally financed runaway programs have been started in many cities. Organized by church groups or concerned individuals and locally financed and supported, these runaway projects have developed as community solutions to a community problem. Often these programs start very small, possibly as a hot line or day time "rap" place. As resources increase, a temporary shelter facility is obtained. Eventually professional psychological services are arranged, usually a separate drug program is begun, and a permanent group foster home is organized for children who should not go home.

Programs of this sort did not exist five years ago. Yet, in that time, thirty to forty runaway facilities developed to meet the growing problems. The best known of these projects is Huckleberry House in San Francisco. Opened in Haight-Ashbury to provide help for the flood of flower children who came in the summer of 1967, Huckleberry House now serves five hundred to six hundred runaways each year. Additionally, thousands of children are served by a drop-in counseling service, neighborhood drug program, free school, and legal services. In this way, Huckleberry House has grown far beyond the runaway house concept and now serves a variety of community needs.

At the present time, there is no Federal program which is designed specifically to aid private, local groups in meeting the problems of juvenile delinquency on the local level. This is one reason why almost no runaway

17. *Id.* at 196.
18. *See* note 3 *supra.*
19. *Id.* at 20.

programs are federally sponsored. I have introduced specific legislation to meet the runaway problem. The Runaway Youth Act[20] authorizes the expenditure of $10,000,000 a year for three years to establish runaway facilities. The Act relies heavily on local groups and agencies by funding such efforts directly, instead of utilizing a State or regional planning mechanism.

These runaways are the most tragic victims of our juvenile institutions because their punishment is so disproportionate to their offense. While in the reformatory they inevitably come into contact with tougher girls. They are often brutally beaten. Homosexual attacks are frequent. When they leave, the family and personal problems which caused them to run away usually have not been solved; and their experience has probably toughened them and made them more likely to begin a life of crime.

B. The Brutalization of Juvenile Offenders

Another aspect of the problem of juvenile status offenders is the incarceration of extremely young children in juvenile institutions. One lawyer from Illinois told of the incarceration of a young child whom he represented in a *habeas corpus* proceeding:

> We had one boy who was 8 years of age who broke into a neighbor's house and took $60, which is a bad act. I am not saying it is good, but he went to the local candy store and he bought candy and ice cream and goodies, and he was found in the dog house about 3 in the morning with all of these goodies and a very sick stomach. He was incarcerated for that act and spent 2½ years in the State prison for children, and then we got him out on *habeas corpus*, which frequently happens, especially with children from very disoriented families and families who cannot cope with the problem of raising children for one reason or another. Something should be done in this case, but I question very much if incarceration is ever an answer. When this boy came out of St. Charles, 2 years later, at the age of 10, he was a very, very knowledgeable little boy about the ways of the world.[21]

This child was incarcerated in the Illinois State Training School for Boys, a particularly dismal institution in St. Charles, Illinois. Nearly 70 years old, in 1970 the institution had a population of 542, which included felons, misdemeanants, and delinquents. It is shocking that eight-year-old children are placed in such an environment. But the lack of resources has left courts

20. S. 2829, 92d Cong., 1st Sess. (1971).
21. *See* note 15 *supra*, at 202.

and correction officials without alternative to the old, overcrowded, and dilapidated training schools which were an earlier generation's panacea for the problem of juvenile delinquency.

Compounding this deplorable situation are frequent instances of brutality by members of the staff of such institutions. Until recently many states officially sanctioned corporal punishment for incarcerated juveniles. The strap was authorized punishment in Florida, Indiana and Arkansas; but broken hoe handles were used in South Carolina, and the policy of open-handed slaps to the head occasionally caused broken ear drums in Delaware.[22] While corporal punishment has been officially terminated in most places, it continues to be utilized frequently. Moreover, other forms of physical punishment or deprivation are common. A well publicized case in Illinois involved two boys who were punished for homosexual acts by being tied spread-eagle on their beds for 77½ hours. They were given a bedpan and allowed to shower once a day but otherwise could not move. A similarly shocking case involved a girl at another Illinois institution who was tied to her bed for 30 consecutive days as punishment for being unmanageable.[23]

Solitary confinement is a universal sanction in American training schools. Official theory usually claims that the "quiet room" provides a period of meditation for a child who has done wrong. This is a cruel and senseless rationalization and reflects a lack of insight and compassion on the part of many institution officials. Solitary confinement is a primitive treatment which at best defers and at worst aggravates the problem which caused the young person's unmanageability. In no sense is it a means of rehabilitation. The treatment in North Carolina, revealed by the Subcommittee hearings, is typical of the use of solitary confinement in many large training schools. As one witness from North Carolina testified:

> The facilities in the training school concern themselves primarily with custody and control. The harshest form of punishment involves being placed in solitary confinement in the quiet room or, as the boys and staff call it, the jug. The debilitating effect of isolation upon an adult has been documented. I leave you to conclude the effect on a child. If a child attempts to run away, is caught smoking, is acting out in a class, or is involved in related offenses, he is placed in the jug. The jug itself consists of a small room in which a slab of rock serves as a bed. An offender must strip down to his underwear. He may only read the Bible; he has only two meals a day. At 5 o'clock in the evening he is given a mattress on which to sleep; at 6 o'clock the

22. H. JAMES, CHILDREN IN TROUBLE: A NATIONAL SCANDAL, *passim* (1969).
23. *See* note 15 *supra*, at 199.

V. THE FEDERAL RESPONSE

A number of different legislative proposals have been developed by the Subcommittee to Investigate Juvenile Delinquency. One proposal, the Juvenile Delinquency Prevention and Rehabilitation Act of 1971,[27] is designed to redirect the emphasis of the Law Enforcement Assistance Administration in the Department of Justice in its approach to the problems of crime control. Established in 1968 to administer the Federal assistance program to State criminal justice systems, LEAA has grown spectacularly from a 1969 appropriation of $63 million to a 1972 appropriation of almost $700 million.[28] The proposed legislation is designed to concentrate a large proportion of LEAA's rapidly expanding resources on the problems of juvenile delinquency by requiring that 40% of all grants to the States be allocated to the fight against delinquency. Additionally, the bill outlines important guidelines to direct the expenditure of juvenile delinquency funds.

First, 50% of the Federal assistance received for juvenile programs must be spent to encourage the diversion of young people from training schools, reform schools, correctional institutions, and detention facilities as a means of eliminating the terrible overcrowding which exists. Second, all juvenile status offenders must be treated in separate facilities. Thus, the commingling of serious offenders and minor offenders, which produces much of the brutality in institutions, would be curtailed. Third, community-based treatment, expanded use of probation, and comprehensive drug-abuse education, prevention, and rehabilitation programs would all be required in the State plan. The Subcommittee's investigation indicates that these programs would be far more effective at preventing and controlling delinquency than the traditional approaches.

Another legislative proposal, examined by the Subcommittee, concerns the establishment of an Institute for Continuing Studies of Juvenile Justice.[29] This bill creates an independent agency which would serve as a central clearinghouse for all information relating to juvenile delinquency as well as a center for training personnel working in the juvenile delinquency field. The Institute could be an important first step in ending the fragmentation and confusion so apparent in the Federal approach to the delinquency problem. A similar measure was reported favorably by the House Judiciary Committee in October of 1971.[30]

---

27. S. 2148, 92d Cong., 1st Sess. (1971), introduced by Senators Mathias, Bayh, and Cook.

28. *See Hearings on S. 1428 Before the* Subcomm., 92d Cong., 2d Sess. (1972).

29. S. 1428, 92d Cong., 1st Sess. (1971), introduced by Senator Percy, R-Ill.

30. H.R. 45, 92d Cong., 1st Sess. (1971).

VI. The Need for a Centralized Federal Effort

Despite the proliferation of agencies dealing with the juvenile crime problem, there is no single agency charged with the responsibility of systematically collecting juvenile delinquency data and disseminating it to individuals and agencies concerned with juveniles and juvenile offenders. Instead, such information is collected only incidentally, as an adjunct to more general data-gathering by agencies which are not concerned exclusively—or even primarily—with the special problems of juvenile delinquency. Efficient gathering and dissemination of research data is the basic first step necessary to improve the quality of State planning and administration of juvenile justice.

Just as there is no information service completely devoted to juvenile delinquency, very little effort is expended on training the personnel who work with juveniles. The average police recruit receives seven and a half hours of training on the problems of juveniles and delinquency.[31] Since there are no national training standards, the quality of this training is uncertain. While training for all who work with juveniles is essential, the Federal government has neglected this aspect. Only 2% of LEAA grants to the States were spent on training during the fiscal year 1971.[32] The training of personnel is clearly not a priority concern of LEAA administrators or of the States applying for funds. The Department of Health, Education and Welfare has done no better.[33] In the fiscal year 1971, only 12.9 percent of the meager funds HEW expended on juvenile delinquency were allocated for training. In the fiscal year 1972, HEW intended to spend only 7% of its budget for training; and, as of January 1, only $100,000 had been spent.[34]

These figures demonstrate in specific areas what I believe to be a general unwillingness or inability of the Federal government to focus either adequate attention or resources on the problems of delinquency. While the Institute is a laudable attempt to solve certain problems, I believe that there is a desperate need for a new agency independent of existing departmental structures. This agency should have the authority to direct and coordinate the entire Federal juvenile delinquency effort as well as additional resources to implement effective new programs.

---

31. *Hearings on S. 1428 Before the* Subcomm., 92d Cong., 2d Sess., at 3 (1972).
32. *Id.*
33. *Id.* at 101 (statement of M. Rector, Executive Director of the National Council on Crime and Delinquency).
34. *Id.* at 110.

VII. Proposals for Restructuring the Federal Approach

As the culmination of the Subcommittee's investigations, I have introduced the Juvenile Justice and Delinquency Prevention Act of 1972.[35] It is a comprehensive proposal to restructure the Federal approach to the problems of juvenile delinquency under a new National Office of Juvenile Justice and Delinquency Prevention in the Executive Office of the President. By placing the power to supervise, coordinate, and evaluate all federally assisted delinquency programs in the Office of the President, the inadequacies of the Federal effort revealed during Subcommittee hearings will be remedied. Priorities will be better defined, responsibilities among agencies will be assigned, and a careful check on the progress of programs will be maintained. In addition to exercising supervisory power over existing Federal programs, the National Office would provide substantial new resources to develop and implement effective delinquency prevention, diversion, treatment, and rehabilitation programs. One billion dollars would be authorized over a four-year period for these programs.

While the National Office is the central concept of the Bill, two additional institutions are proposed to complement the Federal effort. First, a National Institute for Juvenile Justice under the control of the National Office is created. The Institute, though similar to the Institute for Continuing Studies of Juvenile Justice, would be completely integrated into the unified Federal program. It would work closely with the National Office, serving as an information clearinghouse, a research center, a major source of technical assistance to the States, and as a training unit for personnel in the juvenile justice system. The Institute would receive far greater funding than the Institute for Continuing Studies of Juvenile Justice. An authorization of $500 million over a four-year period is proposed.

Second, a National Commission on Standards for Juvenile Justice would be created to conduct a two-year study of the administration of juvenile justice at the Federal, State and local level. The study would focus upon juvenile court procedure and conditions of confinement in juvenile detention and correctional facilities. The recommendations of the Commission would be reported to Congress and widely publicized. State and local governments would be urged to adapt their practices and procedures to conform to the national standards. The recommendations of the Commission would be used by the National Office as guidelines in establishing funding priorities as well as in making individual funding decisions. For example, the Director of the National Office might determine that an applicant agency or institution would require additional funds to bring it up to national standards established by the Commission, or in

---

35. S. 3148, 92d Cong., 2d Sess. (1972), introduced by Senator Bayh.

the alternative, should not receive funds at all since it is merely perpetuating outmoded, ineffective practices.

VIII. THE PRIORITY OF LOCAL PARTICIPATION

This article began with a description of the Morrisania program as a new approach to the problems of juvenile delinquency. I do not advocate Morrisania as the universal solution to the problems of our youth. The specific components were developed to meet the needs of a community in New York City. What is universally applicable is the approach: recognition of delinquency as a local, community problem and the development of a community-based project to meet that problem. The Federal government can be most effective in the fight against delinquency by encouraging the development of community approaches like Morrisania. However, it has not as yet chosen to commit substantial resources to developing that kind of program.

The legislation which I have developed, including the Runaway Youth Act, the Juvenile Justice and Delinquency Prevention Act of 1972, and the Juvenile Delinquency Prevention and Rehabilitation Act of 1971, are all designed to direct more Federal assistance to the local level. We need more programs like Morrisania and Huckleberry House if we are going to control the explosion of juvenile delinquency which has occurred in the past decade. Thus far, State, local, and private resources have not proved sufficient to meet this need.

Recently, I visited the San Francisco area to investigate on a first hand basis innovative community-based juvenile delinquency and drug treatment programs which have been developed. San Francisco is a relatively compact city which provides many striking contrasts, yet none was more forceful than the simple fact that Huckleberry House is a mere fifteen minute drive from San Quentin Penitentiary. When a young person runs away or commits some other minor offense he is perilously close to the path of crime which leads inevitably to San Quentin. As long as we, as a society, refuse to face that fact, we will continue to live with an unmanageable problem of crime in the streets.

3 | THE CASE FOR REPEAL OF SECTION 383 OF THE NEW YORK SOCIAL SERVICES LAW

JONATHAN WEISS*
and OSCAR CHASE**

In New York State, parents who feel that transient circumstances prevent them from giving proper care to their children have the option of executing a temporary surrender of custody to a state welfare agency.[1] Often, however, parents sign such surrender agreements under duress and unaware of the nature of the document. The state assumes custody of the child until, presumably, the natural parent regains the capacity to furnish an adequate domestic environment, at which time custody of the child may be returned. However, under New York's current statutory scheme governing the care and custody of dependent children, Section 383 of the SOCIAL SERVICES LAW,[2] a parent who either chooses, or is coerced, to exercise this option may unknowingly relinquish his ability to unilaterally determine the child's future status. Under § 383, once custody has been transferred, the

---

* Director, Legal Services for the Elderly Poor; formerly Managing Attorney, MFY Legal Services; Yale, B.A., 1960, LL.B., 1963.

** Professor of Law, Brooklyn Law School.

The authors would like to thank Paul E. Levine, a Columbia Law School student, for his research and editorial assistance.

1. N.Y. Soc. SERV. LAW § 398 (McKinney's 1960), which reads in relevant part: Commissioners of public welfare and city public welfare officials . . . shall have power and perform duties as follows:
>   1. As to destitute children: Assume charge of and provide support for any destitute child who cannot be properly cared for in his home.
>   * * *
>   5. As to children born out of wedlock:
>   a. Provide care in a family free or boarding home, in an agency boarding home or in an institution for any child born out of wedlock . . . when in the judgment of such commissioner . . . needed care cannot be provided in the mother's home.

2. Id., § 383, which reads in relevant part:
> (a) The parent of a child remanded or committed to an authorized agency shall not be entitled to the custody thereof, except upon consent of the court, public board, commission or official responsible for the commitment of such child, or in pursuance of an order of a court or judicial officer of competent jurisdiction, determining that the interest of such child will be promoted thereby and that such parent is fit, competent and able to duly maintain, support and educate such child.

subsequent decision as to the parent's fitness[3] for resumption of parental obligations rests with the state welfare agency. The manner in which the right to secure return of custody on demand is thus lost poses a serious constitutional question arising from a possible conflict with the requirements of due process. This article sets forth the contention that deprivation of an interest as vital as control over one's child can be consistent with due process only if preceded by an evidentiary hearing,[4] and that therefore § 383 is of dubious constitutional validity as well as unjustified in terms of public policy.

The factual setting which generates the issue is not uncommon to major urban centers.[5] A divorced parent in a financial bind, an unwed adolescent mother still too immature to rear a child, or a welfare mother confronted with hospitalization and therefore temporarily incapable of caring for her child, require a temporary custodian for their children. In order to effect a transfer of custody to a local state welfare agency,[6] the parent must sign a consent form,[7] under the terms of which he voluntarily surrenders the child. Parents on welfare may be coerced into surrendering the child as a condition of continued receipt of welfare benefits. Although the legal technicality of its phraseology renders the surrender document impenetrable to lay comprehension, its signing is normally not accompanied by the aid of counsel. The nature and extent of the custodial rights surrendered are often not understood by the parent. Hence, believing he will be able to reacquire custody when he adjudges himself ready, the parent, unawares, relinquishes the right to the child's return on demand.

Indeed when the parent later requests the agency to turn over his child, he may be flatly refused, on the grounds that the agency believes him still unfit to care for the child. This refusal is authorized by § 383.[8] Under the terms of the statute the parent is *not* entitled to custody *except* by the agency's consent or by court order determining parental fitness. When the agency refuses the parent's request, it has cut off the right of parental control on the basis of its own judgment, having afforded the parent no opportunity to be heard. His only recourse is to invoke the aid of a court[9]

---

3. *Id.*

4. *See,* text accompanying notes 27-39, *infra.*

5. The following sequence of events represents a generalization abstracted from the authors' experience in this field.

6. In New York City, the agency is the Child Welfare Bureau of the Department of Social Services.

7. The agreement is authorized by § 384 of the N.Y. Soc. SERV. LAW. *See* note 1, *supra.* Section 384 provides in relevant part:

> 1 . . . guardianship may be committed by written instrument signed (in the case of illegitimate children) by the mother.
>
> 2 . . . the instrument shall be upon such terms, for such time, and subject to such conditions as may be agreed upon by the parties thereto.

8. *See* note 2, *supra.*

9. The New York State Supreme Court has jurisdiction over custody controversies. Boone v. Wyman, 295 F. Supp. 1143 (S.D.N.Y. 1969). *See* note 12, *infra.*

by initiating a *habeas corpus* proceeding, at which a judicial determination of whose guardianship best serves the child's interests is made.[10] In the meantime, the parent has lost the custody and society of his child against his will.

The effect of § 383 then, may be to permit an administrative agency to deprive an individual of an interest[11] deserving of constitutional protection without the benefit of a hearing on the facts. It further imposes the burden of going forward with remedial litigation on the parent, who is usually in cases of this sort the party least able to shoulder it. Finally, it prolongs the separation of parent and child, with deleterious consequences for both.

These contentions were advanced when the constitutionality of the statute was challenged on due process grounds in *Boone v. Wyman*,[12] a class action brought on behalf of parents seeking to regain custody of children where state agencies had refused under § 383.[13] An intervening plaintiff was Lourdes Gonzales, an 18 year old mother of an illegitimate child. Three years previous to the suit, she had surrendered the child to New York City's Department of Social Services. At the time of birth, Miss Gonzales was informed she was unable to care for the baby. With the intention of assuming parental responsibility at some future date, she signed an agreement authorizing the Department to maintain temporary custody of her child. She was allegedly induced to sign the surrender form by the assurance of a representative of the Child Welfare Bureau that she could secure the

---

10. 39 AM. JUR. 2d § 148:
Generally, where the writ of habeas corpus is prosecuted for the purpose of determining the right to custody of a child, the controversy does not involve the question of personal freedom, because the infant is presumed to be in the custody of someone until it attains its majority . . . . Therefore, these cases are decided, not on the legal right of the petitioner to be relieved of unlawful imprisonment or detention, as in the case of an adult, but on the court's view of the best interests of those whose welfare requires that they be in custody of one person or another; and here a court is not bound to deliver a child into the custody of any claimant or of any person, but should, in the exercise of a sound discretion, . . . leave it in such custody as its welfare at the time appears to require. In short, the child's welfare is the supreme consideration, irrespective of the rights and wrongs of its contending parents . . . . An application by a parent, through the medium of a habeas corpus proceeding, for custody of a child is addressed to the discretion of the court, and custody may be withheld from the parent where it is made clearly to appear that by reason of unfitness . . . the permanent interests of the child would be sacrificed by a change of custody.

11. In certain cases the parent's right to care and control of a child is an interest which may not be denied by the state unless the requisites of due process are complied with. *See* cases discussed in text accompanying notes 20-26, 36; *infra*.

12. 295 F. Supp. 1143 (S.D.N.Y. 1969); *aff'd*, 412 F.2d 857 (2d Cir. 1969); *cert. denied*, 396 U.S. 1024 (1970). The author represented an intervening plaintiff in *Boone*.

13. The class representative was a father seeking the return of an illegitimate son who had been surrendered to the state by the mother. The agency had refused him custody under § 383.

return of the child whenever she wished. Some two years later the mother considered her situation sufficiently improved to provide for her infant. Her request for the child's release, however, was refused by the Department. The administrators' decision was predicated on their having adjudged Miss Gonzales unfit to care for the child.[14]

Miss Gonzales, joining the other plaintiff in *Boone*, sought an injunction in federal court against agency officials' refusal to return custody of her child without a prior evidentiary hearing on parental fitness. The substance of plaintiff's claim was that this refusal to turn over the child in the absence of such a hearing constituted a denial of procedural due process. She claimed her right to parental custody had been terminated by the state under § 383 in violation of the Due Process clause of the 14th Amendment. In addition, it was argued that § 383 was superfluous, given the state's capacity to take the child by neglect proceedings.

The Court, however, did not agree. The complaint was dismissed on the grounds that plaintiffs had no substantial constitutional claim on which the federal court's jurisdiction could be founded. Judge Mansfield concluded that § 383 procedure did not contravene the dictates of the Due Process clause. He pointed to what he saw as plaintiff's erroneous assumption that the agency's refusal to return the child amounted to a permanent committal and that this interim decision was binding on plaintiffs.[15] Since § 383 provides that a parent can obtain custody by court order, defendant's decision was neither binding nor final. A binding, final determination of custody can emanate only from the independent decision by a court in a *de novo*[16] *habeas corpus* proceeding in which the agency would have the burden of proving the parent's lack of fitness.[17] The Court emphasized that the existence of this prompt judicial remedy imposing the burden of proof on the state assured procedural due process to the parent in any dispute arising under § 383.[18]

The opinion in *Boone*, although not a wholly incorrect interpretation of the mandate of due process at the time, remains a triumph of form over substance. It is indeed a sanguine view of due process which stresses the lack of finality of the agency refusal plus defendant's burden of proof at the *habeas corpus* proceeding when the reality of the situation determines that in many, if not most, cases, the judicial proceeding shall never be initiated. For the consequences of § 383 largely affect ghetto residents who

14. Agency refusal in this case was not put into an official text.

15. 295 F. Supp. at 1149.

16. In a *de novo* proceeding, the court is not bound by agency findings of fact, but reaches an independent conclusion on the basis of evidence presented by both sides. Hence the parent cannot be prejudiced by a prior agency determination.

17. 295 F. Supp. at 1149, *citing* People ex rel. Anonymous v. N.Y. Foundling Hospital, 12 N.Y.2d 863.

18. 295 F. Supp. at 1150, *citing* Bourjois, Inc. v. Chapman, 301 U.S. 183 (1937).

have little or no access to courts and counsel.[19] Further, although the technical burden of proof may be on the state in a *habeas corpus* proceeding, the parent is obligated to affirmatively prove his fitness in order to have any chance of regaining custody through such court action. (The parent must prove his fitness because the test in *habeas corpus* proceedings of this nature is "best interests of the child.") The imposition here, of the burden of going forward with litigation upon the parent is thus of equal or greater significance for due process purposes than the agency's burden of proof in *habeas corpus* proceedings. Yet the former went unmentioned in the Court's decision. However, debate over the merits of *Boone* now is perhaps academic. For recent developments in the law of procedural due process seem to have rendered it obsolete as a constitutional legitimation of § 383.

To establish the framework of constitutional principle against which § 383 must be tested requires the identification of two discrete developments in legal doctrine; one, the older and well-settled notion that custody is an interest protected by the Due Process clause; the other, just now reaching fruition, that due process necessitates a prior hearing before the state deprives a person of such an interest.

The Supreme Court directed its attention to the importance of the parental custodial right almost 50 years ago when a state statute forbidding education in any language other than English was challenged in *Meyer v. Nebraska*.[20] The Court found the law unconstitutional as an arbitrary government restriction on the parent's right to bring up his children as he saw fit, a right which was ruled to be an essential part of the "liberty" protected by due process.[21] Similarly, Oregon's legislative attempt to require all children to attend public schools to the exclusion of private institutions was invalidated as an unreasonable interference with this same liberty in *Pierce v. Society of Sisters*.[22] The Court described the parent's substantive right in the following terms:

> The child is not the mere creature of the state; those who nurture him and direct his destiny have the right, coupled with the high duty to recognize and prepare him for additional obligations.[23]

May v. Anderson[24] involved an estranged father's attempt to enforce an ex parte judgment by a Wisconsin court awarding him custody of his children against his wife residing in Ohio. Although the issue raised was whether an Ohio court had to accord the Wisconsin judgment full faith

---

19. *See* Weiss, *The Law and the Poor*, 26 J. OF SOCIAL ISSUES 59 (1970).
20. 262 U.S. 390 (1923).
21. 262 U.S. at 399.
22. 268 U.S. 510 (1925).
23. 268 U.S. at 535.
24. 345 U.S. 528 (1953).

and credit, the Court emphasized the importance of the interest at stake. "The right to custody is far more precious . . . than property rights."[25] In *Armstrong v. Manzo*,[26] a divorced mother and her second husband obtained an adoption decree for her child in a Texas court proceeding, no notice of which was given the father. The Court held this failure to notify him of the pending adoption action a denial of due process. The right to legal custody could not be terminated without adequate notice and an opportunity to contest the termination. Hence, as these cases indicate, it is well established that the right of a parent to control the welfare of his child falls, in many circumstances, within the protective net of the Due Process clause.

This principle becomes meaningful in regard to § 383 and the *Boone* rationale (where it was not at issue) when coupled with a constitutional doctrine fully articulated only in the past three years. After several recent decisions, the rule that interests protected by due process may not be denied by state judicial or administrative organs without a prior hearing on the facts seems well entrenched.

The trend was given impetus by *Sniadach v. Family Finance Corp. of Bay View*.[27] There, a Wisconsin statutory provision for pre-judgment wage garnishment was found to be in contravention of the 14th Amendment. The statute authorized seizure of defendant's wages before he was served with the complaint. Justice Douglas ruled that the interim freezing of wages without a prior chance to be heard is violative of elemental due process requirements. Plaintiffs in *Goldberg v. Kelly*[28] were recipients of financial aid under New York's federally assisted Aid to Families with Dependent Children program. State welfare officials terminated the funds without a hearing. The Court held such action contrary to the mandate of the Due Process clause. Following the reasoning of *Sniadach*, the state officials were instructed that, consistent with due process, an evidentiary hearing on the recipient's eligibility for assistance was a prerequisite to the withholding of benefits already being received. The termination of unemployment compensation without a hearing on the employee's eligibility has instigated a spate of litigation. Of the five district court cases decided, all but one applied the *Goldberg* rule to find such action a denial of due process.[29] Similar rulings

---

25. 345 U.S. at 533.
26. 380 U.S. 545 (1964).
27. 395 U.S. 337 (1969).
28. 397 U.S. 254 (1970).
29. In California Dept. of Human Resources Development v. Java, 317 F. Supp. 875 (N.D. Cal. 1970), *aff'd. on statutory grounds*, 402 U.S. 121 (1971), the *Goldberg* rule was applied in finding a termination of unemployment benefits upon the employer's appeal of the determination of eligibility a violation of due process. *Java* was followed by Crow v. California Dept. of Human Resources, 325 F. Supp. 1314 (N.D. Cal. 1970); Wheeler v. Vermont, 335 F. Supp. 856 (D. Vt. 1971); and Hyatt v. Indiana Employment Security Division, — F. Supp. — (N.D. Ind. 1971) all of which dealt with the summary termination of such benefits upon findings that the recipients had failed either

were rendered in *Bell v. Burson*,[30] involving the suspension of a driver's license in the absence of an adequate prior hearing on potential liability for an accident, and *Wisconsin v. Constantineau*,[31] in which plaintiff's reputation was diminished by the sheriff's posting at all local liquor outlets a prohibition of sale to plaintiff without benefit of hearing determining plaintiff's alcoholism. The Court found in *Bell* that because a license is an important interest,

> It is fundamental, that when a state seeks to terminate such an interest, it must afford notice and an opportunity for hearing before the termination becomes effective.[32]

The expansion of due process continued apace in the very recent decision in *Fuentes v. Shevin*,[33] which reversed the repossession of plaintiffs' property under Florida and Pennsylvania pre-judgment replevin statutes. The laws permitted private parties to obtain pre-judgment writs of replevin via an ex parte application to a court clerk upon posting of bond. The sheriff was required to execute the writ by seizing the property and keeping it for three days, during which time the owner could reclaim possession by also posting bond. Plaintiffs were purchasers of household goods under conditional sales contracts whose property had been repossessed in this manner. The Court held the statutorily prescribed procedure in violation of the Due Process clause which dictated an opportunity for a hearing before the state authorized its agents to seize the property. The fact that the deprivation was conceivably only temporary was held not to mitigate the applicability of the due process requirement. Thus, *Fuentes* has important implications for § 383. The finality issue which so preoccupied Judge Mansfield in *Boone*,[34] is addressed directly by the *Fuentes* Court.

> If the right to notice and a hearing is to serve its full purpose, then it is clear that it must be granted at a time when the deprivation can still be prevented . . . no later hearing can undo the fact that

---

to accept or seek suitable employment. The courts found the agency action, per *Goldberg*, violative of due process in that no hearings were held prior to the termination of funds. In Torres v. New York State Dept. of Labor, 321 F. Supp. 432 (S.D.N.Y., 1970), *vacated and remanded*, 402 U.S. 968 (1971), *opinion on remand*, 333 F. Supp. 341 (S.D.N.Y., 1971), *aff'd. without opinion*, 405 U.S. 949 (1971), the recipient's aid had been cut off when the agency was apprised of new information compromising his eligibility and he was given a personal interview at which he admitted the truth of the new facts. The Court was successful in distinguishing this situation from *Java*, finding the interview adequate for due process purposes as developed in *Goldberg*.

30. 402 U.S. 535 (1971).
31. 400 U.S. 433 (1971).
32. 402 U.S. at 542.
33. 407 U.S. 67 (1972).
34. *See* text accompanying notes 15-17, *supra*.

the arbitrary taking that was subject to the right of procedural due process has already occurred . . . . It is settled that a temporary, non-final deprivation of property is nonetheless a deprivation in terms of the 14th Amendment. (citing *Sniadach* and *Bell*)[35]

The two clear lines of constitutional principle here mentioned, the importance of the custodial right and the necessity of a hearing before a termination of such an interest, have intersected in *Stanley v. Illinois*,[36] a highly significant decision for any assessment of the validity of § 383. An Illinois statute provided that an unwed father's children automatically became wards of the state upon the mother's death. Unfitness of the father was made a legislative presumption, with no provision for a hearing on the actual fact before custody passed immediately to the state. The father's remedies were either adoption or custody proceedings, at which he would have to prove himself fit. In holding the father entitled by due process to a hearing before his children were removed, the Court stressed that the existence of these remedies did not bar an attack on the statute. "This Court has not, however, embraced the general proposition that a wrong may be done if it may be undone."[37] It was recognized that in the delay between the doing and the undoing, the father suffered the deprivation of his children and the children endured uncertainty and dislocation.[38] The opinion concludes with the general proclamation that all parents in Illinois (and by necessary implication, all parents everywhere) are constitutionally entitled to a hearing on fitness before their children are removed from custody.[39]

Of course *Stanley* is distinguished from *Boone* on at least two counts, but they appear insufficient to affect the obvious impact of the decision on the constitutionality of § 383. First, plaintiff in *Stanley* had physical custody of his children when the statutory scheme came into play to take them away. Miss Gonzales had already surrendered her child to the state when § 383 prevented her from securing its return. The status quo upset by the two statutes differed markedly. Secondly, the burden of proving fitness rested with plaintiff in *Stanley* had he resorted to his available remedies, whereas in a *habeas corpus* proceeding in New York, the burden would have been on the state. The *Boone* court considered this factor decisive in upholding § 383.

The former distinction appears inconsequential since, as we saw in *Meyer, Pierce,* and *Armstrong*,[40] it is the right to control the child's welfare, rather than mere physical possession alone, that is protected by due process.

---

35. 407 U.S. at 81-85.
36. 405 U.S. 645 (1972).
37. 405 U.S. at 647.
38. 405 U.S. at 647.
39. 405 U.S. at 658.
40. *See* text accompanying notes 20-26, *supra*.

Section 383 nullifies this right by shifting from parent to agency the determination of the child's custody. The differing burdens of proof also seem inadequate to save *Boone*, for the clear message of *Bell*, *Fuentes*, and *Stanley* is that the availability of ultimate remedies, of whatever nature, is immaterial once a deprivation of interest has occurred. Their import is that an evidentiary hearing must be granted prior to the deprivation, no matter how "nonfinal" that action may be. Hence, the conclusion appears inescapable that in light of *Fuentes* and *Stanley*, the constitutionality of § 383 is now highly questionable, and that *Boone v. Wyman* represents an interpretation of due process no longer in keeping with the full meaning of that clause.

The case against § 383 becomes more compelling when its deficiencies from a public policy perspective are added to its probable constitutional infirmity. One such defect has already been noted[41] in reference to *Boone*, namely the imposition of the burden of going forward with litigation on the parent once the agency has refused to give up custody. This feature of the statutory procedure effectively denies any remedy to many parents who have a right to a judicial inquiry on their fitness, but lack the knowledge, financial resources, initiative or counsel necessary to institute litigation. The nature of the group affected by § 383, mostly poor people, often on welfare, who tend not to be aware of the availability of courts, or indeed are afraid of them, makes the impact of his burden particularly onerous. It is the authors' experience that agencies involved in disputes arising under § 383 seldom inform the parent of either the possibility of judicial relief via a *habeas corpus* proceeding, or his right to counsel. The remedy provided is clearly of little value to the parent without the crucial assistance of counsel,[42] yet there is no provision for assignment of free legal counsel for indigent parents.[43] Those unable to afford an attorney must obtain help from offices offering free legal services. The shortage of this resource, however, makes it an improbable tool in alleviating the problem created by § 383.[44] Thus if an

---

41. *See* text accompanying note 19, *supra*.

42. The right to be heard would be . . . of little avail if it did not comprehend the right to be heard by counsel. Even the intelligent and educated layman has small and sometimes no skill in the science of law. Gideon v. Wainwright, 332 U.S. 335, 344-45 (1963).

43. The New York Court of Appeals has recently held that an indigent parent faced with the loss of a child's custody in a neglect proceeding is entitled to *assigned* counsel. In re Ella B., 30 N.Y.2d 352, 285 N.E.2d 288, 334 N.Y.S.2d 133 (1972). Judge Fuld ruled that a denial of such assistance would be in violation of due process, citing Stanley v. Illinois (*see* note 36, *supra*). Although in an action for neglect the state sues the parent for custody, Fuld's dicta would indicate that the principle should apply to § 383 *habeas corpus* situations as well.

The parent's concern for the liberty of the child, and care and control are too fundamental an interest and right to be relinquished to the state without an opportunity for a hearing with assigned counsel if the parent is indigent. 285 N.E.2d at 290.

44. *See* Weiss, *supra* note 19.

aggrieved parent does manage to obtain counsel, institute a *habeas corpus* proceeding, and ultimately win on the merits, his good fortune has been a triumph over an oppressive system rather than the product of a rational statutory scheme.

Forcing the parent to initiate litigation has the further effect of prolonging the separation of parent and child, along with the deleterious consequences of such separation. This impact was explicitly recognized by Justice White in *Stanley*.[45] In those instances in which the parent is genuinely able and willing to provide a proper home, no environment provided by a welfare agency can equal the intimate care which can come from the natural parent.[46] In such cases, obviously, the child's interests require the renewal of its relationship with the natural parent as soon as possible.[47] Although no one would argue that all parents will in fact afford their children the necessary attention if custody is returned as demanded, it is clear that § 383 defeats an important social objective where a fully responsible parent is involved. As we may assume there are as many fit parents as not, a presumption of unfitness by the state, as allowed by § 383, seems unjustifiable. It should also be remembered that after *Stanley*, it is probably unlawful as well.[48]

One corollary to the delay effects exacerbated by § 383 is that the parent has insufficient opportunity prior to the *habeas corpus* determination to affirmatively demonstrate his fitness, for at no time will he have possession of the child. If the burden of initiating legal action were on the state, through neglect proceedings,[49] the parent would be able to utilize the period between return of the child and commencement of the court action to establish his fitness. While it is true that at both the *habeas corpus* proceeding necessitated by § 383 and a standard neglect action the technical burden of proving lack of fitness rests with the state, parental custody prior to the judicial remedy could provide the parent with valuable evidence in rebuttal to agency findings.

Finally, § 383 is indefensible because it is unnecessary. The legitimate interest of the state in safeguarding children would not be defeated by allowing the natural parent to regain custody on demand, for the state retains two effective alternative means of intervention in the home to protect this interest. Under the emergency removal provision of the Family Court Act,[50]

---

45. 405 U.S. at 647.
46. J. BOWLBY, MATERNAL CARE AND HEALTH 67 (1952).
47. The relationship between natural parent and child is so important for the latter's development that "children thrive better in bad homes than in good institutions . . ." J. BOWLBY, *supra* note 46, at 68.
48. 405 U.S. at 652-56.
49. *See* note 43, *supra*, and text accompanying note 51, *infra*.
50. N.Y. FAMILY COURT ACT § 1024 (McKinney's 1972 Pocket Supp.). This section reads in relevant part:

the state may remove a child from its home without either a court order or the parent's consent if conditions there present an imminent danger to the child's life or health. Since the state thus maintains its ability to retake temporary custody unencumbered by court proceedings if the situation so requires, there appears little justification for refusal to release the child upon the parent's demand.

Of course even in the absence of emergency conditions the parent's custody is always subject to state intervention through normal neglect proceedings in the Family Court.[51] In these proceedings, roughly equivalent to a regular civil action, the state sues the parent for custody, alleging parental unfitness. As plaintiff, the state has the burden of proof. After an evidentiary hearing, the court holds a dispositional hearing, at which point it decides on the preponderance of the evidence either to keep the child in the possession of the parent or award custody to the state. Given the availability of these remedies, there seems no reason why § 383 could not be replaced with a system which allowed the parent to recover the child on demand or required a hearing upon the parent's request.[52] Such an arrangement might benefit parent and child without hampering the state's ability of protect the child.

Although the Department of Social Services does not release figures on the quantity of temporary surrender agreements signed, it has been the authors' observation that a not insignificant number of parents are subjected to the consequences of § 383 each year. A statute which imposes such hardships and is unsound both in terms of social policy and the constitutional mandate of due process represents a needless threat to family unity in New York. Section 383 should be repealed and replaced with a provision that requires either an evidentiary hearing before an agency decision withholding custody, or release of custody on demand.

(a) A peace officer . . . or a designated employee of a city or county department of social services may remove a child from the place where he is residing . . . without an order under § 1022 (which authorizes a court order of temporary state custody before filing of neglect proceedings) and without the consent of the parent . . . if (i) the child is in such condition that his continuing in said place of residence or in the care and custody of the parent or person legally responsible for the child's care presents an imminent danger to the child's life or health. . . .

51. *Id.*, § 1031-48, and *see* note 43, *supra*.

52. Precisely this scheme is recommended in the *Standards for Services of Civil Institutions* promulgated by the Child Welfare League of America. Section 2.1 of these proposals provides in part:

When a parent enters into a voluntary agreement with a child welfare agency for placement of his child, he retains his full rights and duties with the exception of those he delegates to the agency and that the agency undertakes to provide in his stead. In situations of voluntary placement, the parent has full right to have the child returned to him on request. If the agency decides it is contrary to the welfare of the child to permit discharge, it has responsibility in such instances to take proper legal action.

4 | A CHILDREN AND YOUTH COURT: A Modest Proposal

LOIS G. FORER*

INTRODUCTION

Since the turn of the century and the enactment of the first Juvenile Court Act,[1] juvenile courts have relied increasingly on the values inherent in sociology, psychology and psychiatry, rather than law.[2] This fact, combined with a natural paternalism towards juveniles, has caused an almost complete disregard by the juvenile courts of the constitutional rights and legal safeguards to which, as American citizens, children ought to be entitled. The sociological approach, though well intentioned, has been unsuccessful, resulting not only in indiscriminate incarceration of children in jail-like institutions but also in contributing to disrespect for the rule of law.[3] The

---

*Judge, Court of Common Pleas of Philadelphia; author, No ONE WILL LISSEN: HOW OUR LEGAL SYSTEM BRUTALIZES THE YOUTHFUL POOR, John Day Co. (1970), Universal Library (1971).

1. Act of April 21, 1899, ILLINOIS LAWS § 21 (1899).
2. "The early juvenile court statutes showed a surprising solicitude for the child's legal rights." Clark, *Why Gault: Juvenile Court Theory and Impact in Historical Perspective,* in GAULT—WHAT NOW FOR THE JUVENILE COURT 5 (V. Nordin ed. 1968).
3. The dimensions of this failure are startling. The Senate Subcommittee to Investigate Juvenile Delinquency reported:
We know that over 100,000 children across the country are detained in jails or jail-like facilities, often together with adult felons, contrary to accepted correctional standards and, in many cases, contrary to State and local laws.
We know that less than five percent of our institutional personnel are involved in

shortcomings of the juvenile justice system can best be ameliorated by ensuring that children receive the full privileges and protections of the due process clause,[4] and by establishing a comprehensive bill of rights for children, with adequate procedures to enforce these rights.

The child, as I view him, is a citizen. The law must provide for him *both* the full panoply of constitutional rights guaranteed to adults (including those rights which one can extrapolate as coming into legal recognition), *and* the benefits which contemporary society owes to those members who are vulnerable and incapable of providing for themselves. This present juvenile justice system has largely ignored the former and assumed that the latter would be provided through its ministrations.[5]

Unfortunately, it is time consuming, wasteful and inefficient to attempt the reform of the juvenile justice system through litigation. Both federal and state courts properly refrain from rewriting state laws, and the decisions of the Supreme Court are but slowly and grudgingly being effectuated. It is almost five years since the *Gault* decision and, except for the increased presence of lawyers, the outmoded juvenile system has changed very little.[6] In order to have meaningful reform, the State legislatures must repeal the present juvenile court laws and enact new laws providing for a coherent system based on the realities of life in the seventies. They must create a court for children which functions like a court, its powers clearly defined and limited.

This article will present a new model law for children—the *Child and Youth Act*—designed to meet the needs and aspirations of young people today, predicated both upon a different concept of the Juvenile Court and upon a different concept of the rights and needs of children. It will begin

---

treatment or are even professionally qualified for rehabilitation. (92nd Cong. 1st Sess. Report No. 92-176)

Richard W. Velde, Associate Administrator of the Law Enforcement Assistance Administration, before that same subcommittee stated that 72 percent of those arrested at age 20 or under were rearrested within five years (March 31, 1971). Other studies indicate that more than half of the children now in correctional institutions are not even accused of a criminal offense. (Mangel, *How to Make a Criminal out of a Boy*, LOOK MAGAZINE, June 29, 1971.) In addition to the failure to produce a better record of rehabilitation, this "socialized" judicial system—designed to ameliorate the harsh effects of criminal law upon juveniles—has often delivered harsher penalties to juveniles than they would have received in traditional criminal courts. Finally, as Justice Fortas noted in In re Gault, 387 U.S. 1 (1966), the benefit of the juvenile court system in preventing juvenile indiscretions from unnecessarily haunting juvenile defendants in later years, has often not been realized.

4. In re Gault, 387 U.S. 1 (1966), although a significant breakthrough in establishing that children do have some rights, leaves many serious problems still undecided.

5. Waite, *How Far Can Court Procedure Be Socialized Without Impairing Individual Rights?* 12 J. CRIM. L. & CRIM. 339 (1922); H. LOU, JUVENILE COURTS IN THE UNITED STATES (1927); F. Allen, *The Borderland of Criminal Justice*, 11 WAYNE L. REV. 676 (1965).

6. Lefsteing, Stapleton & Teitlebaum, *In Search of Juvenile Justice: Gault and Its Implementation*, 3 LAW & SOC'Y REV. 491 (1966); Nordin, *supra*, note 2.

with a short explanation of the new court's scheme, followed by a survey of the procedures governing its operations, and an outline of a juvenile bill of rights. The final section will be the act itself, with citations to the existing *Uniform Juvenile Court Act* submitted in 1968 by the National Conference of Commissioners for Uniform State Law to the American Bar Association.[7]

The Courts

The CYA's most visible change is in its court structure. The proposed law establishes two separate fora—criminal and civil—with appropriate procedures and remedies (§ 3). This separation gives structural recognition to the difference in philosophy and technique required for a judicial proceeding to determine guilt or innocence of a delinquent act and one to determine such civil matters as custody, health, school attendance and the like.

The Civil Division. In the past the juvenile court, despite claims that it acts in the best interests of the child and community, has never seen its function as that of providing a forum where a child could bring an action to assert his claims against those who are allegedly infringing on his rights.[8] Therefore, in addition to the traditional civil subject-matter jurisdiction of juvenile courts—adoption and custody, mental health and parental rights— the civil division of the Child and Youth Court will be empowered to entertain "actions brought by or on behalf of a child to obtain redress for abuse, denial of rights or entitlements" (§ 4-B-1). This will enable the child to assert his rights against those who fail in their duty to him.

To accomplish this novel purpose, the civil division will have all the powers of any other court of record including the power to issue injunctions, mandamus and writs of habeas corpus (§ 6-B-6), and the power to cite witnesses for contempt.

The Criminal Division. The criminal division of the CYA will provide for children the substance of due process safeguards of adult criminal courts. *In re Gault* requires in juvenile delinquency proceedings the minimum components of a "fair and equitable hearing."[9] The CYA implements those minimum rights and provides further safeguards which are found in other areas of law.

---

7. Enacted almost verbatim in N.D. CENT. CODE § 27-30 (1969).

8. In most jurisdictions a juvenile must go to the civil division of the court and establish a traditional cause of action. This is difficult both because juveniles lack many rights that "citizens" have and also because their parents or guardians are protected by law from being penalized for their violations of the juvenile's rights. *Cf.* In re Holmes, 175 Pa. Super. 137, 103 A.2d 454, (1954) *aff'd.* 379 Pa. 599, *cert. den.* 348 U.S. 973. The court reiterated the traditional law that juveniles do not have a right to liberty but only to custody.

9. *Gault* made (1) proper notice, (2) the right to counsel, (3) the right to confrontation and cross-examination of witnesses, and (4) the right against self-incrimination, constitutionally required in criminal juvenile cases.

The Gault Rights

Notice. The Supreme Court responded most emphatically to the lack of notice given Gerald Gault and his parents. Justice Fortas, writing for the majority, said, "written notice [must] be given at the earliest practical time, and in any event sufficiently in advance of hearing to permit preparation."[10] But a timely petition of notice is unsatisfactory if it is not sufficiently particular to enable the child and his representative to meet the issues intelligently and competently. The CYA replaces the vague petition requirement of the UJCA which asks only for:

a statement that it is in the best interest of the child and the public that the proceedings be brought and, if delinquency or unruly conduct is alleged, that the child is in need of treatment or rehabilitation. (§ 21)

with a petition specifying, with particularity:

the offense allegedly committed by the child—including the date, time and place of the alleged crime or delinquent act. (§ 7-A-1).

Such particularity serves not only to put the defendant on notice of the charges lodged against him but properly limits the jurisdiction of the court to those specific charges.

Counsel. Consistent with *Gault*, the CYA requires that counsel be present at all adjudicatory proceedings "which may result in commitment to an institution in which the juvenile's freedom is curtailed,"[11] and that the child must be notified of this right and of his right to appointed counsel if he cannot afford his own (§§ 6-B-4; 6-D). In fact, the CYA requires that the petition include notice of these rights (§ 7-A-2). However, since representation of children is relatively new, many members of the bar have, themselves, not discarded the notion of *parens patriae*.[12] As a result they continue to make social judgments rather than legal ones. Thus the CYA, standing alone will not be enough; the judge must insure that the child not only have counsel, but that he have one that will defend him "effectively."

Confrontation and Cross-examination. The same rationale of "fair and equitable hearing" led the Supreme Court to require confrontation by and cross-examination of accusatory witnesses in juvenile actions.[13] Many traditional juvenile courts either lack the necessary contempt power to compel

10. 387 U.S. 1, 33.

11. *Id.* at 41; See also Powell v. Alabama, 287 U.S. 55 (1932); Gideon v. Wainwright, 372 U.S. 335 (1963).

12. The state has the power, under this concept of guardianship, over persons under disability such as minors, insane and incompetent persons.

13. *Cf.* UJCA § 58; ILL. REV. STAT. 1969, Ch. 37 § 704-6; People v. Y. O. 2404, 47 Misc.2d 30, 291 N.Y.S.2d 510 (1968).

witnesses to appear or choose only to exercise that power to require the accused child and his parents to appear. Few, if any, juvenile courts make available to the child subpoena power to obtain witnesses in his own defense.

Privilege Against Self-incrimination. Gault also extends the privilege against self-incrimination to juvenile delinquency proceedings. The arguments against "judicializing" the juvenile courts assert that the introduction of due process interferes with the informal, "helping" nature of the courts and violates the principle of *parens patriae*. The specific content of this claim, as to the privilege against self-incrimination, is that juvenile confessions are somehow therapeutic and should be encouraged.

Rather than rely on the statistics of general failure of the juvenile court system, Justice Fortas attacks this argument directly. Citing a study by Wheeler, Cottrell and Romasco, Fortas points out that juvenile confessions, when followed by retribution, may cause a "hostile and adverse reaction by the child" rather than having the supposed "cleansing effect."[14] Furthermore, the veracity of a juvenile confession is even more questionable than an adult's, often coming, as it does, from a frightened child seeking approval from his elders.[15]

The other half of the traditional argument against "judicializing" juvenile proceedings is that they are not criminal in nature but merely civil inquiries, leading to the conclusion that the Fifth Amendment does not apply. The court wisely assays the reality of juvenile proceedings and says:

> A proceeding where the issue is whether the child will be found
> to be "delinquent" and subject to the loss of his liberty for years
> is comparable in seriousness to a felony prosecution[16] . . . (and
> later) . . . to hold otherwise is to disregard substance because of
> the feeble enticement of the "civil" label-of-convenience attached
> to juvenile proceedings.[17]

The CYA clearly recognizes that juvenile proceedings in its criminal division are more than "comparable" to criminal cases, but are equivalent.[18]

Beyond Gault

The Supreme Court limited its consideration of juvenile court practice to these minimal rights. It chose not to consider the pre-trial procedures,[19]

---

14. 387 U.S. 1, 51; *cf. also* RUSSEL SAGE FOUNDATION, JUVENILE DELINQUENCY—ITS PREVENTION AND CONTROL (1966).

15. Gallegos v. Colorado, 370 U.S. 49 (1962); Haley v. Ohio, 332 U.S. 596 (1948). Cases holding exclusionary rule applicable to certain juvenile confessions.

16. 387 U.S. at 36.

17. *Id.* at 50.

18. But see Appendix A of Pee v. United States, 107 U.S.App.D.C. 47, 274 F.2d 556 (1959) (cites decisions in 51 jurisdictions holding that juvenile cases are civil and not criminal).

19. 387 U.S. at 36.

post-trial penalties, and many aspects of the trial itself. The CYA provides specific procedures to cover the entire spectrum of the delinquency proceeding.

Pretrial. Absent a new statute, there is nothing to protect the child's rights during the early "critical stages" of a delinquency action.

The CYA changes the operative statutory language of offense from "delinquent act," a phrase so miscomprehended and imprecise as to threaten due process,[20] to "crime" (§ 2-2). It also substitutes the constitutional requirement for arrest—a warrant or probable cause—for the less demanding and vague standards of the other codes (UJCA § 13—"reasonable grounds").

The Act abolishes the "intake interview" and limits the pre-trial hearing to determining (1) whether a *prima facie* case has been proven and (2) if it has, whether it is of such seriousness to warrant a trial rather than counseling (§ 7-B). If a *prima facie* case has not been made out or if the offense is trivial, then the juvenile cannot be put to trial.

Trial. From *In re Winship*[21] the code takes for its criminal division cases the now constitutional standard of proof—proof beyond a reasonable doubt. In *Winship*, the Supreme Court, again recognizing that the essence of the action was criminal, said that this standard is an "essential of due process and fair treatment."[22] More importantly, perhaps, Justice Brennan's majority opinion noted that the use of a more demanding standard would have no effect on the informality, flexibility or speed of the child's trial.[23] For the same reason the CYA requires the application of all the rules of evidence in its criminal division ("No hearsay or other inadmissible evidence shall be received.") (§ 7-E-9).

Jury Trials. The need for an act such as the CYA is nowhere more evident than in the discussion of the right to a jury for children charged with a serious crime. In *McKeiver v. Pennsylvania*,[24] the Supreme Court reverted to the discredited *"parens patriae"* concept, declaring: (1) that the jury trial would "remake the juvenile procedure into a fully adversary process, and [would] put an effective end to what has been the idealistic prospect of an intimate, informal, protective proceeding,"[25] and (2) that a juvenile trial is not criminal, but civil. In addition, Mr. Justice Blackmun's plurality opinion (joined by Chief Justice Burger, and Justices White and Stewart) based its decision on the conclusion that a jury is not a "necessary component of

---

20. *See* Gesicki v. Oswald, 336 F. Supp. 371 (S.D.N.Y. 1971), *aff'd without opinion* 406 U.S. 913 (1972).

21. 397 U.S. 358 (1970).

22. *Id.* at 361.

23. Opponents of the judicialization of juvenile courts consistently cite increase in cost of certain measures, both in time and money. This argument is not persuasive in regard to adult proceedings, and in juvenile cases, where the court is avowedly going out of its way to protect the interests of the child, it has even less weight.

24. 403 U.S. 528 (1971).

25. *Id.*

accurate fact finding" and that a juvenile defendant's rights will be sufficiently protected so long as there are conditions which guarantee his right to a public trial.

McKeiver v. Pennsylvania, supra, has been the subject of extensive criticism.[26] Significantly, in 1968, the United States Supreme Court in *Duncan v. Illinois* upheld the importance of the jury in criminal trials. The Court declared:

> A right to jury trial is granted to criminal defendants in order to prevent oppression by the government . . . to provid[e] . . . an estimable safeguard against the corrupt or overzealous prosecutor and against the compliant, biased or eccentric judge . . . Beyond this the jury trial provisions reflect a fundamental decision about the exercise of official power—a reluctance to entrust plenary power over life and liberty of the citizen to one judge . . .[27]

The saliency of this reasoning is no less strong in a trial of a child who by reason of his youth, inexperience and lack of resources is especially vulnerable to any abuse of power.

Public Trials. "[T]he right of the defendant to a public trial has long been regarded as fundamental in criminal procedure."[28] Many juvenile courts operate *in camera,* limiting the presence in the court room to the child, his parents and persons granted permission by the trial judge. In many juvenile courts the press is excluded by statute or by court practice (UJCA § 24(d)). The reason given for *in camera* juvenile court trials is the protection of the child from unfavorable publicity. The CYA would give the juvenile the right to a public trial in delinquency (criminal) charges. In civil matters, the child may request that the hearing be closed (§ 6-E-5). Thus, the abused child or the child with family problems could at his discretion avoid the publicity of a public hearing.

Speedy Trials. The CYA is committed to the right to a "speedy trial." The effect of a long trial period upon a young person can be overwhelming and the disruption of the child's life by incarceration can interfere not only with his schooling but also with his general development.[29] To minimize this effect, the CYA goes beyond Chief Judge Fuld's rule in New York

---

26. *Juvenile Jury Trial Case—A Regrettable 'Policy' Decision,* 32 LA. L. REV. 133 (1971); *Juries for Juveniles—A Rehabilitative Tool,* 11 J. FAM. L. 107 (1971); McKeiver v. Pennsylvania—*Juries and Juveniles—Parens Patriae Revived,* 5 IND. LEG. F. 197 (1971).

27. 391 U.S. 145, 156 (1968). Since fewer than 5% of adults accused of a crime demand jury trials, it is unlikely that the right to a jury trial would impose an excessive burden on the Children and Youth Court.

28. People v. Jelke, 308 N.Y. 56, 61 (1954).

29. *Cf.* Appendix to Justice Douglas' dissent in *McKeiver,* 403 U.S. 523, 563 (1970).

(which requires that criminal defendants be brought to trial within six months),[30] and requires that children be brought to trial within sixty days if they are not in detention and within ten days if they are (§ 7-E-1). Again, the argument against such a plan is the unconvincing claim for judicial economy. The Supreme Court's unanimous decision in *Barker v. Wingo*[31] not to set a "specified time period" which satisfies the constitutional requirement of speed for fear that it would be legislating or rule-making does not impinge upon the right and duty of the state legislatures to make their own judgments as to that requirement.[32]

Transcripts and Appeals. The CYA grants the right to appeal and to receive the transcripts of the trial in juvenile criminal cases (§ 8-B-1, 2). In *Gault* the Supreme Court refrained from passing on whether these protections were constitutionally required under the Due Process Clause. However, a recent Supreme Court decision indicates that the Court might not find that an appeal and a transcript of the trial are essential elements of due process.[33]

The right to an appeal, which is granted to all adults accused of a crime, is a necessary component of procedural due process. It provides an essential means for correcting error, bias, or prejudice which are inherent in all human institutions. When a child is deprived of his liberty, the need for the right to an appeal would appear to be obvious.

Bill of Rights. Procedural rights are worthless, however, without substantive rights. Section 5 of the CYA establishes definite substantive rights for juveniles, designed both to grant them rights as citizens and to insure them proper care, treatment and education.

First, the Act grants generally all of the privileges, immunities and protections guaranteed to adults under the Constitution, thereby statutorily, at least, eliminating any distinction between a child and a "citizen" (§ 5-8). Secondly, several provisions establish a broad array of personal rights ex-

---

30. In the spring of 1971 Chief Judge Fuld of the New York Court of Appeals proposed an Administrative Rule which would have required that any defendant held in detention for over 90 days be released on bail if the state could not bring its case (Judicial Administrative Rule 29.1). This rule was to go into effect on May 1, 1972, but the state legislature passed Chapter 184 of the 1972 New York Session Laws to supersede Judge Fuld's rule. The legislature's rule calls for the prosecutor to bring his case to the court within six months for a felony, 90 days for a misdemeanor punishable by over three months imprisonment and 30 days for a less serious misdemeanor. If the defendant is in detention, he must be released on bail in 90, 30 and 15 days respectively. However, the legislature's bill only requires that the state's case be ready; the trial may be delayed for a longer period if the court deems it necessary.

31. 407 U.S. 514 (1970).

32. *See* note 23, *supra.*

33. *See* Griffin v. Illinois, 351 U.S. 12, 14 (1959). *Griffin* did hold, however, that once a state grants the right to appeal generally, it cannot discriminate against some convicted defendants because of their poverty.

clusively for children: "the right to bodily safety and integrity and freedom from physical and mental abuse" (§ 8-1);[34] the right to medical, psychiatric and dental care (§ 8-2); the right to an education (§ 8-3); the right "to a home which provides food, shelter, clothing, care and recreation" (§ 8-4). More than mere policy statements, these rights set the groundwork for civil actions by the child himself to remedy the deficiencies in his life.

The Act specifically establishes rights and standards for the treatment of children incarcerated or removed from their homes pursuant to court order. The CYA extends the right to treatment doctrine[35] to require the provision of educational facilities and appropriate medical, dental and psychiatric care to the child who is in custody (§ 7-F-5).

The Act also implements the equal protection concept by providing in section 7-F-3 that "No order shall exceed the maximum period for which an adult could be incarcerated for the same offense."[36]

The common practice in juvenile courts is to use indeterminate sentencing. This practice reflects a philosophy which does not attempt to make the punishment fit the crime but attempts to make the punishment fit the criminal. The use of indeterminate sentencing both of children and of adults has caused much dissatisfaction.[37] Neither the prisoner nor the state knows the duration of the commitment nor the standards of conduct required for release. In an effort to permit the early release of children whose continued custody is not required either for the safety of the community or the rehabilitation of the child, the CYA requires that any order calling for over six months' confinement be reviewed by the court every six months (§ 7-F-4).

The Youth Services Board. An essential component of the Act is a comprehensive board composed of the Chief Judge of the Court, the county secretary of Welfare, representatives of the various professions involved,

---

34. This right combined with section 6 (the civil division subject-matter jurisdiction) will allow a juvenile the unprecedented right to sue to be released from parents or guardians who fail to provide these basic amenities. Although this may seem radically dangerous, the wisdom of the juvenile court judge should be sufficient to limit these actions to cases where a benefit for the child could be achieved.

35. *See* Wyatt v. Stickney, 325 F. Supp. 781 (M.D.Ala. 1971).

36. *Cf.* In re Charles Wilson, 264 A.2d 614 (Pa. Super. 1970) in which the court held that a child may be imprisoned longer than an adult only if three factors are present: (1) the juvenile must have notification at the outset of the proceedings of any and all factors upon which the state proposes to base its adjudication of delinquency, (2) the ultimate conditions upon which the findings of delinquency are based, and the facts supporting each of them, must be clearly found and set forth in the adjudication, and (3) it must be clear that the longer commitment will result in the juvenile's receiving appropriate rehabilitative care and not just in his being deprived of his liberty for a longer time.

37. A. M. Schrieber, *Indeterminate Therapeutic Incarceration of Dangerous Criminals: Perspectives and Problems,* 56 VA. L. REV. 602 (1970); D. A. Thomas, *Current Developments in Sentencing—The Criminal Justice Act in Practice,* 1969 CRIM. L. R. 235 (1969); *Dilemmas of Sentencing,* 44 CALIF. S.B.J. 332 (1969); D. Meure, *Indeterminate Sentencing in Tasmania,* 3 TASMANIA U.L. REV. 329 (1970).

and children. This board would be responsible for overseeing the institution to which children are committed and the effectiveness of the various rehabilitation programs, homes, training courses, and other social services utilized by the Court. The board would provide for coordination of services and institutions and accountability to the community.

PROPOSAL: CHILDREN AND YOUTH COURT ACT

Section 1. Purpose

The purpose of this Act shall be to establish a court for the adjudication of rights and remedies of children and transgressions of the law by children, to declare the rights of children and to provide procedures for the enforcement of said rights, and to provide interstate procedures to effectuate such rights and remedies.

COMMENT

This section eliminates the social welfare phraseology which may well be unduly vague as a standard. See *Gesicki v. Oswald*, 336 F. Supp. 371 (S.D.N.Y. 1971), *aff'd without opinion*, 406 U.S. 913 (1972). "Wholesome moral development", e.g., fails to meet the accepted tests of statutory precision. The purpose clause clearly establishes the court as a court to adjudicate civil rights and prosecute violations of law.

UJCA

SECTION 1. [*Interpretation.*] This Act shall be construed to effectuate the following public purposes:

(1) to provide for the care, protection, and wholesome moral, mental, and physical development of children coming within its provisions;

(2) consistent with the protection of the public interest, to remove from children committing delinquent acts the taint of criminality and the consequences of criminal behavior and to substitute therefor a program of treatment, training, and rehabilitation.

(3) to achieve the foregoing purposes in a family environment whenever possible, separating the child from his parents only when necessary for his welfare or in the interest of public safety;

(4) to provide a simple judicial procedure through which this Act is executed and enforced and in which the parties are assured a fair hearing and their constitutional and other legal rights recognized and enforced; and

(5) to provide simple interstate procedures which permit resort to cooperative measures among the juvenile courts of the several states when required to effectuate the purposes of this Act.

Section 2. Definitions

1. "Child" means an individual (1) who is under the age of 18 years.

COMMENT

This limits the jurisdiction of the court to the age of 18 rather than 21, and follows recent statutes establishing 18 as the age of majority.

UJCA

SECTION 2. [*Definitions.*] As used in this Act:
(1) "child" means an individual who is:
      (i) under the age of 18 years; or
      (ii) under the age of 21 years who committed an act of delinquency before reaching the age of 18 years; [or]
      [(iii) under 21 years of age who committed an act of delinquency after becoming 18 years of age and is transferred to the juvenile court by another court having jurisdiction over him;]

2. "Crime" means an act designated a crime under the law, including local ordinances of this state, except summary motor vehicle violations, or under Federal law.

COMMENT

Crime is defined as a violation of the statute and is similar to the Model Act's definition of "delinquent act." However, summary motor vehicle violations are excluded from the jurisdiction of the Children and Youth Court.

UJCA

SECTION 2 (2) "delinquent act" means an act designated a crime under the law, including local [ordinances] [or resolutions] of this state, or of another state if the act occurred in that state, or under federal law, and the crime does not fall under paragraph (iii) of subsection (4) [and is not a juvenile traffic offense as defined in section 44] [and the crime is not a traffic offense as defined in [Traffic Code of the State] other than [designate the more serious offenses which should be included in the jurisdiction of the juvenile court such as drunken driving, negligent homicide, etc.];

COMMENT

One of the difficulties of the present law is semantics. The court is predicated upon the theory that it is not a criminal court, that children do not commit crimes and that they are not punished. These are patently legal fictions. To clarify the role of the child and the court, obfuscating words are eliminated and the usual legal terminology is used.

3. "Delinquent Acts." Any child shall be guilty of a delinquent act who

1) Without cause repeatedly runs away from home; but there shall be recognized justifiable runaway from an unsuitable home.

UJCA

SECTION 2 (3) "delinquent child" means a child who has committed a delinquent act and is in need of treatment or rehabilitation;
(4) "unruly child" means a child who:
(i) while subject to compulsory school attendance is habitually and without justification truant from school;
(ii) is habitually disobedient of the reasonable and lawful commands of his parent, guardian, or other custodian and is ungovernable; or
(iii) has committed an offense applicable only to a child; and
(iv) in any of the foregoing is in need of treatment or rehabilitation;

2) Without cause habitually refuses to attend school.

COMMENT

This section is in lieu of the "unruly child" provision of the Model Act. It is strictly defined and permits a runaway child to raise the defense that his home conditions are unsuitable and also that the school conditions are improper, illegal, or unconstitutional.

4. "Deprived Child" means a child who
a) is without adequate physical care, subsistence, education or medical and psychiatric care.

COMMENT

This subsection permits the court to take jurisdiction of a child who is denied necessary care by reason of the poverty of the parents. It does not permit a child to be removed from his home solely because of poverty but to obtain proper medical and other care.

b) has been placed for care or adoption in violation of law.

c) has been abandoned, abused or mistreated by his parents, guardian, or other custodian.

d) is without a parent, guardian, or legal custodian.

UJCA

SECTION 2 (5) "deprived child" means a child who:

(i) is without proper parental care or control, subsistence, education as required by law, or other care or control necessary for his physical, mental, or emotional health, or morals, and the deprivation is not due primarily to the lack of financial means of his parents, guardian, or other custodian;

(ii) has been placed for care or adoption in violation of law; [or]

(iii) has been abandoned by his parents, guardian, or other custodian; [or]

[(iv) is without a parent, guardian, or legal custodian;]

5. "Shelter Care" means temporary care of a child who is not accused of or convicted of delinquency.

COMMENT

This prohibits the mingling of non-delinquent children with those accused or convicted of crime.

UJCA

(6) "Shelter Care" means temporary care of a child in physically unrestricted facilities;

6. "Detention" means temporary care of a child who is accused of crime or delinquency and awaiting trial or placement.

UJCA

SECTION 2 (7) "protective supervision" means supervision ordered by the court of children found to be deprived or unruly;

7. "Next Friend" means any person over the age of 18 who appears on behalf of a child for the purposes of litigation, protection, or care.

COMMENT

This section specifically permits someone other than the court officers or welfare department to act on behalf of a child. See Sec. 6-A-1, *infra*.

8. "Children and Youth Court" means the Children and Youth Court of this State.

UJCA

SECTION 2 (9) "juvenile court" means the [here designate] court of this state.

9. "Representative" means a parent, guardian, or custodian whose interest is not adverse to the child, a next friend or counsel.

COMMENT

This section recognizes that the interest of the parent, foster parent or agency may be adverse to the child and authorizes another party to represent the child.

UJCA

SECTION 2 (8) "custodian" means a person, other than a parent or legal guardian, who stands in *loco parentis* to the child or a person to whom legal custody of the child has been given by order of a court;

10. "Youth Services Board" means the Board established under Sec. 13 of this Act.

11. "Mental Disability" means such defect of intellect, emotional or psychiatric disorder which prevents the child from leading a normal life and requires special treatment.

Section 3. Court

The Children and Youth Court shall be composed of one or more judges learned in the law. It shall sit in two divisions—a civil division and a criminal division. The hearings of the two divisions shall be separate and apart. The dockets and records of the divisions shall be kept separately and labeled civil docket and criminal docket.

COMMENT

This establishes two divisions of the court with separate procedures and standards of proof.

Section 4. Jurisdiction

A. The jurisdiction of the Court shall be confined to children under the age of 18 and to persons charged with violating their rights or contributing to their delinquency. The jurisdiction of the Court shall cease when the child reaches the age of 18 and no order issued by the Court shall be effective against a child after his 18th birthday.

B. The civil division shall have exclusive original jurisdiction over:

(1) All actions brought by or on behalf of a child to obtain redress for abuse, denial of rights or entitlements.

COMMENT

This is an entirely new provision. It would permit a child to bring an action for abuse, denial of care, change of custody, property rights, welfare rights, etc.

(2) adoption,

(3) mental disability,

COMMENT

A court for children is the appropriate forum to make such determinations and placements of mentally disturbed children.

UJCA

SECTION 3. [*Jurisdiction.*]

(a) The juvenile court has exclusive original jurisdiction of the following proceedings, which are governed by this Act:

(1) proceedings in which a child is alleged to be delinquent, unruly, or deprived [or to have committed a juvenile traffic offense as defined in section 44;]

(2) proceedings for the termination of parental rights except when a part of an adoption proceeding; and

(3) proceedings arising under section 39 through 42.

(b) The juvenile court also has exclusive original jurisdiction of the following proceedings, which are governed by the laws relating thereto without regard to the other provisions of this Act:

[(1) proceedings for the adoption of an individual of any age;]

(2) proceedings to obtain judicial consent to the marriage, employment, or enlistment in the armed services of a child, if consent is required by law;

(3) proceedings under the Interstate Compact of Juveniles; [and]

(4) proceedings under the Interstate Compact on the Placement of Children; [and]

[(5) proceedings to determine the custody or appoint a guardian of the person of a child.]

[SECTION 4. [*Concurrent Jurisdiction.*] The juvenile court has concurrent jurisdiction with [_____] court of proceedings to treat or commit a mentally retarded or mentally ill child.]

(4) judicial consent to the marriage, employment or enlistment in military services, or medical, surgical or psychiatric treatment of a child if consent is required by law,

(5) proceedings under Interstate Compact on Placement of Children,

(6) proceedings to determine custody or appoint a guardian of the person of a child,

(7) proceedings under the Interstate Compact of Juveniles if the Juvenile is not alleged to be delinquent,

(8) proceedings for the termination of parental rights or emancipation of minor,

(9) proceedings for a writ of habeas corpus, unless the child is charged with or adjudicated guilty of an act of delinquency.

COMMENT

Many juvenile courts assume that they do not have the authority or jurisdiction to issue a writ of habeas corpus.

(10) all adults and institutions and organizations against whom a child has filed a pleading under this Act.

The Civil Division shall have concurrent jurisdiction with [. . .] court for the appointment of a guardian of the estate or property of a child and proceedings in which a child claims a right, interest, or entitlement in property.

COMMENT

This is a new provision and permits the court to act to protect the property interests of children.

C. The Criminal Division shall have exclusive original jurisdiction over:

(1) all criminal acts allegedly committed in this State by a child under the age of 18,

(2) all acts denominated delinquent under this statute and allegedly committed in this State by a child under the age of 18,

(3) proceedings under the Interstate Compact of Juveniles in which delinquency or crime is alleged,

(4) proceedings for a writ of habeas corpus arising out of detention or a charge of delinquency or adjudication for an act of delinquency,

COMMENT

Many juvenile courts have assumed that they lacked the power or jurisdiction to issue writs on behalf of children illegally confined.

The court would have the right and duty to determine whether a child committed to an institution is in fact receiving education, therapy and rehabilitation treatment.

(5) all adults alleged to have contributed to the delinquency of a minor.

Nothing in this section shall deprive a federal court of jurisdiction to determine the rights of a child.

Section 5. Bill of Rights [New]

Every child is guaranteed certain rights, privileges, immunities and entitlements which shall be provided by the State if the child's parents or guardian are unable or unwilling to do so, and which shall be enforceable by appropriate proceedings in the Children and Youth Court.

(1) Every child shall have the right to bodily safety and integrity and freedom from physical or mental abuse.

COMMENT

This permits a child to leave an intolerable home or institution and/or bring a proceeding to compel his removal and transfer to a suitable place.

(2) Every child shall have the right to medical, psychiatric and dental care.

COMMENT

If the parents are financially able to provide health care for their child, the court may order them to do so. If they are not, the court may require the appropriate public authorities to do so.

(3) Every child shall have the right to an education suitable to his intellectual, emotional and physical capacities.

COMMENT

This section would require the public schools to provide or purchase educational facilities for educable children who are retarded, emotionally disturbed, physically handicapped, or intellectually superior.

(4) Every child shall have the right to a home which provides food, shelter, clothing, care and recreation in a non-coercive, non-penal setting.

COMMENT

A child who has not been convicted of a crime or delinquent act could not be placed in a security institution. Group homes, foster parents and other substitute facilities will have to be provided for such children. The prohibition against peonage is significant since many institutions for children fail to provide the equivalent of a public school education and require the children to do the maintenance work of the institution, work in a factory within the institution or bind the child out to work on a farm, as a domestic servant or in industry without any compensation or at substandard rates of pay. The other provisions are necessary since it is not clear that children are protected by the Bill of Rights and the 14th Amendment.

(5) No child shall be arrested or apprehended without a warrant and no warrant shall issue except upon probable cause.
(See Section 7.)
(6) Every child shall have access to the courts for enforcement of his rights and to recover damages for wrongs suffered and for deprivation of rights, privileges, immunities, entitlements and property.

COMMENT

This section is an entirely new provision. In view of recent U.S. Supreme Court opinions and opinions of state courts, the legislature must declare that children have specific substantive and procedural rights and not rely on the assumption that the rights and privileges guaranteed under the U.S. Constitution to all "persons" will be extended to children under the equal protection clause or the due process clause.

Section 6. Procedures under Civil Division [New]

A. *Commencement of Action*

(1) Every action by or on behalf of a child shall be commenced by a pleading. A child may file a pleading on his own behalf or by a next friend. He may appear by next friend and/or counsel or *pro se.*

COMMENT

The entire civil proceeding brought by or on behalf of the child is new. Actions on behalf of deprived children are the closest approximation of this function.

(2) The Court shall provide for service of the pleading on the respondent and the subpoena of witnesses when the child, friend or counsel certifies that the testimony of such witness is necessary to the presentation or substantiation of the child's case.

COMMENT

Since most children are indigent or not in control of their own property, they will be unable to obtain witnesses unless subpoenas and service are provided by the court.

(3) The Court shall provide simple forms and assist the child in preparing his pleadings.

B. *Hearings*

(1) The rules of civil procedure shall apply.

COMMENT

There is no provision for procedural rules in the Model Uniform Juvenile Court Act. Few Juvenile Courts have adopted procedural rules.

(2) Unless the child is ill or too young to be brought to court, the child shall be present at all hearings.

(3) The child and/or his representative shall have the right to present evidence, to compel testimony and to cross-examine witnesses.

(4) The child and/or his representative shall be represented by counsel unless there is a knowing and intelligent waiver of the right to counsel. In any case in which it is alleged that the rights of a child under Sec. 5 of this Act, or under the Constitution of the United States or the Constitution of this state have been violated, and the child cannot afford to retain counsel, the Court shall appoint counsel for him. The child and/or his representative may request the appointment of any member of the bar, which request shall be honored unless good reason for not doing so is found.

The provision of counsel for a battered baby or an abused adolescent for protection of his life and safety, seems to be a proper extension of *Gault* and *Gideon*.

(5) All hearings shall be open to the press and public unless the child or his representative requests that the hearing be closed.

(6) The Court may issue injunctions, mandamus, writs of habeas corpus or take any other appropriate action to protect the rights and interests of a child.

(7) The Court may appoint a referee to take testimony and report to the Court. In all proceedings before a referee, the rules and procedures established for hearings before the Court shall apply and all the rights and privileges guaranteed to a child under this Act shall obtain.

(8) Decisions shall be made upon the preponderance of evidence adduced in court.

(9) The Court may where appropriate order psychiatric tests for the child and/or any adult subject to its jurisdiction and social investigations. All test results and reports shall be presented in court and made available to counsel for the child and other parties.

C. *Adjudications*

The court shall have authority to order appropriate parties (1) to provide medical, psychiatric and dental care, (2) to provide a suitable education, (3) to place the child in a suitable, safe non-penal home or shelter, (4) to remove the child from the home in which he was mistreated, (5) to terminate parental rights, (6) to appoint a guardian of the person and/or property of the child, (7) to award damages, and (8) to issue such writs and orders as may be appropriate to enforce the rights of the child and to carry out the purposes of this Act.

D. *Protective Custody*

(1) A child may be taken into protective custody:

(a) pursuant to an order of the Civil Division of the Court entered after a hearing.

(b) pursuant to an order of the Civil Division of the Court prior to a hearing.

(c) upon the verified petition of any responsible adult alleging that the child is being or has been abused, mistreated, neglected or abandoned and that the child's health and welfare will be jeopardized if the child is not taken into custody prior to a court hearing.

UJCA

See § 13(3), *infra*.

(d) by any responsible citizen who sees a child being abused, mistreated or endangered.

UJCA

SECTION 53. [*Protective Order.*] On application of a party or on the court's own motion the court may make an order restraining or otherwise controlling the conduct of a person if:

(1) an order of disposition of a delinquent, unruly, or deprived child has been or is about to be made in a proceeding under this Act;

(2) the court finds that the conduct (1) is or may be detrimental or harmful to the child and (2) will tend to defeat the execution of the order of disposition; and

(3) due notice of the application or motion and the grounds therefor and an opportunity to be heard thereon have been given to the person against whom the order is directed.

(2) A child taken into protective custody shall be placed in a hospital or shelter. His parent, guardian, custodian, or next friend shall be promptly notified. The child shall be permitted to communicate with counsel and friends. No child taken into protective custody shall be held in a jail, prison, correctional institution, or detention facility for delinquent children.

Section 7. Procedures under Criminal Division

A. Initiation of Proceedings

(1) Every proceeding shall commence with the filing of a verified petition specifying with particularity the offense allegedly committed by the child—including the date, time, and place of the alleged crime or delinquent act and a statement of the whereabouts of the child.

UJCA

SECTION 8. [*Commencement of Proceedings.*] A proceeding under this Act may be commenced:

(1) by transfer of a case from another court as provided in section 9;

[(2) as provided in section 44 in a proceeding charging the violation of a traffic offense;] or

(3) by the court accepting jurisdiction as provided in section 40 or accepting supervision of a child as provided in section 42; or

(4) in other cases by the filing of a petition as provided in this Act. The petition and all other documents in the proceeding shall be entitled "In the interest of _____, a [child] [minor] under [18] [21] years of age."

SECTION 21. [*Contents of Petition.*] The petition shall be verified and may be on information and belief. It shall set forth plainly:

(1) the facts which bring the child within the jurisdiction of the court, with a statement that it is in the best interest of the child and the public that the proceeding

be brought and, if delinquency or unruly conduct is alleged, that the child is in need of treatment or rehabilitation;

(2) the name, age, and residence address, if any, of the child on whose behalf the petition is brought;

(3) the names and residence addresses, if known to petitioner, of the parents, guardian, or custodian of the child and of the child's spouse, if any. If none of his parents, guardian, or custodian resides or can be found within the state, or if their respective places of residence address are unknown, the name of any known adult relative residing within the [county,] or, if there be none, the known adult relative residing nearest to the location of the court; and

(4) if the child is in custody and, if so, the place of his detention and the time he was taken into custody.

(2) The petition shall be personally served on the child and his parent, guardian or custodian. Attached to the petition shall be a statement informing the child, his parent, guardian or custodian of his right to counsel and how to obtain counsel if he is indigent.

(3) If the child is in detention, a preliminary hearing shall be held before a judge or referee within 24 hours. If the child is not in detention, the preliminary hearing shall be held not sooner than 3 days nor later than 10 days after the filing of service of the petition.

B. *Arrest*

A child may be arrested:

(1) Pursuant to an order of the Delinquency Division.

(2) Pursuant to the laws of arrest for a violation of the penal code of this Act. Except for sight arrest, no child shall be arrested or apprehended without a warrant.

(3) Every child who is arrested shall be notified of his right to remain silent, his right to counsel and of the charges against him.

(4) Every child shall have the right to call a lawyer and his representative.

(5) The police shall immediately notify the child's parent, guardian, custodian or representative that the child has been arrested, his place of confinement and the charges against him.

(6) No statement given by a child who has been arrested shall be admissible unless made in the presence of his counsel or representative.

COMMENT

The laws of arrest are made applicable to juveniles under both statutes. There is no reason to use the circumlocution "taking into custody."

The legal standards for release on bail of adults are made applicable to arrest of juveniles. Under Uniform Juvenile Court Act, Sec. 14, a child may be held in detention (jail), *inter alia*, "to protect the property of others" or because he has no person able to provide supervision and care. Protection of property is not a legally cognizable ground for detention of an adult. If a child has no suitable home, he should be placed under the "deprived child" rubric through the Civil Division.

UJCA

SECTION 13. [*Taking into Custody.*]
(a) A child may be taken into custody:
    (1)pursuant to an order of the court under this Act;
    (2) pursuant to the laws of arrest;
    (3) by a law enforcement officer [or duly authorized officer of the court] if there are reasonable grounds to believe that the child is suffering from illness or injury or is in immediate danger from his surroundings, and that his removal is necessary; or
    (4) by a law enforcement officer [or duly authorized officer of the court] if there are reasonable grounds to believe that the child has run away from his parents, guardian, or other custodian.
(b) The taking of a child into custody is not an arrest, except for the purpose of determining its validity under the constitution of this State or of the United States.

SECTION 14. [*Detention of Child.*] A child taken into custody shall not be detained or placed in shelter care prior to the hearing on the petition unless his detention or care is required to protect the person or property of others or of the child or because the child may abscond or be removed from the jurisdiction of the court or because he has no parent, guardian, or custodian or other person able to provide supervision and care for him and return him to the court when required, or an order for his detention or shelter care has been made by the court pursuant to this Act.

SECTION 15. [*Release or Delivery to Court.*]
(a) A person taking a child into custody, with all reasonable speed and without first taking the child elsewhere, shall:
    (1) release the child to his parents, guardian, or other custodian upon their promise to bring the child before the court when requested by the court, unless his detention or shelter care is warranted or required under section 14; or
    (2) bring the child before the court or deliver him to a detention or shelter care facility designated by the court or to a medical facility if the child is believed to suffer from a serious physical condition or illness which requires prompt treatment. He shall promptly give written notice thereof, together with a statement of the reason for taking the child into custody, to a parent, guardian, or other custodian and to the court. Any temporary detention or questioning of the child necessary to comply with this subsection shall conform to the procedures and conditions prescribed by this Act and rules of court.
    (3) If a parent, guardian, or other custodian, when requested, asks to bring the child before the court as provided in subsection (2) the court may issue its warrant directing that the child be taken into custody and brought before the court.

C. Detention

(1) No child shall be held in detention pending an adjudicatory hearing unless:

(a) the offense charged is non-bailable, or

(b) there is substantial reason to believe that the child will flee the jurisdiction, or

(c) there is substantial reason to believe that the child is a danger to himself, or

(d) the child has no home.

COMMENT

This establishes the same standards for pre-trial detention of children as the release of adults on bail. Since few children have financial resources, bail for children would operate even more harshly and inequitably than it does with respect to adults.

(2) While in detention a child shall have the right to communicate with parents, friends and counsel and to receive regular visits at reasonable times. No child shall be held in solitary confinement.

(3) No child shall be held in detention in a place where adults accused or convicted of crime are incarcerated.

UJCA

Section 16(d) A child alleged to be deprived or unruly may be detained or placed in shelter care only in the facilities stated in paragraphs (1), (2), and (4) of subsection (a) and shall not be detained in a jail or other facility intended or used for the detention of adults charged with criminal offenses or of children alleged to be delinquent.

D. Preliminary Hearings

At the preliminary hearing the court or referee shall determine (a) if a prima facie case has been established, (b) if so, whether the offense is of such seriousness that an adjudicatory hearing is required, (c) if the charge is not serious, the referee may refer the child to the Youth Services Board for voluntary counselling and services. No referral to the Youth Services Board shall constitute an adjudication of crime or delinquency or be deemed a waiver of the child's rights. Any child may refuse the referral and no adverse implications or consequences shall attach. If the Court determines that the case should proceed to an adjudicatory hearing, the Court shall inform the child of his right to counsel. If the child has no counsel and is indigent, the Court shall appoint counsel. If the child requests the appointment of a designated member of the bar, the request shall be honored by the Court unless good reason is shown for not doing so.

COMMENT

Since representation of children is relatively new, many members of the bar are not prepared to defend a child but continue to make social judgments as to their views of the best interests of the child. The child's need for counsel who will defend him is of crucial importance.

UJCA

SECTION 10. *[Informal Adjustment.]*

(a) Before a petition is filed, the probation officer or other officer of the court designated by it, subject to its direction, may give counsel and advice to the parties with a view to an informal adjustment if it appears:

(1) the admitted facts bring the case within the jurisdiction of the court;

(2) counsel and advice without an adjudication would be in the best interest of the public and the child; and

(3) the child and his parents, guardian or other custodian consent thereto with knowledge that consent is not obligatory.

(b) The giving of counsel and advice cannot extend beyond 3 months from the day commenced unless extended by the court for an additional period not to exceed 3 months and does not authorize the detention of the child if not otherwise permitted by this Act.

(c) An incriminating statement made by a participant to the person giving counsel or advice and in the discussions or conferences incident thereto shall not be used against the declarant over objection in any hearing except in a hearing on disposition in a juvenile court proceeding or in a criminal proceeding against him after conviction for the purpose of a presentence investigation.

SECTION 19. *[Petition—Preliminary Determination.]* A petition under this Act shall not be filed unless the [probation officer,] the judge or other person authorized by the court has determined and decided upon the petition that the filing of the petition is in the interest of the public and the child.

SECTION 20. *[Petition—Who May Make.]* Subject to section 19 the petition may be made by any person, including a law enforcement officer, who has knowledge of the facts alleged or is informed and believes that they are true.

E. *Trials*

(1) Trials shall be held no later than 10 days after the preliminary hearing if the child is in detention. If the child is not in detention, the adjudicatory hearing shall be held no later than 60 days after the preliminary hearing. Unless the child requests a continuance or good cause is shown for the delay, the criminal petition shall be dismissed and the record expunged if the trial is not held within the times specified.

COMMENT

This follows the rule of the New York courts which requires dismissal of criminal charges if the case is not brought to trial.

(2) Guilt shall be found only upon proof beyond a reasonable doubt.

(3) In all cases in which the child may be deprived of his liberty for a period in excess of six (6) months he shall have the right to trial by jury.

COMMENT

The U.S. Supreme Court has held in *McKeiver v. Pennsylvania*, *403 U.S. 528* (1971), that the U.S. Constitution does not *require* a jury trial in cases of juvenile delinquency. The legislatures of the states are not precluded from granting a jury trial and, insofar as possible, providing substantive and procedural safeguards for children which approximate those Constitutionally guaranteed to adults.

(4) All hearings shall be stenographically transcribed and the record made available to the child and his representative without cost if the child is indigent.

UJCA

Section 24(c) If requested by a party or ordered by the court the proceedings shall be recorded by stenographic notes or by electronic, mechanical, or other appropriate means. If not so recorded full minutes of the proceedings shall be kept by the court.

(5) All hearings shall be open to the press and the public.

UJCA

Section 24(d) Except in hearings to declare a person in contempt of court, [and in hearings under section 44,] the general public shall be excluded from hearings under this Act. Only the parties, their counsel, witnesses, and other persons accompanying a party for his assistance, and any other persons as the court finds have a proper interest in the proceeding or in the work of the court may be admitted by the court. The court may temporarily exclude the child from the hearing except while allegations of his delinquency or unruly conduct are being heard.

(6) At the commencement of the hearing, the judge shall ascertain that the child knows and understands the nature of the charges against him and if he is not represented that he has knowingly and understandingly waived his right to counsel.

(7) The state shall present its evidence against the child after which the child may move for a dismissal of the charges.

(8) The child shall have the right to call witnesses on his behalf, to cross-examine the witnesses and shall have the right to remain silent. No inferences shall be drawn from the child's failure to testify.

UJCA

SECTION 27. [*Other Basic Rights.*]

(a) A party is entitled to the opportunity to introduce evidence and otherwise be heard in his own behalf and to cross-examine adverse witnesses.

(b) A child charged with a delinquent act need not be a witness against or otherwise incriminate himself. An extra-judicial statement, if obtained in the course of violation of this Act or which would be constitutionally inadmissible in a criminal proceeding, shall not be used against him. Evidence illegally seized or obtained shall not be received over objection to establish the allegations made against him. A confession validly made by child out of court is insufficient to support an adjudication of delinquency unless it is corroborated in whole or in part by other evidence.

(9) No hearsay or other inadmissible evidence shall be received.

(10) The rules of criminal procedure shall apply. The child shall have the right to file pre-trial motions and to subpoena witnesses. If the child is indigent the court shall provide without cost subpoenas and service of process.

UJCA

[SECTION 18. [*Subpoena.*] Upon application of a party the court or the clerk of the court shall issue, or the court on its own motion may issue, subpoenas requiring attendance and testimony of witnesses and production of papers at any hearing under this Act.]

(11) Upon conclusion of the trial the court shall make a finding of guilt or innocence. If the court finds the child is innocent, he shall be promptly released and the record of his arrest expunged.

UJCA

SECTION 29. [*Hearing—Findings—Dismissed.*]

(a) After hearing the evidence on the petition the court shall make and file its findings as to whether the child is a deprived child, or if the petition alleges that the child is delinquent or unruly, whether the acts ascribed to the child were committed by him. If the court finds that the child is not a deprived child or that the allegations of delinquency or unruly conduct have not been established it shall dismiss the petition and order the child discharged from any detention or other restriction theretofore ordered in the proceeding.

(12) If the court finds the child guilty, the court may call for a pre-commitment investigation and require such medical, psychological, and psychiatric tests as may be appropriate. No such tests or investigation shall be made prior to a finding of guilt. Pending such investigation the child may be held in detention for a period not in excess of 30 days. The reports of all investigations and tests shall be available to the child's counsel and representative. Upon a finding of guilt the Court shall inform the child of his right to appeal and his right to have counsel and, if he is indigent, to have counsel provided for him.

UJCA

Section 29(b) If the court finds on proof beyond a reasonable doubt that the child committed the acts by reason of which he is alleged to be delinquent or unruly it shall proceed immediately or at a postponed hearing to hear evidence as to whether the child is in need of treatment or rehabilitation and to make and file its findings thereon. In the absence of evidence to the contrary evidence of the commission of acts which constitute a felony is sufficient to sustain a finding that the child is in need of treatment or rehabilitation. If the court finds that the child is not in need of treatment or rehabilitation it shall dismiss the proceeding and discharge the child from any detention or other restriction theretofore ordered.

(c) If the court finds from clear and convincing evidence that the child is deprived or that he is in need of treatment or rehabilitation as a delinquent or unruly child, the court shall proceed immediately or at a postponed hearing to make a proper disposition of the case.

(d) In hearings under subsections (b) and (c) all evidence helpful in determining the questions presented, including oral and written reports, may be received by the court and relied upon to the extent of its probative value even though not otherwise competent in the hearing on the petition. The parties or their counsel shall be afforded an opportunity to examine and controvert written reports so received and to cross-examine individuals making the reports. Sources of confidential information need not be disclosed.

F. Pre-disposition Investigation

The Court may order an investigation of the child's background, family, and school record prior to disposition and require psychiatric and other tests where appropriate. No investigation or testing shall be made prior to a finding of guilt. All such records shall be available to the child and his representative and the child may require the presence of any person making such reports and cross-examine him.

COMMENT

The investigation of children and their families prior to an adjudication is a gross waste of money and an invasion of privacy. Often the results are made available to the court prior to the hearing and affect the determination of guilt or innocence. There is at present no requirement that such reports be made available to the child's representative.

UJCA

Section 6. [Powers and Duties of Probation Officers.]

(a) For the purpose of carrying out the objectives and purposes of this Act and subject to the limitations of this Act or imposed by the Court, a probation officer shall

(1) make investigations, reports, and recommendations to the juvenile court;

(2) receive and examine complaints and charges of delinquency, unruly conduct or deprivation of a child for the purpose of considering the commencement of proceedings under this Act;

(3) supervise and assist a child placed on probation or in his protective supervision or care by order of the court or other authority of law;

(4) make appropriate referrals to other private or public agencies of the community if their assistance appears to be needed or desirable;

(5) take into custody and detain a child who is under his supervision or care as a delinquent, unruly or deprived child if the probation officer has reasonable cause to believe that the child's health or safety is in imminent danger, or that he may abscond or be removed from the jurisdiction of the court, or when ordered by the court pursuant to this Act. Except as provided by this Act a probation officer does not have the powers of a law enforcement officer. He may not conduct accusatory proceedings under this Act against a child who is or may be under his care or supervision; and

(6) perform all other functions designated by this Act or by order of the court pursuant thereto.

(b) Any of the foregoing functions may be performed in another state if authorized by the court of this state and permitted by the laws of the other state.

G. *Penalties*

(1) Upon a finding of guilt the Court shall have the authority (a) to commit a child to a suitable institution, (b) to place the child on probation, (c) suspend sentence, (d) refer him to the Youth Services Board, and/or (e) to order restitution within the financial capabilities of the child and/or a reasonable amount of public service within the physical, mental and emotional capacities of the child.

UJCA

SECTION 31. [*Disposition of Delinquent Child.*] If the child is found to be a delinquent child the court may make any of the following orders of disposition best suited to his treatment, rehabilitation, and welfare:

(1) any order authorized by section 30 for the disposition of a deprived child;

(2) placing the child on probation under the supervision of the probation officer of the court or the court of another state as provided in section 41, or [the Child Welfare Department operating within the county,] under conditions and limitations the court prescribes;

(3) placing the child in an institution, camp, or other facility for delinquent children operated under the direction of the court [or other local public authority;] or

(4) committing the child to [designate the state department to which commitments of delinquent children are made or, if there is no department, the appropriate state institution for delinquent children].

(2) Any order of commitment or probation may require the child to attend school and be conditioned upon the child attaining reasonable standards of educational proficiency and skills.

COMMENT

The Uniform Juvenile Court Act does not authorize restitution or service. Although many courts require restitution and some juvenile courts order work such as the removal of graffiti and repair of vandalized property, the statutes authorize only incarceration and probation.

(3) No order shall exceed the maximum period for which an adult could be incarcerated for the same offense. The penalty for a delinquent act shall not exceed six months commitment, probation or order requiring service.

COMMENT

This act does not require a state to maintain juvenile correctional institutions. Any state adopting the proposed act may follow the example of Massachusetts and abolish such juvenile jails substituting community based treatment centers. Whatever institution or supervision is provided, this limits the period of control to the maximum penalty for an adult. See *In re Charles Wilson, supra,* holding that a child may be incarcerated for a longer period than an adult.

UJCA

SECTION 36. *[Limitations of Time on Orders of Disposition.]*
  (a) An order terminating parental rights is without limit as to duration.
  (b) An order of disposition committing a delinquent or unruly child to the [State Department of Corrections or designated institution for delinquent children] continues in force for 2 years or until the child is sooner discharged by the [department or institution to which the child was committed]. The court which made the order may extend its duration for an additional 2 years, subject to like discharge, if:
    (1) a hearing is held upon motion of the [department or institution to which the child was committed] prior to the expiration of the order;
    (2) reasonable notice of the hearing and an opportunity to be heard is given to the child and the parent, guardian, or other custodian; and
    (3) the court finds that the extension is necessary for the treatment or rehabilitation of the child.
  (c) Any other order of disposition continues in force for not more than 2 years. The court may sooner terminate its order or extend its duration for further periods. An order of extension may be made if:
    (1) a hearing is held prior to the expiration of the order upon motion of a party or on the court's own motion;
    (2) reasonable notice of the hearing and opportunity to be heard are given to the parties affected;
    (3) the court finds that the extension is necessary to accomplish the purposes of the order extended; and
    (4) the extension does not exceed 2 years from the expiration of prior order.
  (d) Except as provided in subsection (b) the court may terminate an order of disposition or extension prior to its expiration, on or without an application of a party, if it appears to the court that the purposes of the order have been accomplished. If a party may be adversely affected by the order of termination the order may be made only after reasonable notice and opportunity to be heard have been given to him.
  (e) Except as provided in subsection (a) when the child reaches 21 years of age

all orders affecting him then in force terminate and he is discharged from further obligation or control.

(4) Any order exceeding 6 months shall be reviewed every 6 months. Thirty days before the expiration of the six month period the child and his representative shall be notified of the forthcoming review and shall have the right to appear before the court to request a modification of the order and to present evidence with respect thereto or to submit the request in writing with supporting information. Upon review the court may modify the order but shall not increase the period of time in which the child is under its orders.

COMMENT

At present there is no system of review of juvenile sentences, no parole board, and no pardon for children. Their prolonged detention in jail or a jail-like facility is recognized to be detrimental and counter-productive.

UJCA

SECTION 37(b) Except an order committing a delinquent child to the [State Department of Corrections or an institution for delinquent children,] an order terminating parental rights, or an order of dismissal, an order of the court may also be changed, modified, or vacated on the ground that changed circumstances so require in the best interest of the child. An order granting probation to a child found to be delinquent or unruly may be revoked on the ground that the conditions of probation have not been observed.

(5) No child shall be placed in a detentional facility or a correctional institution in which adults are held. Every child shall have educational facilities and appropriate medical, dental and psychiatric care while in detention and correctional institutions.

Section 8. Appeals

A. *Civil* [New]
(1) Every person aggrieved by an order of the Civil Division shall have the right to appeal. A notice of appeal shall be filed within 45 days of the adjudication.
(2) The Court shall have jurisdiction to grant a stay pending appeal.

B. *Criminal Division*

(1) A child shall have the right to appeal any order of the Criminal Division, including the adjudication of guilt and/or the penalty imposed.

The appeal shall be filed within 45 days of the adjudication and shall specify the grounds for appeal.

COMMENT

An appeal on excessive sentencing has been recommended in adult cases for many years to correct gross inequities.

UJCA

SECTION 59. [*Appeals.*]

(a) An aggrieved party, including the state or a subdivision of the state, may appeal from a final order, judgment, or decree of the juvenile court to the [Supreme Court] [court of general jurisdiction] by filing written notice of appeal within 30 days after entry of the order, judgment, or decree, or within any further time the [Supreme Court] [court of general jurisdiction] grants, after entry of the order, judgment, or decree. [The appeal shall be heard by the [court of general jurisdiction] upon the files, records, and minutes of transcript of the evidence of the juvenile court, giving appreciable weight to the findings of the juvenile court.] The name of the child shall not appear on the record on appeal.

(b) The appeal does not stay the order, judgment, or decree appealed from, but the [Supreme Court] [court of general jurisdiction] may otherwise order on application and hearing consistent with this Act if suitable provision is made for the care and custody of the child. If the order, judgment or decree appealed from grants the custody of the child to, or withholds it from, one or more of the parties to the appeal it shall be heard at the earliest practicable time.

(2) The Court shall have jurisdiction to grant a stay pending appeal and/or to release the child from detention pending appeal.

The transcript of any civil and/or criminal trial shall be made available to the child without cost for the purposes of appeal upon certification by counsel that the child cannot afford the cost of the transcript.

COMMENT

There is no reason to grant a trial de novo if the original trial has been properly conducted and a transcript made. Retrial of a case imposes an undue burden on the child and his counsel. Since the rules of civil and criminal procedure are made applicable, appropriate post trial motions are available.

Section 9. Records

A. No adjudication of crime or delinquency shall be considered a criminal conviction. The records of the court shall not be released to any individual, organization, institution, or governmental agency without the consent of the child and his representative if he is under the age of 18, or without the consent of the child if he is over the age of 18.

UJCA

SECTION 33. [*Order of Adjudication—Non-Criminal.*]

(a) An order of disposition or other adjudication in a proceeding under this Act is not a conviction of crime and does not impose any civil disability ordinarily resulting from a conviction or operate to disqualify the child in any civil service application or appointment. A child shall not be committed or transferred to a penal institution or other facility used primarily for the execution of sentences of persons convicted of a crime.

(b) The disposition of a child and evidence adduced in a hearing in juvenile court may not be used against him in any proceeding in any court other than a juvenile court, whether before or after reaching majority, except in dispositional proceedings after conviction of a felony for the purposes of a pre-sentence investigation and report.

B. No civil records shall be made public or released to any individual or agency, public or private, without the written consent of the child if he is 18 years of age or older or with the written consent of the child's parent or representative if he is under the age of 18.

UJCA

SECTION 57. [*Sealing of Records.*]

(a) On application of a person who has been adjudicated delinquent or unruly or on the court's own motion, and after a hearing, the court shall order the sealing of the files and records in the proceeding, including those specified in sections 55 and 56, if the court finds:

(1) 2 years have elapsed since the final discharge of the person;

(2) since the final discharge he has not been convicted of a felony, or of a misdemeanor involving moral turpitude, or adjudicated a delinquent or unruly child and no proceeding is pending seeking conviction or adjudication; and

(3) he has been rehabilitated.

(b) Reasonable notice of the hearing shall be given to:

(1) the [prosecuting attorney of the county];

(2) the authority granting the discharge if the final discharge was from an institution or from parole; and

(3) the law enforcement officers or department having custody of the files and records if the files and records specified in sections 55 and 56 are included in the application or motion.

(c) Upon the entry of the order the proceeding shall be treated as if it never occurred. All index references shall be deleted and the person, the court, and law enforcement officers and departments shall properly reply that no record exists with respect to the person upon inquiry in any matter. Copies of the order shall be sent to each agency or official therein named. Inspection of the sealed files and records thereafter may be permitted by an order of the court upon petition by the person who is the subject of the records and only by those persons named in the order.

Section 10. Expungement

Upon application of a child the record of his apprehension, arrest, preliminary hearing, hearing and/or adjudication may be expunged. Upon the entry of such an order the records shall be physically destroyed and a certification of that fact shall be made to the court.

COMMENT

There is no right to a pardon for delinquency. This provision will protect a child from having his juvenile records prejudice him in adult life.

Section 11. Probation

The court of each jurisdiction shall appoint a chief probation officer who shall be qualified by training, experience and temperament. He shall be in charge of the probation services of the Delinquency Division of the Court and shall employ, subject to the civil service laws, such probation officers, assistants and supporting personnel as are authorized by law. The Chief Probation Officer shall be responsible to the court and to the Chief Juvenile Probation Officer of the state. Probation services shall be borne by the state.

The duties of the Probation Officers shall be to supervise children placed on probation by the Criminal Division of the court, to render reports to the court and to make pre-disposition investigations.

No social or other investigation of a child shall be made until after an adjudication of crime or delinquency by the court.

COMMENT

The role of the probation officer is limited to pre-sentence investigations and supervision of children found guilty who are placed on probation. The present practice continued in the Uniform Juvenile Court Act of having the probation officer conduct investigations for the prosecution, social investigations and act as the "friend" of the child places incompatible and excessive powers in the probation officer.

UJCA

SECTION 5. [Probation Services.]

[(a) [In [counties] of over _____ population] the [_____] court may appoint one or more probation officers who shall serve [at the pleasure of the court] [and are subject to removal under the civil service laws governing the county]. They have the powers and duties stated in section 6. Their salaries shall be fixed by the court with the approval of the [governing board of the county]. If more than one probation officer is appointed, one may be designated by the court as the chief probation officer or director of court services, who shall be responsible for the administration of the probation services under the direction of the court.]

[(b) In all other cases the [Department of Corrections] [state [county] child welfare department] [or other appropriate state agency] shall provide suitable probation services to the juvenile court of each [county.] The cost thereof shall be paid out of the general revenue funds of the [state] [county]. The probation officer or other qualified person assigned to the court by the [Department of Corrections] [state [county] child welfare department] [or other appropriate state agency] has the powers and duties stated in section 6.]

Section 12. Revocation of Probation [New]

A probation officer may file a petition to revoke probation specifying with particularity the violations of law and/or the violations of the terms of probation. Such petition shall be personally served on the child and his parents or representative and shall contain a notice informing the child that he is entitled to be represented by counsel at the hearing to revoke probation and, if he cannot afford to retain counsel, how to obtain free legal representation. Not less than 3 nor more than 10 days after the service of such petition a hearing shall be held in the Criminal Division of the Court. The procedures and rules applicable to all hearings in Criminal Division shall apply. Upon a finding that the child has committed a crime or violated a material condition of probation, the court may revoke the order of probation and require the child to serve the penalty which could have been imposed. An order of revocation shall be appealable in the same manner as any other adjudication or order by the Criminal Division.

COMMENT

This follows recent court decisions requiring a due process hearing for the revocation of parole of an adult.

Section 13. Youth Services Board [New]

A Youth Services Board shall be established in each judicial jurisdiction of the state. It shall be composed of the Chief Judge of the Children and Youth Court or his delegate, the County Secretary of Welfare, three (3) adults designated by the Mayor, (county commissioners) one of whom shall be a lawyer, one a doctor, and one a social worker or educator, three (3) adults designated by the Governor, one of whom shall be a lawyer, one a doctor, and one a social worker or educator, three (3) children between the ages of 15 and 18 designated by the Superintendent of Public Schools in consultation with the heads of the non-public schools of the jurisdiction.

It shall be the duty of the Board:

(1) To visit and oversee all institutions and facilities in which children are placed or committed by the courts and to issue a public report annually.

(2) To recommend the establishment or purchase of such services as may be needed including, but not limited to, drug rehabilitation programs, half-way houses, youth homes, recreational programs, vocational training, psychiatric and counselling services.

(3) To oversee the operations of all services for children referred or committed by the Court.

The Youth Services Board shall examine the needs of the children of the community for group homes, foster homes, recreation, supplemental and remedial education, employment and training, crime prevention, physical and mental health care and render annual written reports to the governor which shall be public.

Upon the request of any child, parent, school teacher, social worker, doctor, lawyer or other person, or upon referral by the court, the Board shall ascertain the needs of the child and on a purely voluntary basis provide such shelter, care, medical care, treatment, education and training as the child requires. The Board may operate homes and shelters for children or contract with other agencies to provide such facilities. It shall contract with hospitals, mental health clinics, schools and other qualified agencies and individuals to provide necessary services.

The Board shall maintain accurate records of the children served and the services rendered. Such records shall be open to inspection but the identities of the children shall remain confidential.

Section 14. Mental Disability [New]

A petition may be filed by any responsible person over the age of 21, asking that a child be declared mentally disabled and that suitable education, medical and psychiatric care be provided for him. If the child denies that he is medically disabled or if the petition seeks to have the child placed in an institution, the court shall appoint counsel to represent the child.

Section 15. Immunity of Next Friend

Any person who files a pleading on behalf of a child as next friend, guardian, custodian or representative shall have immunity for any allegations contained in said pleadings, testimony or exhibits. Such person shall have access to the hospital records, school records, and other confidential information germane to the pleading to the same extent as a natural parent or legal guardian.

UJCA

SECTION 51. [Guardian ad litem.] The court at any stage of a proceeding under this Act, on application of a party or on its own motion, shall appoint a guardian ad litem for a child who is a party to the proceeding if he has no parent, guardian, or custodian appearing on his behalf or their interests conflict with his or in any other case in which the interests of the child require a guardian. A party to the proceeding or his employee or representative shall not be appointed.

Section 16. Counselling [New]

The Court shall appoint a Chief Counsellor who shall be qualified by education, training and temperament to advise and assist non-delinquent children. He shall be responsible to the Civil Division of the Court. The Chief Counsellor shall appoint such assistants, and supporting personnel as are authorized by law, who shall be qualified and subject to the civil service law. The cost of counselling services shall be borne by the state.

The duties of the counsellors shall be, upon direction of the Court, to investigate cases of alleged child abuse, dependency, neglect, mental disability and such cases in which the child and/or his representative seeks the assistance of the counsellor in connection with any matter before the Civil Division of the Court. The counsellors shall report to the court. The counsellors shall at the direction of the court investigate suitable homes, care, education, treatment and employment and assistance for children whose cases are before the Civil Division and make reports to the court. Such reports shall be available to the child's representative and counsel.

Section 17. Institutions [New]

Every child in an institution, foster home or other facility shall receive the equivalent of public school education, medical, and dental care, and psychiatric care if needed. Upon the request of the Chief Administrator of the institution, or upon petition by the child and/or his representative, the court shall conduct a mental health hearing. Upon finding that a child is mentally disabled, the court shall order the child transferred to a suitable mental institution. Children in institutions shall have the right to have visitors and to communicate with counsel and next friend without censorship.

Any responsible citizen group shall have the right to visit and inspect every institution for children at reasonable times. The privacy of the children shall be respected.

Section 18. Referees

The Court may appoint referees learned in the law to conduct preliminary hearings under the Criminal Division and under the Civil Division to take testimony and report to the Court.

COMMENT

Note that the Model Act permits referees not learned in the law to conduct hearings and make final dispositions and adjudications. Many juvenile court laws prohibit preliminary hearings. E.g., Pa. 11 P.S. § 246(3). However, most courts have a preliminary procedure called "intake" which is conducted by social workers or probation officers not learned in the law. There are no rules or standards by which proceedings are governed.

UJCA

[SECTION 7. [Referees.]

(a) The judge may appoint one or more persons to serve at the pleasure of the judge as referees on a full or part-time basis. A referee shall be a member of the bar [and shall qualify under the civil service regulations of the County]. His compensation shall be fixed by the judge [with the approval of the [governing board of the County] and paid out of [_____]].

(b) The judge may direct that hearings in any case or class of cases be conducted in the first instance by the referee in the manner provided by this Act. Before commencing the hearing the referee shall inform the parties who have appeared that they are entitled to have the matter heard by the judge. If a party objects the hearing shall be conducted by the judge.

(c) Upon the conclusion of a hearing before a referee he shall transmit written findings and recommendations for disposition to the judge. Prompt written notice and copies of the findings and recommendations shall be given to the parties to the proceeding. The written notice also shall inform them of the right to a rehearing before the judge.

(d) A rehearing may be ordered by the judge at any time and shall be ordered if a party files written request therefor within 3 days after receiving the notice required in subsection (c).

(e) Unless a rehearing is ordered the findings and recommendations become the findings and order of the court when confirmed in writing by the judge.]

Section 19. Transfer of Cases to Adult Court

The Criminal Division may, after a hearing, transfer the case of any child over the age of 15 who is accused of crime to the adult court. Before making such a transfer, the Criminal Division shall find:

(1) That the child is mentally and emotionally able to understand the charges against him and intelligently cooperate in his defense.

(2) That the charge is sufficiently serious to warrant prosecution as an adult.

COMMENT

This section codifies the ruling in Kent v. United States, 383 U.S. 541 (1966), and establishes appropriate standards.

UJCA

SECTION 34. [*Transfer to Other Courts.*]

(a) After a petition has been filed alleging delinquency based on conduct which is designated a crime or public offense under the laws, including local ordinances, [or resolutions] of this state, the court before hearing the petition on its merits may transfer the offense for prosecution to the appropriate court having jurisdiction of the offense if:

(1) the child was 16 or more years of age at the time of the alleged conduct;

(2) a hearing on whether the transfer should be made is held in conformity with sections 24, 26, and 27;

(3) notice in writing of the time, place, and purpose of the hearing is given to the child and his parents, guardian, or other custodian at least 3 days before the hearing;

(4) the court finds that there are reasonable grounds to believe that

(i) the child committed the delinquent act alleged;

(ii) the child is not amenable to treatment or rehabilitation as a juvenile through available facilities;

(iii) the child is not committable to an institution for the mentally retarded or mentally ill; and

(iv) the interests of the community require that the child be placed under legal restraint or discipline.

(b) The transfer terminates the jurisdiction of the juvenile court over the child with respect to the delinquent acts alleged in the petition.

(c) No child, either before or after reaching 18 years of age. shall be prosecuted for an offense previously committed unless the case has been transferred as provided in this section.

(d) Statements made by the child after being taken into custody and prior to the service of notice under subsection (a) or at the hearing under this section are not admissible against him over objection in the criminal proceedings following the transfer.

(e) If the case is not transferred the judge who conducted the hearing shall not over objection of an interested party preside at the hearing on the petition. If the case is transferred to a court of which the judge who conducted the hearing is also a judge he likewise is disqualified from presiding in the prosecution.

Section 20. Transfer of Cases from Adult Court

Whenever it appears that a defendant in a criminal proceeding is under the age of 18 the court (or magistrate, or alderman, or other judicial officer) shall forthwith transfer the defendant together with a copy of all papers to the Children and Youth Court, which shall promptly conduct a waiver hearing under the provisions of Sec. 19 of this Act. If the defendant has reached the age of 18 by the time of his hearing in Adult Court, that court shall retain jurisdiction.

COMMENT

The Children and Youth Court has no jurisdiction over children who have reached the age of 18. Compare U.J.C.A. § 3.

UJCA

SECTION 9. [*Transfer from Other Courts.*] If it appears to the court in a criminal proceeding that the defendant [is a child] [was under the age of 18 years at the time the offense charged was alleged to have been committed], the court shall forthwith transfer the case to the juvenile court together with a copy of the accusatory pleading and other papers, documents, and transcripts of testimony relating to the case. It shall order that the defendant be taken forthwith to the juvenile court or to a place of detention designated by the juvenile court, or release him to the custody of his parent, guardian, custodian, or other person legally responsible for him, to be brought before the juvenile court at a time designated by that court. The accusatory pleading may serve in lieu of a petition in the juvenile court unless that court directs the filing of a petition.

Section 21. Emancipation [New]

A child may petition the Civil Division Court to be emancipated. If the court shall find that the child is mentally, physically and emotionally able to choose his own residence, to maintain himself, intelligently to direct his education and training and employment, the court shall enter an order of emancipation. An emancipated child shall be entitled to retain his own earnings, choose his own residence and receive directly any rights, entitlements and benefits to which he may legally be entitled. An order of emancipation shall not terminate parental obligations.

COMMENT

This section permits a child of sufficient maturity to live without parental supervision if the court shall permit him to do so. Such emancipated child shall be entitled to receive his own public assistance payment.

Section 22. Venue

A. Criminal Division

A proceeding in the Criminal Division shall be instituted in the county in which the offense allegedly occurred. Upon request of the child and/or his representative, the proceedings may be transferred to the county of the child's residence. With or without the consent of the child, after conviction, the case may be transferred to the county of the child's residence for disposition. Certified copies of all documents and records pertaining to the case shall accompany the transfer.

COMMENT

No social investigations or records are made prior to conviction contrary to the procedure mandated under the U.J.C.A. The trial must be held where the offense allegedly occurred.

UJCA

SECTION 11. [*Venue.*] A proceeding under this Act may be commenced in the [county] in which the child resides. If delinquent or unruly conduct is alleged, the proceeding may be commenced in the [county] in which the acts constituting the alleged delinquent or unruly conduct occurred. If deprivation is alleged, the proceeding may be brought in the [county] in which the child is present when it is commenced.

SECTION 12. [*Transfer to Another Juvenile Court Within the State.*]

(a) If the child resides in a [county] of the state and the proceeding is commenced in a court of another [county], the court, on motion of a party or on its own motion made prior to final disposition, may transfer the proceeding to the county of the child's residence for further action. Like transfer may be made if the residence of the child changes pending the proceeding. The proceeding shall be transferred if the child has been adjudicated delinquent or unruly and other proceedings involving the child are pending in the juvenile court of the [county] of his residence.

(b) Certified copies of all legal and social documents and records pertaining to the case on file with the clerk of the court shall accompany the transfer.

B. *Civil Proceedings* [New]

A civil proceeding may be initiated by or on behalf of a child in any county in which the child is physically present, in the county of the child's residence or in the county in which the events giving rise to the proceeding occurred. The Court may transfer the proceeding to any other county in which venue lies unless the transfer will work hardship or inconvenience on the parties.

Section 23. *Non-resident Child*

A. The Criminal Division upon finding that a child who has been convicted is a resident of another State may transfer the child to the Juvenile Court of that jurisdiction for disposition. The Court may not commit a child to an institution in another state. Whenever possible a child shall be committed to an institution in the county in which he lives.

If a child, while on probation, becomes a resident of another state, the Court may request the appropriate court of that state to accept jurisdiction and to continue supervision.

B. The Civil Division upon finding that a child who is under its jurisdiction has moved or is about to move to another county or state, or who is placed in the custody of a non-resident, may request the appropriate court of that jurisdiction to provide supervision and/or services. With the written consent of the child's representative or counsel, the court may request such court to assume jurisdiction.

Whenever possible, a child shall be placed in an institution, in the county in which he lives. Placement with relatives or friends, whether within the same state or not, shall be preferred to institutionalization.

C. Upon acceptance of jurisdiction by the Court of another county or another state, the jurisdiction of the Children and Youth Court shall cease. All records and certified copies of the orders of the court shall accompany the transfer. All appeals or other petitions shall be addressed to the court accepting jurisdiction.

D. Where out of county or out of state supervision, care and protection is requested and granted, the requesting county shall bear the reasonable costs of such services including transportation.

UJCA

SECTION 39. [Disposition of Non-Resident Child.]

(a) If the court finds that a child who has been adjudged to have committed a delinquent act or to be unruly or deprived is or is about to become a resident of another state which has adopted the Uniform Juvenile Court Act, or a substantially similar Act which includes provisions corresponding to sections 39 and 40, the court may defer hearing on need for treatment or rehabilitation and disposition and request by any appropriate means the juvenile court of the [county] of the child's residence or prospective residence to accept jurisdiction of the child.

(b) If the child becomes a resident of another state while on probation or under protective supervision under order of a juvenile court of this State, the court may request the juvenile court of the [county] of the state in which the child has become a resident to accept jurisdiction of the child and to continue his probation or protective supervision.

(c) Upon receipt and filing of an acceptance the court of this State shall transfer custody of the child to the accepting court and cause him to be delivered to the person designated by that court to receive his custody. It also shall provide that court with certified copies of the order adjudging the child to be a delinquent, unruly, or deprived child, of the order of transfer, and if the child is on probation or under protective supervision under order of the court, of the order of disposition. It also shall provide that court with a statement of the facts found by the court of this State and any recommendations and other information it considers of assistance to the accepting court in making a disposition of the case or in supervising the child on probation or otherwise.

(d) Upon compliance with subsection (c) the jurisdiction of the court of this State over the child is terminated.

SECTION 41. [Ordering Out-of-State Supervision.]

(a) Subject to the provisions of this Act governing dispositions and to the extent that funds of the [county] are available the court may place a child in the custody of a suitable person in another state. On obtaining the written consent of a juvenile court of another state which has adopted the Uniform Juvenile Court Act or a substantially similar Act which includes provisions corresponding to sections 41 and 42 the court of this State may order that the child be placed under the supervision of a probation officer or other appropriate official designated by the accepting court. One certified copy of the order shall be sent to the accepting court and another filed with the clerk of the [Board of County Commissioners] of the [county] of the requesting court of this State.

(b) The reasonable cost of the supervision including the expenses of necessary travel shall be borne by the [county] of the requesting court of this State. Upon receiving a certified statement signed by the judge of the accepting court of the cost incurred by the supervision the court of this State shall certify if it so appears that the sum so stated was reasonably incurred and file it with [the appropriate officials] of the [county] [state] for payment. The [appropriate officials] shall thereupon issue a warrant for the sum stated payable to the [appropriate officials] of the [county] of the accepting court.

Section 24. Non-resident Child

If the appropriate court of another state or county requests the Children and Youth Court to assume supervision, protection or jurisdiction over a child who has moved or is about to move into the territorial jurisdiction of the Children and Youth Court, the Court may do so. Such child shall have the right to petition the court for any remedies, relief or protection which would be available to a child under order of this court and shall be entitled to all the procedural and substantive rights under the Act.

The reasonable expenses of supervision, enforcement and protection shall be borne by the requesting jurisdiction.

COMMENT

This section avoids the difficulties of "residence" and enforcement of orders which would not be legally permissible under this Act. All transfers must be handled through the Children and Youth Court and cannot be made by and between probation officers. A child who has been transferred is guaranteed access to the Court where he is physically present. There is no provision for return of runaways, incorrigibles, etc., without court order. See, especially, U.J.C.A. § 43 which vests broad powers in the probation officer.

UJCA

SECTION 40. [*Disposition of Resident Child Received from Another State.*]

(a) If a juvenile court of another state which has adopted the Uniform Juvenile Court Act, or a substantially similar Act which includes provisions corresponding to sections 39 and 40, requests a juvenile court of this State to accept jurisdiction of a child found by the requesting court to have committed a delinquent act or to be an unruly or deprived child, and the court of this State finds, after investigation that the child is, or is about to become, a resident of the [county] in which the court presides, it shall promptly and not later than 14 days after receiving the request issue its acceptance in writing to the requesting court and direct its probation officer or other person designated by it to take physical custody of the child from the requesting court and bring him before the court of this State or make other appropriate provisions for his appearance before the court.

(b) Upon the filing of certified copies of the orders of the requesting court (1) determining that the child committed a delinquent act or is an unruly or deprived child, and (2) committing the child to the jurisdiction of the juvenile court of this State, the court of this State shall immediately fix a time for a hearing on the need for treatment or rehabilitation and disposition of the child or on the continuance of any probation or protective supervision.

(c) The hearing and notice thereof and all subsequent proceedings are governed by this Act. The court may make any order of disposition permitted by the facts and this Act. The orders of the requesting court are conclusive that the child committed the delinquent act or is an unruly or deprived child and of the facts found by the court in making the orders, subject only to section 37. If the requesting court has made an order placing the child on probation or under protective supervision, a like order shall be entered by the court of this State. The court may modify or vacate the order in accordance with section 37.

SECTION 42. [*Supervision Under Out-of-State Order.*]

(a) Upon receiving a request of a juvenile court of another state which has adopted the Uniform Juvenile Court Act, or a substantially similar act which includes provisions corresponding to sections 41 and 42 to provide supervision of a child under the jurisdiction of that court, a court of this State may issue its written acceptance to the requesting court and designate its probation or other appropriate officer who is to provide supervision, stating the probable cost per day therefor.

(b) Upon the receipt and filing of a certified copy of the order of the requesting court placing the child under the supervision of the officer so designated the officer shall arrange for the reception of the child from the requesting court, provide supervision pursuant to the order and this Act, and report thereon from time to time together with any recommendations he may have to the requesting court.

Section 25. Children without Proper Care

A. The Civil Division of the Court shall upon finding that a child is without a proper home or lacks necessary care, after notice to the natural parents, legal guardian or person with whom the child was residing, shall enter an order placing the child in a suitable home and/or requiring that necessary services shall be provided for him. In making such an order the court shall be guided by (a) the best interests and needs of the child, (b) the preference of the child, and (c) the desirability of placing a child with relatives, friends, or in a home rather than in an institution.

Every order removing a child from his home shall be reviewed every six months. Every order requiring the furnishing of services to a child shall require regular reports to the court respecting the services rendered and the condition of the child.

UJCA

SECTION 30. [*Disposition of Deprived Child.*]

(a) If the child is found to be a deprived child the court may make any of the following orders of disposition best suited to the protection and physical, mental, and moral welfare of the child.

(1) permit the child to remain with his parents, guardian, or other custodian, subject to conditions and limitations as the court prescribes, including supervision as directed by the court for the protection of the child;

(2) subject to conditions and limitations as the court prescribes transfer temporary legal custody to any of the following:

(i) any individual who, after study by the probation officer or other person or agency designated by the court, is found by the court to be qualified to receive and care for the child;

(ii) an agency or other private organization licensed or otherwise authorized by law to receive and provide care for the child; or

(iii) the Child Welfare Department of the [county] [state,] [or other public agency authorized by law to receive and provide care for the child;]

(iv) an individual in another state with or without supervision by an appropriate officer under section 40; or

(3) without making any of the foregoing orders transfer custody of the child to the juvenile court of another state if authorized by and in accordance with section 39 if the child is or is about to become a resident of that state.

(b) Unless a child found to be deprived is found also to be delinquent he shall not be committed to or confined in an institution or other facility designed or operated for the benefit of delinquent children.

If the child has no suitable relative or next friend, the court may appoint an individual, voluntary or public agency to act as next friend of the child and to report regularly to the court with respect to his condition. The court appointment of a next friend shall not preclude the later appearance of another individual or agency who wishes to act as next friend of the child.

B. The Criminal Division, whenever it finds that a child is not guilty of the offense with which he is charged but it appears that he is without proper care, shall transfer the matter to the Civil Division for appropriate proceedings.

No child shall be placed pursuant to an order of the Civil Division in a place of detention or institution for children charged with or convicted of criminal offenses or delinquent acts.

UJCA

SECTION 38. [*Rights and Duties of Legal Custodian.*] A custodian to whom legal custody has been given by the court under this Act has the right to the physical custody of the child, the right to determine the nature of the care and treatment of the child, including ordinary medical care and the right and duty to provide for the care, protection, training, and education, and the physical, mental, and moral welfare of the child, subject to the conditions and limitations of the order and to the remaining rights and duties of the child's parents or guardian.

(See UJCA § 30.)

Section 26. Mentally Disabled Child

If, at any time, it appears that a child under the jurisdiction of the Civil or Criminal Division is suffering from such severe mental disability as to require commitment, the court shall notify the appropriate authorities to institute mental health commitment proceedings or appoint a guardian ad litem for this purpose and shall suspend action on all pending matters. If the child does not have counsel, the Court shall appoint counsel to represent him in the mental health proceedings.

UJCA

SECTION 35. [*Disposition of Mentally Ill or Mentally Retarded Child.*]
(a) If, at a dispositional hearing of a child found to be a delinquent or unruly child or at a hearing to transfer a child to another court under section 34, the evidence indicates that the child may be suffering from mental retardation or mental illness the court before making a disposition shall commit the child for a period not exceeding 60 days to an appropriate institution, agency, or individual for study and report on the child's mental condition.

(b) If it appears from the study and report that the child is committable under the laws of this state as a mentally retarded or mentally ill child the court shall order the child detained and direct that within 10 days after the order is made the appropriate authority initiate proceedings for the child's commitment.

(c) If it does not so appear, or proceedings are not promptly initiated or the child is found not to be committable, the court shall proceed to the disposition or transfer of the child as otherwise provided by this Act.

Section 27. Termination of Parental Rights

The Court may, upon petition by a child, his representative or any responsible private or public agency, order termination of parental rights when

1) the parent has abandoned the child or

2) the parent has willfully and repeatedly abused the child.

The parents shall be personally served with a copy of the petition and notice of hearing and shall be informed of their rights to counsel. If the child is illegitimate and the father has acknowledged paternity, the father shall be notified. The child shall be represented by counsel. If the child does not have a representative, the court shall appoint a guardian ad litem to retain counsel and to protect the child pending the proceedings and to assure his appropriate care and placement if parental rights are terminated. Any responsible individual or public or private agency may serve as guardian ad litem.

An order of termination of parental rights shall terminate all rights of the parent to custody and control. The parent shall not be entitled to notice of any future proceedings affecting the child and the parent's consent shall not be required in any adoption proceedings. Such order shall not deprive the child of any rights of inheritance or other benefits to which he may be legally entitled from his natural parents.

COMMENT

Note that contrary to U.J.C.A. a child whose parental rights have been terminated will continue to inherit from his parent and receive social security, military, pension and other benefits.

UJCA

SECTION 47. [*Termination of Parental Rights.*]

(a) The court by order may terminate the parental rights of a parent with respect to his child if:

(1) the parent has abandoned the child;

(2) the child is a deprived child and the court finds that the conditions and causes of the deprivation are likely to continue or will not be remedied and that by reason thereof the child is suffering or will probably suffer serious physical, mental, moral, or emotional harm; or

(3) the written consent of the parent acknowledged before the court has been given.

(b) If the court does not make an order of termination of parental rights it may grant an order under section 30 if the court finds from clear and convincing evidence that the child is a deprived child.

SECTION 48. [*Proceeding for Termination of Parental Rights.*]

(a) The petition shall comply with section 21 and state clearly than an order for termination of parental rights is requested and that the effect thereof will be as stated in the first sentence of section 49.

(b) If the paternity of a child born out of wedlock has been established prior to the filing of the petition the father shall be served with summons as provided by this Act. He has the right to be heard unless he has relinquished all parental rights with reference to the child. The putative father of the child whose paternity has not been established, upon proof of his paternity of the child, may appear in the proceedings and be heard. He is not entitled to notice of hearing on the petition unless he has custody of the child.

SECTION 49. [*Effect of Order Terminating Parental Rights.*] An order terminating the parental rights of a parent terminates all his rights and obligations with respect to the child and of the child to him arising from the parental relationship. The parent is not thereafter entitled to notice of proceedings for the adoption of the child by another nor has he any right to object to the adoption or otherwise to participate in the proceedings.

SECTION 50. [*Commitment to Agency.*]

(a) If, upon entering an order terminating the parental rights of a parent, there is no parent having parental rights, the court shall commit the child to the custody of [the State (County) Child Welfare Department] or a licensed child-placing agency, willing to accept custody for the purpose of placing the child for adoption, or in the absence thereof in a foster home or take other suitable measures for the care and welfare of the child. The custodian has authority to consent to the adoption of the child, his marriage, his enlistment in the armed forces of the United States, and surgical and other medical treatment for the child.

(b) If the child is not adopted within 2 years after the date of the order and a general guardian of the child has not been appointed by the [_____] court, the child shall be returned to the court for entry of further orders for the care, custody, and control of the child.

Section 28. Records

All records and files with respect to a child under the Civil and Criminal Divisions of this Court shall be kept separate and apart from the records and files of adults under the jurisdiction of the Court. The records of the child shall not be open to public inspection and their contents shall not be disclosed to any individual or public or private agency without the authorization of the Court.

UJCA

SECTION 54. [*Inspection of Court Files and Records.*] [Except in cases arising under section 44] all files and records of the court in a proceeding under this Act are open to inspection only by:

(1) the judge, officers, and professional staff of the court;

(2) the parties to the proceeding and their counsel and representatives;

(3) a public or private agency or institution providing supervision or having custody of the child under order of the court;

(4) a court and its probation and other officials or professional staff and the attorney for the defendant for use in preparing a presentence report in a criminal case in which the defendant is convicted and who prior thereto had been a party to the proceeding in juvenile court;

(5) with leave of court any other person or agency or institution having a legitimate interest in the proceeding or in the work of the court.

SECTION 55. [*Law Enforcement Records.*] Law enforcement records and files concerning a child shall be kept separate from the records and files of arrests of adults. Unless a charge of delinquency is transferred for criminal prosecution under section 34, the interest of national security requires, or the court otherwise orders in the interest of the child, the records and files shall not be open to public inspection or their contents disclosed to the public; but inspection of the records and files is permitted by:

(1) a juvenile court having the child before it in any proceeding;

(2) counsel for a party to the proceeding;

(3) the officers of public institutions or agencies to whom the child is committed;

(4) law enforcement officers of other jurisdictions when necessary for the discharge of their official duties; and

(5) a court in which he is convicted of a criminal offense for the purpose of a pre-sentence report or other dispositional proceeding, or by officials of penal institutions and other penal facilities to which he is committed, or by a [parole board] in considering his parole or discharge or in exercising supervision over him.

Section 29. Expungement of Childhood Record [New]

When a child reaches the age of 18 and any time thereafter he may petition the Court to have his record expunged. An order of expungement shall operate to void and nullify the arrest and conviction.

COMMENT

This permits an individual, in effect, to obtain a pardon for childhood offenses. At present, since there is technically no crime, there can be no pardon and an adult cannot rid himself of his juvenile record.

Section 30. Costs and Expenses for Care of Child

(a) The following expenses shall be a charge upon the funds of the county upon certification thereof by the court:

(1) the cost of medical and other examinations and treatment of a child ordered by the court;

(2) the cost of care and support of a child committed by the court to the legal custody of a public agency other than an institution for delinquent children, or to a private agency or individual other than a parent;

(3) reasonable compensation for services and related expenses of counsel appointed by the court for a party;

(4) reasonable compensation for a guardian ad litem;

(5) the expense of service of summons, notices, subpoenas, travel expense of witnesses, transportation of the child, and other like expenses incurred in the proceedings under this Act.

(b) If, after due notice to the parents or other persons legally obligated to care for and support the child, and after affording them an opportunity to be heard, the court finds that they are financially able to pay all or part of the costs and expenses stated in paragraphs (1), (2), (3), and (4) of subsection (a), the court may order them to pay the same and prescribe the manner of payment. Unless otherwise ordered payment shall be made to the clerk of the juvenile court for remittance to the person to whom compensation is due, or if the costs and expenses have been paid by the (county) to the (appropriate officer) of the (county).

(Cf. UJCA Sec. 52 for identical provision.)

Section 31. Children's Fingerprints, Photographs

(a) No child under 14 years of age shall be fingerprinted in the investigation of a crime except as provided in this section. Fingerprints of a child 14 or more years of age who is referred to the court may be taken and filed by law enforcement officers in investigating the commission of a felony.

(b) Fingerprint files of children shall be kept separate from those of adults. Copies of fingerprints known to be those of a child shall be maintained on a local basis only and not sent to a central state or federal depository unless needed in the interest of national security.

(c) Fingerprint files of children may be inspected by law enforcement officers when necessary for the discharge of their official duties. Other inspections may be authorized by the court in individual cases upon a showing that it is necessary in the public interest.

(d) Fingerprints of a child shall be removed from the file and destroyed if:

(1) the child is not convicted of a criminal offense; or

(2) the child reaches 18 years of age and there is no record that he committed a criminal offense after reaching 16 years of age.

(e) If latent fingerprints are found during the investigation of an offense and a law enforcement officer has probable cause to believe that they are those of a particular child he may fingerprint the child regardless of age or offense for purposes of immediate comparison with the latent fingerprints. If the comparison is negative the fingerprint card and other copies of the fingerprints taken shall be immediately destroyed. If the comparison is positive and the child is referred to the court, the fingerprint card and other copies of the fingerprints taken shall be delivered to the court for disposition. If the child is not referred to the court, the fingerprints shall be immediately destroyed.

(f) Without the consent of the judge, a child shall not be photographed after he is taken into custody unless the case is transferred to another court for prosecution.

(Cf. UJCA Sec. 56 for identical provision.)

Section 32. Rules of Court

The Supreme Court of this State shall within 6 months after the enactment of this Statute adopt rules of procedure not in conflict with this Act governing proceedings under it.

COMMENT

Many juvenile courts now function without rules of procedure.

UJCA

SECTION 60. [*Rules of Court.*] The [Supreme] Court of this State may adopt rules of procedure not in conflict with this Act governing proceedings under it.

Section 33. Short Title

This Act may be cited as the Children and Youth Law.

Section 34. Repeal

The following Acts and Parts of Acts are repealed. (Juvenile Court Law)

Section 35. Time of Taking Effect

This Act shall take effect 60 days after its adoption.

COMMENT

Summary motor vehicle violations are excluded from the jurisdiction of the Children and Youth Court. Other motor vehicle violations are dealt with in the same manner as other violations of law.

UJCA

[SECTION 44. [*Juvenile Traffic Offenses.*]

(a) *Definition.* Except as provided in subsection (b), a juvenile traffic offense consists of a violation by a child of:

(1) a law or local ordinance [or resolution] governing the operation of a moving motor vehicle upon the streets, highways of this State, or the waterways within or adjoining this State; or

(2) any other motor vehicle traffic law or local ordinance [or resolution] of this State if the child is taken into custody and detained for the violation or is transferred to the juvenile court by the court hearing the charge.

(b) A juvenile traffic offense is not an act of delinquency unless the case is transferred to the delinquency calendar as provided in subsection (g).

(c) *Exceptions.* A juvenile traffic offense does not include a violation of: [Set forth the sections of state statutes violations of which are not to be included as traffic offenses, such as the so-called negligent homicide statute sometimes appearing in traffic codes, driving while intoxicated, driving without, or during suspension of, a driver's license, and the like].

(d) *Procedure.* The [summons] [notice to appear] [or other designation of a ticket] accusing a child of committing a juvenile traffic offense constitutes the commencement of the proceedings in the juvenile court of the [county] in which the alleged violation occurred and serves in place of a summons and petition under this Act. These cases shall be filed and heard separately from other proceedings of the court. If the child is taken into custody on the charge, sections 14 to 17 apply. If the child is, or after commencement of the proceedings becomes, a resident of another [county] of this State, section 12 applies.

(e) *Hearing.* The court shall fix a time for hearing and give reasonable notice thereof to the child, and if their address is known to the parents, guardian, or custodian. If the accusation made in the [summons] [notice to appear] [or other designation of a ticket] is denied an informal hearing shall be held at which the parties have the right to subpoena witnesses, present evidence, cross-examine witnesses, and appear by counsel. The hearing is open to the public.

(f) ·*Disposition.* If the court finds on the admission of the child or upon the evidence that he committed the offense charged it may make one or more of the following orders:

(1) reprimand or counsel with the child and his parents;

(2) [suspend] [recommend to the [appropriate official having the authority] that he suspend] the child's privilege to drive under stated conditions and limitations for a period not to exceed that authorized for a like suspension of an adult's license for a like offense;

(3) require the child to attend a traffic school conducted by public authority for a reasonable period of time; or

(4) order the child to remit to the general fund of the [state] [county] [city] [municipality] a sum not exceeding the lesser of $50 or the maximum applicable to an adult for a like offense.

(g) In lieu of the preceding orders, if the evidence indicates the advisability thereof, the court may transfer the case to the delinquency calendar of the court and direct the filing and service of a summons and petition in accordance with this Act. The judge so ordering is disqualified upon objection from acting further in the case prior to an adjudication that the child committed a delinquent act.]

•

[SECTION 45. [*Traffic Referee.*]

(a) The court may appoint one or more traffic referees who shall serve at the pleasure of the court. The referee's salary shall be fixed by the court [subject to the approval of the [Board of County Commissioners]].

(b) The court may direct that any case or class of cases arising under section 44 shall be heard in the first instance by a traffic referee who shall conduct the hearing in accordance with section 44. Upon the conclusion of the hearing the traffic referee shall transmit written findings of fact and recommendations for disposition to the judge with a copy thereof to the child and other parties to the proceedings.

(c) Within 3 days after receiving the copy the child may file a request for a rehearing before the judge of the court who shall thereupon rehear the case at a time fixed by him. Otherwise, the judge may confirm the findings and recommendations for disposition which then become the findings and order of disposition of the court.]

[SECTION 46. [*Juvenile Traffic Offenses—Suspension of Jurisdiction.*]

(a) The [Supreme] court, by order filed in the office of the [_____] of the [county,] may suspend the jurisdiction of the juvenile courts over juvenile traffic offenses or one or more classes thereof. The order shall designate the time the suspension becomes effective and offenses committed thereafter shall be tried by the appropriate court in accordance with law without regard to this Act. The child shall not be detained or imprisoned in a jail or other facility for the detention of adults unless the facility conforms to subsection (a) of section 16.

(b) The [Supreme] court at any time may restore the jurisdiction of the juvenile courts over these offenses or any portion thereof by like filing of its order of restoration. Offenses committed thereafter are governed by this Act.]

5 | THE CHILDREN AND THE STATE:
Adversaries in the Juvenile Justice System

STEPHEN WIZNER*

> Did we win or lose?
> We won.
> Yeah? What did we win?[1]

When the child and the state confront each other in the juvenile justice system, no amount of benevolent intentions, studied informality, or euphemistic terminology should be allowed to obscure the fact that they are, in fact, adversaries. What is at stake in juvenile delinquency proceedings is the child's right to liberty and his right to continue in the custody of his parents against the state's power to control crime and enforce morality.

Despite this fact, the juvenile justice system created by legislation in virtually every state was empowered to disregard customary procedures for protecting the accused from the power of the state. It was allowed to employ instead a non-adversary, rehabilitative, parental approach in "treating" children, both those charged with special juvenile offenses[2] (e.g., incorrigibility, truancy) and those charged with offenses criminal for adults.[3]

Such a departure was based on good intentions. Reformers anxious to

---

* B.A., Dartmouth College, 1959; J.D. University of Chicago, 1963; Supervising Attorney and Instructor in Law, Yale Law School; Formerly Managing Attorney, Mobilization for Youth Legal Services, New York City.

The author would like to thank Rona F. Feit, a Columbia Law School student, for her research and editorial assistance.

1. Conversation between a child and this writer after a successful defense to a charge of burglary in a juvenile delinquency hearing.

2. These special juvenile offenses continue today. N. MORRIS & G. HAWKINS, THE HONEST POLITICIANS GUIDE TO CRIME CONTROL 146 (1970):

> Conditions included in the various statutory descriptions of delinquent behavior comprise a medley consisting of anything from smoking cigarettes, truancy, sleeping in alleys, and using vulgar language to major felonies such as rape and homicide. Moreover, such vague imprecise and subjective terms as idleness, loitering, waywardness, stubbornness, incorrigibility and immoral conduct are commonly employed.

3. See, e.g., A.M. PLATT, THE CHILD SAVERS 137-45 (1969). An excellent study of the history of the juvenile court.

102 / STEPHEN WIZNER

save the children were repelled by the rigidities, technicalities, and harshness in the substantive and procedural criminal law.[4] They were convinced that youth crime was not a problem of law enforcement but a social—psychological problem of children and their families requiring interventions of a therapeutic nature, involving state interference with and assumption of the parental function of child rearing.[5] This rationale was reinforced by a legal theory of the state's power to act as parens patriae derived improperly from practices of the English courts of chancery.[6] The lack of formal legal procedures and protections for the children was justified on the ground that nothing "bad" was being done to the children, but rather something "good" was being provided for them. The fact that the result of these proceedings was often the removal of the child from his parents and his placement in an institution was considered a reasonable state extension of parental discipline. The child, never totally at liberty, was simply moved from the inadequate or damaging custody of his parents to the benevolent custody of the state.[7]

Flaws in the system began to show up early. The removal of the child frequently was unjustified, high handed, and cruel.[8] Since the discretion of a juvenile judge was immense, unlimited by anything but his benevolence, parents and children were literally at his mercy.[9] The institutions to which the child was removed were, as often as not, overcrowded, regimented, poorly equipped and inadequately staffed detention centers where nothing really rehabilitative was done for the child.[10] "Delinquent" and "neglected" children were often confined together in bleak and impersonal institutions which were constantly criticized and almost never improved. Since a distinctive feature of the juvenile court was indeterminate sentencing, children frequently remained in these institutions for years for nothing more than truancy.[11]

Though reformist, the juvenile court movement from the beginning had an authoritarian impulse evident both from its belief in the need for firm control of delinquents and its sense of children as helpless depen-

---

4. *See, e.g.*, F.A. ALLEN, THE BORDERLAND OF CRIMINAL JUSTICE 47-48 (1964).
5. *See, e.g.*, Mack, *The Juvenile Court*, 23 HARV. L. REV. 104 (1909); THE CHILD, THE CLINIC AND THE COURT (J. ADDAMS ed. 1925).
6. *See, e.g.*, Cogan, *Juvenile Law Before and After the Entrance of Parens Patriae*, 22 S.C.L. REV. 147 (1970); Rendleman, *Parens Patriae: From Chancery to the Juvenile Court*, 23 S.C.L. REV. 205 (1971). See also discussion *infra* at 392.
7. *See* note 5 *supra*.
8. Rendleman, *supra* note 6, at 237-45; A.M. PLATT, *supra* note 3, at 103-04.
9. A rare, early case holding a parens patriae commitment to reform school unconstitutional was People v. Turner, 55 Ill. 280 (1870), cited in A.M. PLATT, *supra* note 3, at 104.
10. A.M. PLATT, *supra* note 3, at 145-52.
11. *Id.* at 150-51.

dents.[12] Characterized also by middle-class bias, it set high standards of family propriety which it invoked primarily against lower-class families.[13]

As dissatisfaction with the lack of procedural safeguards in juvenile proceedings grew, first the states[14] and then the Supreme Court acted to provide protections. In *In re Gault*,[15] an appeal from a decision in which a 15-year-old boy was sentenced to a state institution until his majority for making a lewd telephone call that he denied making, the Supreme Court at last confronted the claim of the parens patriae doctrine that juveniles were outside the constitutional scheme and rejected it. However, it did not overthrow the juvenile court system, nor indeed, many other aspects of parens patriae. The Court carefully confined its holding to the adjudicatory phase of confinement. For this phase it did not demand exact conformity with adult criminal procedural safeguards but only a standard of "fundamental fairness" combined with four specific procedural protections: the right to adequate and timely notice, confrontation of witnesses, counsel,[16] and the privilege against self-incrimination. Later, in *In re Winship*,[17] the Court carefully added to the list of specific safeguards the requirement of proof beyond a reasonable doubt. However, in *McKeiver v. Pennsylvania*[18] the Court refused to add the right to a jury trial. Because the Court was explicitly concerned that such a right would ". . . remake the juvenile proceeding into a fully adversary process . . . ending what has been the idealistic prospect of an intimate, informal, protective proceeding,"[19] it held that a jury trial was not an essential element of "fundamental fairness."

The language of the Court in the progression of decisions from *Gault* to *McKeiver* shows an increasing fear that the importation of procedural safeguards into the juvenile system will destroy that system by making it fully adversary.[20] This concern with the adversary problem is a shift from

12. *See, e.g.*, A.M. PLATT, *supra* note 3, at 135-36. Some social scientists today stress the need for programs that provide autonomy, responsibility, and a sense of competence in rehabilitating delinquent adolescents. Wheeler, Cottrell & Romasco, *Juvenile Delinquency: Its Prevention and Control*, PRESIDENT'S COMMISSION ON LAW ENFORCEMENT AND ADMINISTRATION OF JUSTICE, TASK FORCE REPORT: JUVENILE DELINQUENCY AND YOUTH CRIME 416 (1967). (Hereinafter called TASK FORCE REPORT.)

13. *Id.*

14. *See, In re* Gault, 387 U.S. 1, 13 (1967).

15. 387 U.S. 1 (1967).

16. *Id.*, at 13. It is regrettable that the right to counsel was confined to the adjudicatory phase. Counsel is crucial to fairness at the intake and dispositional phases of juvenile proceedings as well.

17. 397 U.S. 358 (1970).

18. 403 U.S. 528 (1971).

19. *Id.*, at 545.

20. *In re* Winship, 397 U.S. 358, 366 (showing concern for "the informality, flexibility or speed of the hearing at which the fact-finding takes place.") McKeiver v. Pennsylvania, 403 U.S. 528, 545 (quoted in the text), 550 (relating delay, formality, and clamor to the adversary system).

the reasoning in the *Gault* decision. There the Court stressed that some elements of adversary proceedings in juvenile court were necessary, but that they would leave untouched other distinctive benefits of the juvenile system such as separate treatment of juvenile offenders,[21] no classification as a criminal,[22] no civil disability or disqualification for civil service appointment as a result of conviction,[23] confidentiality of the proceedings,[24] and the presence of "kindly" juvenile judges.[25] *Gault* also noted that much informality could be retained as well, but questioned its value.[26] The later decisions bring back for the legal profession a set of questions that had seemed largely laid to rest by the reasoning in *Gault*. Is the functioning of the juvenile court threatened by vigorous adversary fact-finding, and, if so, what is the meaning of the child's right to counsel?

It is, in truth, an old set of questions. Juveniles had counsel before *Gault*, and the resulting problems were extensively discussed then.[27] *Gault's* emphasis on the need for counsel had apparently only qualified, not abolished, the pervasive paternalistic approach of the juvenile courts. Parens patriae lingers on, obscuring the adversary relation of the court and the child, despite its historical irrelevancy and its danger to libertarian values.

The protective power of the sovereign as parens patriae exercised by the courts of chancery in equity is not the historical basis for power over troublesome children. In English practice, misbehaving children were prosecuted, if at all, under the criminal laws. The chancellors invoked the equitable doctrine of parens patriae only in resolving disputes between private parties over guardianship and property matters affecting "infants and idiots" who were deemed to be incapable of caring for themselves.[28]

The juvenile court's delinquency jurisdiction derives from the criminal law,[29] and the Elizabethan Poor Laws (and their American counterparts) relating to the control of paupers and their children.[30]

As Morris and Hawkins have observed:

Historical idiosyncracies gave us a doubtful assumption of power over children. With the quasi-legal concept of parens patriae to brace it, this assumption of power blended well with the earlier

---

21. *See*, 387 U.S. at 22.
22. *Id.*, at 23.
23. *Id.*, at 24.
24. *Id.*
25. *Id.*, at 27.
26. *Id.*, 25-27.
27. *See, e.g.*, THE NATIONAL COUNCIL OF JUVENILE COURT JUDGES, COUNSEL FOR THE CHILD (1966). This is a symposium on the role of the lawyers in Juvenile Court together with an extensive bibliography.
28. Rendleman, *supra* note 6.
29. *See*, R. POUND, INTERPRETATIONS OF LEGAL HISTORY 134-35 (1923).
30. Rendleman, *supra* note 6.

humanitarian traditions in the churches and other charitable organizations regarding child care and childsaving. The juvenile court is thus the product of paternal error and maternal generosity, which is a not unusual genesis of illegitimacy.[31]

The point is not that the juvenile courts have no legal right to exist. It is rather that their claim to be free of the need for an adversary balancing of interests is based on their asserted identity of interest with the child. They argue that the parens patriae approach to juvenile delinquency cases removes the apparent conflict between the misbehaving child's desire for liberty and his "obvious" need for corrective custody and guidance, by asserting that the court does not deprive children of a right to liberty, but rather grants them the right to parental care and discipline.[32] The history of the court reveals, however, that it has always been concerned with the identification and control of wayward children as much in the interests of public order as in the interests of the children.[33] Whatever its benevolent intentions, the juvenile system's concern for the "best interests" of the child has been clearly affected by the demands made upon it to deal with the crime problem posed by juveniles.[34] Roughly half of the serious crimes in the United States are committed by children of juvenile court age, although this age group constitutes less than one-fifth of the total population.[35] Responsibility for dealing with the problem of crime is as much that of the juvenile courts as it is of adult criminal courts. Indeed, one of the main functions of the juvenile justice system is law enforcement.[36]

---

31. N. MORRIS & G. HAWKINS, *supra* note 2, at 157.
32. *See, e.g.*, Mack, *supra* note 5.
33. A.M. PLATT, *supra* note 3, at 137-41.
34. F.A. ALLEN, *supra* note 4, at 43-50.
35. 118 *Congressional Record* (daily ed. February 8, 1972), S. 1331 (remarks of Senator Birch Bayh).
    Mr. President, juvenile crime in this country is reaching crisis proportions. During the past decade, arrests of juveniles for violent crimes increased by 148 percent, and arrests of juveniles for property crimes, such as burglary and auto theft, jumped 85 percent.
    I am deeply alarmed by these rapidly accelerating arrest rates for young people. But I am even more alarmed by the fact the juveniles now represent almost half the crime population in this country. Children between the ages of 10 and 17 compose only 16 percent of the national population, yet they account for more than 48 percent of all arrests for serious crimes. And the problem is even worse than the figures indicate, because a larger proportion of adult arrests for serious crimes are those we failed to rehabilitate as young offenders.
    Our dismal failure to rehabilitate is dramatically clear from the recidivism rate for juvenile delinquents estimated at 74 percent to 85 percent. Our attempts to redirect young lives by the traditional means of incarceration in large training schools simply do not work; they succeed only in producing more sophisticated, more alienated young criminals.
36. TASK FORCE REPORT 1 (1967):
    The juvenile court has become the primary judicial agency for dealing with

Furthermore, the fallacy of any easy analogy of the state's role to that of the parent is immediately pointed up by the state's own interest in the control and discipline of disruptive youth. There is a fundamental difference between a parent's disciplining a child by placing limits on his behavior and the state's punishing the child by imposing sanctions such as arrest, detention, prosecution, stigmatization, probation and institutionalization. Parents may not imprison children; the state can and does.[37] State institutions for children are notoriously far from home-like.[38] The state, as parent, subjects the child to cultural influences that may be both foreign and unacceptable to the real parent and even to the child.[39] Intervention in family life is destructive of family solidarity, which is frequently of more importance to minorities and the poor than those in power are willing to admit.[40] The state's concept of itself as parent can lead to the idea that it should assume custody of children whose parents are unconventional by dominant community standards.[41] These are all considerations of great social and political sensitivity, exposing the dangers inherent in parens patriae.

Constitutional interpretation has consistently recognized that the parents' claim to authority in the rearing of their children is basic to our society.[42] It is also clear that the state has an independent interest in protecting the welfare of children and safeguarding them from abuses.[43] Certainly in the adjustment of these two interests our political commitment to the value of individual liberty demands scrupulous procedural safeguards for individual rights. This is particularly true now that we are

---

juvenile criminality, the singlemost pressing and threatening aspect of the crime problem in the United States. One in every nine children will be referred to juvenile courts for an act of delinquency before his 18th birthday. Considering boys alone, the ratio is one in every six. Arrests of persons under 18 for serious crimes increased 47 percent in 1965 over 1960; the increase in that age group population for the same period was 17 percent. In 1965 persons under 18 referred to juvenile court constituted 24 percent of all persons charged with forcible rape, 34 percent of all persons charged with burglary, 45 percent of all persons charged with larceny, 61 percent of all persons charged with auto theft. It is apparent that responsibility for meeting the problems of crime rests more heavily on no other judicial institution.

37. *Id.*, at 6.
38. *Id.*, at 23.
39. *See e.g.*, Rendleman *supra* note 6.
40. *Id.*, at 205-06, making reference to Dandridge v. Williams, 397 U.S. 471 (1970), in which the Supreme Court found acceptable the "attenuation" of parent-child relationships resulting from state welfare legislation that indirectly promoted the farming out of children in large, poor families to relatives.
41. *Id.*, at 252-53. *See, Book Review*, Katz, *When Parents Fail*, 4 COLUM. HUMAN RIGHTS L. REV. 497 (1972).
42. *See, e.g.*, Ginsberg v. New York, 390 U.S. 629, 639, 640, 641 (1967).
43. *Id.*; *see also*, Paulsen, *The Legal Framework of Child Protection*, 66 COLUM. L. REV. 679 (1966).

witnessing a massive shift from private to public efforts to provide child protective services and an increasing push to make them universally available.[44] Easy analogies of the state to the parent will not and should not serve to legitimize the state's power over children. If such a rationale is relied on, it seems reasonable to expect those affected by that power, frequently the nation's newly militant poor, to confront it in court and demand that the state's performance be as parental as advertised.[45] Perhaps we will see an increase in the number of cases using the writ of habeas corpus to free juveniles from confinement in institutions demonstrably not rehabilitative or parental.[46]

The expressed concern of the Supreme Court for allowing the benevolent experiment of the juvenile justice system to go on without the clamor, formality and delay of a fully adversary proceeding may or may not be warranted. But any impairment of the freedom of defense counsel to wage a vigorous adversary defense should be firmly opposed. It is a serious political problem that many in the juvenile justice system and many lawyers neither accept nor understand that the state and the child are in fact adversaries in juvenile delinquency cases, and that regardless of the benevolent intentions of the judge, probation officers and institutional personnel, involuntary "treatment" of young offenders as a "cure" for their misbehavior and rebellious tendencies is to those who do not wish to receive it nothing less than punishment, a coercive exercise of the police power of the state.

Apparently, despite *Gault*, the right to counsel is viewed as an unnecessary safeguard in many juvenile courts. Two post-*Gault* studies revealing widespread waiver of the right to counsel found that most of the waivers by children and parents were uninformed and inadvertent.[47] The court involved had simply failed to give proper, adequate and unprejudiced notice that the state would provide counsel if the parents could not afford it.[48] One recent study found that attorneys were present in

44. Paulsen, *supra* note 43, at 710.
45. *Id.*, at 709.
46. This line of attack is suggested in Weiss, *Defense of a Juvenile Court Case*, in 2 CRIMINAL DEFENSE TECHNIQUES (R.M. CIPES ed. 1969) 60-15. He cites Fulwood v. Stone, 394 F.2d 939 (D.C. Cir. 1967). *See also*, reasonable statutory purpose cases, *e.g.*, Shelton v. Tucker, 364 U.S. 479 (1960); Nebbia v. New York, 291 U.S. 502 (1924); and Wyatt v. Stickney, 344 F. Supp. 373 (M.D. Ala. 1972).
47. *See*, Lefstein, Stapleton & Teitelbaum, *In Search of Juvenile Justice: Gault and Its Implementation*, 3 L. & Soc. REV. 491 (1969); Ferster, Courtless & Snethen, *The Juvenile Justice System: In Search of the Role of Counsel*, 39 FORD. L. REV. 375, 376-80 (1971).
48. For example, the court's language frequently downplayed the need for counsel, failed to advise that free counsel was available, or showed the court's impatience with the idea of counsel. For a holding that a lower court's failure to give proper notice of right to counsel resulted in an invalid waiver of the right, see *In re* Ella B., 30 N.Y.2d 352, — N.E.2d — (1972).

only 24% of the juvenile delinquency cases in a particular jurisdiction.[49] Another study of 24 counties, in states where children were allowed jury trials, found that in 2 of those counties there were lawyers in only 50% of the cases, in 6 other counties, in less than 25% of the cases, and in another 3 counties in less than 10%.[50]

Only in jurisdictions where the public defender or "law guardian" system operates in the juvenile courts are children assisted by counsel as a matter of course. In such jurisdictions there remain built-in problems for vigorous adversary defense because the defender is an employee of the system with a continuing close relationship to the bench and probation officers.[51] It would be preferable for a pool of community based lawyers to be available for such work, but the practice generally does not pay well, and the most able members of the Bar usually know nothing about the procedures in the juvenile court system.[52] Even the experienced criminal lawyer must adapt to the informality, lack of standards, less stringent rules of evidence, child-saving rhetoric and other imponderables.[53]

In cases where juvenile counsel is present, lingering and unwarranted trust by counsel and others in unchallenged benevolence continues to complicate counsel's performance and effectiveness.[54] The hostility of the courts, legislators and commentators to an adversary approach in juvenile court is widespread.[55] The advocate faces long-held assumptions that the necessary fact-finding can be done better by trained social workers and paternalistic judges than by lawyers out to "beat the rap" for their clients.[56]

Counsel must not only contend with hostility. He or she shares the general confusion over the nature of children's rights, which has been only partly allayed by court decisions. Although the Supreme Court stated in *Gault* that "neither the Fourteenth Amendment nor the Bill of Rights is for adults alone," further language in *Gault* and opinions else-

---

49. Ferster, Courtless & Snethen, *supra* note 47, at 386, n.65.
50. *Id.*
51. *See e.g.*, A.M. PLATT, *supra* note 3, at 168-72.
52. *Id.*, 165-67.
53. *See* Weiss, *supra* note 46, for an excellent, detailed and practical guide to effective counselling in the post-Gault juvenile court.
54. *See* Steinfeldt, Kerper & Friel, *The Impact of the Gault Decision in Texas*, 20 JUV. CT. JUDGES J. 154 (1969) discussed and cited in Ferster, Courtless & Snethen, *supra* note 47, at 388.
55. A.M. PLATT, *supra* note 3, at 165.
56. *Id.* Fact-finding solely by the inquisitorial rather than the adversary method has a long history of fallibility in juvenile court. See the discussion *infra* at 397. However, it is also true that adversary fact-finding breaks down. It breaks down completely when counsel has information not otherwise available to the court that the child is guilty but does not offer it. In such a case, the adversary system is justified primarily as a control on state power and not as a fact-finding method. Our system of criminal law has traditionally chosen to put the control of state power first, despite the fact that some of the guilty get away. *See* ABA Canons of Professional Ethics No. 5. This choice is equally appropriate in the juvenile system.

where make it clear that children so far are not the constitutional equivalents of adults.[57]

Effective advocacy is also hindered by the role conflict inevitable in a system in which individuals may be subjected to involuntary treatment and the deprivation of liberty for their own good. "The basis of the adversary system is the separation of roles . . ."[58] and yet the structure of the juvenile court system requires that the judge act as judge, prosecutor and protector,[59] the probation officer as social worker, investigator and law enforcement officer,[60] and the defense attorney as both advocate and guardian.[61]

If we are truly concerned about "fundamental fairness" to the child in juvenile court proceedings, and adequately sensitive to the need for standards and controls on the state's power to intervene in private lives, it is difficult to escape the conclusion that the juvenile court must move away from attitudes and practices which dilute the adversariness of the proceedings.

Whatever else is needed in the juvenile court system, and reforms of many kinds are called for, one clear need is for accurate fact-finding. Neither surmise nor conjecture is an adequate basis for governmental interference with liberty. The question of what facts need to be shown in juvenile court is unsettled.[62] The court's concern for rehabilitation has focused its attention not only on the commission of specific acts but on facts of the juvenile's total personality and its interaction with the environment.[63] Whatever the focus, fact-finding is the primary task of the adjudicatory phase of the juvenile court proceedings. One-sided investigations by social workers and police have led to reports which contain questionable data. Juveniles' social files, often introduced at the adjudicatory hearing, typically contain rumor, gossip and prejudicial school and probation reports,[64] as well as psychiatric reports full of professional jargon that impresses judges.[65] Psychiatric testing done under court auspices has produced results which differ significantly and prejudicially from test results obtained by defense

57. 387 U.S. at 13. *See e.g.*, Prince v. Massachusetts, 321 U.S. 158, 170 (1944); Tinker v. Des Moines Independent School District, 393 U.S. 503, 515 (1969) (Justice Stewart concurring).

58. Handler, *The Juvenile Court and the Adversary System: Problems of Function and Form*, 1965 WISC. L. REV. 7, 43.

59. *See e.g.*, Note, *Rights and Rehabilitation in the Juvenile Courts*, 67 COLUM. L. REV. 281, 297-309 (1967).

60. TASK FORCE REPORT, *supra* note 12, at 6.

61. *See, e.g.*, Note, *supra* note 59, at 327; Dyson & Dyson, 9 J. FAM. L. 1, 58 (1969).

62. For a discussion of the issues, *see* F.A. ALLEN, *supra* note 4, at 18-22.

63. A.M. PLATT, *supra* note 3, at 141-42.

64. *See e.g.*, Note, *supra* note 59, at 337-38.

65. Lemert, *The Juvenile Court—Quest and Realities*, TASK FORCE REPORT *supra* note 12, at 103.

experts.[66] No judge should be expected to weigh such evidence without help from adversary challenge and the presentation of a case for the defense.[67] If the long history of the common law has illustrated that full adversary proceedings are necessary for the protection of adults in criminal proceedings, how can we deny that protection to the juvenile facing delinquency charges and incarceration?[68] Indeed, since the broad discretion of the juvenile court in defining delinquency and in setting sentence lengths poses special threats, should not the juvenile have greater protection than adults?[69]

Full adversary proceedings do not mean that counsel must employ a rigidly technical approach, bitterly contesting every point and issue. The adversary system has always had room for compromise according to the client's best interest. Our adversary system does not ". . . . excessively seek for truth, but rather seek[s] to strike a decent balance between the quantum of proof of guilt and the values of individual freedom."[70] The need for full adversariness probably does mean, however, that there must be clearer role separation in the juvenile courts, a skeptical approach to benevolent pretensions, and vigorous and scrupulous deference by counsel to the wishes of his client, the child.[71]

Some lawyers believe that it is not possible to counsel, relate to, and represent a child as one does an adult. There are, of course, situations involving children of very young age, or limited intelligence, who will not understand legal proceedings. The lawyer's role in such cases might more nearly approach that of guardian than advocate, but even in such cases he should put the state to its proof. The exchange quoted at the outset of this article took place between the writer and a nine year old child after a trial in which he was found innocent of burglary. When it was explained

---

66. Dyson & Dyson, *supra* note 61, at 59-61.

67. *See e.g.,* Handler, *supra* note 58, at 49; Note *supra* note 58, at 336. *But see* dicta of Justice White concurring in McKeiver v. Pennsylvania, 403 U.S. at 550, expressing remarkable trust in the juvenile court's ability to avoid prejudgment in such a situation.

68. *See e.g.,* Dissent of Justice Douglas in McKeiver v. Pennsylvania, 403 U.S. at 559.

69. TASK FORCE REPORT, *supra* note 12, at 23: Juveniles receive ". . . not infrequently . . . sanctions more severe than those an adult would receive for like behavior . . . ."

70. N. MORRIS & G. HAWKINS, *supra* note 2, at 161.

71. For reports and discussion on the role of defense counsel in the juvenile system at or since the time of the *Gault* decision, *see generally,* N. LEFSTEIN & V. STAPLETON, COUNSEL IN JUVENILE COURTS: AN EXPERIMENTAL STUDY, NATIONAL COUNCIL OF JUVENILE COURT JUDGES (1967); Stapleton, *A Social Scientist's View of Gault and a Plea for the Experimenting Society,* 1 YALE REV. OF L. & SOC. ACTION 72 (1970); Wizner, *Juvenile Justice and the Rehabilitative Ideal: A Response to Mr. Stapleton,* 1 YALE REV. OF L. & SOC. ACTION 82 (1970); Teitelbaum, *Gault and the "Experimenting Society": A Response to Mr. Stapleton,* 1 YALE REV. OF L. & SOC. ACTION 86 (1970); Wizner, *The Defense Counsel: Neither Father, Judge, Probation Officer, or Social Worker,* 7 TRIAL, September/October 1971, at 30.

to him what he had "won" was a decision that he "didn't do it" he replied, "but I *didn't* do it." Obviously, the arresting officer, intake worker and prosecutor did not believe him, and only by cross examination of the state's witnesses, and testimony of witnesses in support of the child's story, did the matter reach a just result. The child clearly did not comprehend all that was going on in the trial, but he benefited from the result.

Most youngsters, however, do understand what is at stake in juvenile delinquency proceedings. They understand that they are in trouble, why they are in trouble, and what can happen to them once they are found to be juvenile delinquents. They are not too innocent to play the role of criminal defendant.[72] Most children charged with juvenile delinquency wish to be "acquitted," or to get the lightest "sentence" possible, even if supervision, counselling treatment or institutionalization promises to benefit them.[73] The lawyer should certainly act as an interpreter of the juvenile court to the child, trying to make as clear as possible to him the significance, both good and bad, of what might happen to him there. But it is not counsel's role, necessarily, to achieve for the child what the counsel or judge or prosecutor thinks is best for him. The lawyer's role is to be the child's advocate, to give mature, articulate, intelligent and persuasive voice to the child's expressed wishes with respect to the "best" outcome of the case.

Gault provided the right to counsel as the principal check on the abuses of parens patriae.[74] If counsel limits the defense of the child because of parens patriae assumptions that the court and the child are not adversaries, that check is undermined. Counsel indeed becomes part of the problem instead of part of the solution. If the presence of independent counsel is "the keystone of the whole structure of guarantees that a minimum system of procedural justice requires,"[75] then counsel must vigorously maintain an independent stance. He or she must speak unequivocally for the child's legal rights.[76] The child's right to be heard requires no less.

72. N. MORRIS & G. HAWKINS, *supra* note 2, at 163-64:
". . . [S]ome experience with children's courts and juvenile institutions leads one rapidly to eschew the belief in the innate innocence of children. Indeed, when one includes the incompetent, the decrepit, and the lost characters that form so much of the grist of the mill of adult courts, one might suspect that there is a lesser quantum of responsibility per hundred in adult cases than in juvenile cases."
73. This conclusion, a fairly obvious one, is based on the writer's own experience and that of numerous lawyers of his acqaintance who represent children in delinquency cases.
74. 367 U.S. at 38 & n.65.
75. TASK FORCE REPORT, *supra* note 12, at 32, quoted in 367 U.S. at 38, & n.65.
76. This view has been adopted by juvenile court public defenders in San Leandro, California, *see* Note, *supra* note 59, at 327 & n.246, and by the "Law Guardians" serving New York juvenile courts. Dyson & Dyson, *supra* note 60. For a description of the difficulties of public defenders serving as both social workers and advocates, *see* Platt, Schechter & Tiffany, *In Defense of Youth: A Case of the Public Defender in Juvenile Court*, 43 IND. L.J. 619 (1968).

6 | **THE TRAINING OF
COMMUNITY JUDGES:
Rehabilitative Adjudication**

WILLIAM P. STATSKY*

I. Introduction

Gilbert is in his freshman year of High School. One of his teachers, Mr. Huber, suspects him of smoking pot in the school bathroom, but he has never been able to prove it. Mr. Huber speaks to Gilbert about it one day in the corridor. Both soon become very angry with each other. They are shouting. Mr. Huber orders Gilbert to the office of the principal, Mr. Fisher. Gilbert becomes furious. They begin to struggle. Mr. Huber falls to the ground and Gilbert disappears. Mr. Huber immediately calls the police to arrest Gilbert for assault.

In New York City, Gilbert may now be confronted with an array of official proceedings: school suspension hearings, police station interrogation, probation office investigation, Family Court confrontation and possibly Civil Court action. This paper deals with one aspect of a program designed to provide an alternative process of disposition. The experiment, located in the Bronx, New York, is called the Neighborhood Youth Diversion Program. It is the product of joint planning by the Vera Institute of Justice[1] and the Institute for Social Research at Fordham University.[2]

* Adjunct Professor of Law, UCLA School of Law, former Forum Director, Neighborhood Youth Diversion Program; B.A., Boston College 1964; J.D., Boston College 1967; LL.M., New York University 1970.

1. Vera undertakes research and demonstration programs designed to divert individuals out of the criminal justice system into alternative rehabilitation settings. Some of Vera's projects have included the Manhattan Bowery Project, the Court Employment Project, the Bronx Sentencing Project and the Addiction Research and Treatment Program. VERA INSTITUTE OF JUSTICE, THE VERA REPORT 1-5 (1970). See also VERA INSTITUTE OF JUSTICE, PROPOSAL FOR THE NEIGHBORHOOD YOUTH DIVERSION PROJECT 8 (1970).

2. The Institute for Social Research was created by the Departments of Sociology and Anthropology at Fordham University as an operating entity to put into practice

Funds for the project come from the Law Enforcement Assistance Administration of the United States Department of Justice through the Criminal Justice Coordinating Council of New York City.

A major part of the program is the Forum which is essentially a community court where residents of the neighborhood volunteer their evenings several times a week to become Forum Judges.[3] Cases which otherwise would find their way into the regular juvenile justice system are brought before the Forum. This paper does not attempt to argue the merits of this concept, nor to explore the legal ramifications of the program.[4] Rather, it will examine the genesis and execution of a training curriculum for the Forum Judges.

The pilot training cycle consisted of fifteen trainees: one, a minister, had a professional degree, three were enrolled in a community or technical college and the majority had some high school training. All the trainees, except the minister, were Black or Puerto Rican. Among the occupations of the trainees were housewife, community worker and student. The average age of the trainees was approximately twenty-eight.[5] None of the trainees were employed by the Neighborhood Youth Diversion Program. Before coming to the program, no trainee had had any legal training or judicial experience.

II. The Neighborhood Youth Diversion Program as an Alternative

In New York, a youth who gets into trouble can be declared a Juvenile Delinquent, if "over seven and less than sixteen years of age"

---

some of the theories that flow from these departments. See J. Martin & J. Fitzpatrick, Delinquent Behavior: A Redefinition of the Problem (1965) and J. Martin, J. Fitzpatrick & R. Gould, The Analysis of Delinquent Behavior: A Structural Approach (1968) for a description of some of the preplanning conducted by Fordham in the target area of the Neighborhood Youth Diversion Program.

3. Although none of the Forum Judges are paid for their services, they do receive $10.00 for every training session and for every Forum hearing they conduct in order to cover transportation, baby-sitting and similar expenses.

4. For such a discussion of other projects, see Gaines and Skrabut, The Youth Court Concept and Its Implementation in Timpkins County, New York, 52 Cornell L.Q. 942 (1967); Taylor, Building Conflict Resolution Systems, Philadelphia 4-A 4 (a position paper prepared for the National Workshop on Community Crisis Intervention held at the Center for Mediation and Conflict Resolution of New York City, June 16, 1971); National Council on Crime and Delinquency, Teen-age Juries, 12 Crime & Delinquency 305 (1966) and Berman, The Cuban Popular Tribunals, 69 Colum. L. Rev. 1317 (1969).

5. The program planners were anxious to recruit some young Forum Judges with whom the youthful juveniles could identify. The youngest trainee was sixteen. See infra on the plans to recruit younger trainees for the second cycle of training.

and "does any act which, if done by an adult, would constitute a crime,"[6] or a Person in Need of Supervision if "a male less than sixteen years of age and a female less than eighteen years of age" and "is an habitual truant or who is incorrigible, ungovernable or habitually disobedient and beyond the lawful control of parent or other lawful authority."[7] The New York Family Court has jurisdiction over both categories of minors.[8] When a complainant wants to bring a petition against a minor as a Juvenile Delinquent or as a Person in Need of Supervision, the Department of Probation is authorized to attempt to adjust the case before the petition is filed in Family Court.[9] A case is adjusted when the probation service has persuaded all parties concerned to try to resolve the difficulties outside of Family Court. If the case is not adjusted, it goes to Family Court. If the petition charges Juvenile Delinquency, a fact-finding hearing is held to determine whether the minor did the alleged acts, which if done by an adult would constitute a crime. If the petition charges that the minor is a Person in Need of Supervision, the fact-finding hearing determines whether the minor "did the acts alleged to show that he violated a law or is incorrigible, ungovernable or habitually disobedient and beyond the control of his parents, guardian or legal custodian."[10] A dispositional hearing is then conducted to determine whether the minor requires supervision or treatment.[11]

At the adjustment stage, the Department of Probation can refer cases to agencies like the Neighborhood Youth Diversion Program, and the case could then go before the Forum. It is anticipated that referrals also would come from the Family Court itself or from the Police Department, and that complainants who know about the Forum can participate in it before they approach the police, probation or the court. All Forum participants, complainants and youngsters, come to the Forum voluntarily. They remain free at all times to pursue the normal channels of the criminal justice system for minors. If a case is referred from an official agency, it is usually left open for a number of days to determine if the Neighborhood Youth Diversion Program and the Forum can resolve existing conflicts. If resolution is achieved, the referring agency closes the case.[12] Once a case is referred to the Program, its resource-advocacy staff offers counseling and

6. N.Y. FAM. CT. ACT § 712(a) (McKinney 1963).
7. Id. § 712(b). The age distinction made by the law between males and females has been held violative of the equal protection clauses of the Federal and New York State Constitutions in Matter of Patricia A., 31 N.Y.2d 83, 335 N.Y.S.2d 33, 286 N.E.2d 432 (1972).
8. Id. § 713.
9. Id. § 734(a)(ii). See also N.Y. FAM. CT. R. 7.3 (McKinney 1963).
10. N.Y. FAM. CT. ACT § 742 as amended L. 1963, c. 529, § 11.
11. Id. § 743.
12. See W. Statsky, Procedure Manual and Training Materials for Forum Judges, Case Classification 9-26 (1971).

advocacy services designed to provide the youngster and his family with guidance and the resource tools to help solve problems in areas such as housing and medical care. If the case involves a conflict between the youngster and the complainant that could not be resolved by the resource-advocacy staff, it is sent before the Forum.[13]

The Forum Judges have no power to sentence anyone. Their authority is generated from the consent of all the participants and the referring agency. The results of the Judges' deliberations are always phrased as recommendations to the participants and the referring agency. If the Forum develops an effective approach to conflict resolution, it is anticipated that these recommendations will carry great weight with the referring agencies whose caseload pressures make them very receptive to innovative alternatives for the youngsters and their families.

The challenge of the training program was not simply to train people to perform a newly created role. More fundamentally, it sought to define that role within a framework designed to develop confidence in community residents that they had the capacity to cope with the problems of their young adults without having to rely on professional social workers, probation officers and Family Court Judges. There had to be a close working relationship between the program planners who originated the concept of the Forum and the community people who were to execute the concept and integrate it into the design of their own neighborhood organizations. However, the program planners had to be aware of the extent to which their control over the initial phases of the experiment made the community people dependent on their involvement. The training program, therefore, was conducted within the context of two tensions: the need to engender a sense of community "ownership" of the Forum and the anxiety of the program planners to monitor the Forum tightly in order to ensure its success. From a resolution of these tensions a definition of Forum Judgeship evolved.

III. A "Floating" Workshop

At the outset, the program planners had a better sense of what a Forum Judge should *not* be than of what he should be. He should not be an individual who wears a forbidding black robe; who is so overwhelmed by the number of cases on his calendar that it would be almost impossible to give individualized attention to any particular young adult; or who does not understand the young adult or his background. The planners wanted the Forum Judge to be an instrument of change in the young adult's life,

---

13. *Proposal for the Neighborhood Youth Diversion Project, supra* note 1, at 19-24.

but they could only say abstractly what a Forum Judge should be: empathetic, receptive, resourceful, patient, motivated, intelligent, impartial, available. The problem with this approach was that it tended to idealize the Forum Judge and by implication to vilify the Family Court Judge by suggesting that the latter was not in possession of these "noble" traits. Ultimately, the planners admitted that the concept of Forum Judgeship contained many unknowns and that one purpose of the training was the development of a definition of what a Forum Judge should be.

The orientation to the training program as a discovery process had significant pedagogical implications. Given the fact that there were no definitive guidelines on the nature of Forum Judgeship, the trainees would have to be taken into full partnership in the process of determining or approximating such guidelines. Accordingly, the attitude of the passive student who comes to be taught was not going to be accepted. All too often, the teacher projects himself as someone who possesses ultimate knowledge and it is this projection which encourages the student to relax his own creative faculties and to become dependent on the professor. Moreover, students sometimes create an image of the omniscient teacher in order to justify their own learning deficiencies. In such an environment, knowledge is presumptively infused from above rather than mutually generated.

The antidote was an action workshop wherein the challenge was role discovery. Every participant in the training had to feel the pressure of this challenge. No one could sit back and wait to be told how to be a Forum Judge. This created the obvious danger of a highly unstructured "floating" point of reference which could and, in all probability, had to be a painful experience. It is more comfortable for a student to be lectured or taught how to do something than to be cast into a self-teaching role.

The first problem in this approach was determining an effective way of introducing the trainees to the concept. It would not do simply to tell them that they had an important teaching-discovery role to play during the training sessions. This technique would be as impotent as the "this-is-your-park" technique of getting the public not to litter. A setting which structured the trainees into such a role had to be staged. The audio-visual facilities of the Center on Mediation and Conflict Resolution in New York City[14] were summoned for assistance.

Before any formal instructions or training sessions were given, the trainees were asked to enter a room individually where they found two strangers, a youth and an adult, playing the role of disputants in a fabricated fact situation. The trainees were told that these two individuals had

---

14. *See* Institute for Collective Bargaining and Group Relations, *Automation House 10* (published by the American Foundation on Automation and Employment, undated).

a problem and that the role of the Forum Judge was to try to bring the two people together. They were told that they could use any technique which their common sense suggested in attempting to realize this objective. No other instructions were given. Each trainee was arbitrarily given about twenty minutes for this attempt. They knew that they were being televised on a closed circuit system and that at some later date they would be able to view themselves. After all of the screenings were taped, the trainees, as a group, were able to see their individual performances. Theoretically any techniques that seemed to work would have come naturally from the trainees; they could not have been learned from the project since no learning sessions had yet been held.

During the viewings, the trainees were asked to identify those techniques that they and their peers had used which appeared to be effective. This method of identification was used to convince the trainees that they had begun the process of creating their own role. Hopefully, they saw that there was no deep magic in being a Forum Judge; the mystique of judgeship was domesticated. The trainees observed that being a Forum Judge, to a large degree, simply meant a continuation of the normal tendency to draw upon their visceral responses when confronted with two people engaged in a dispute. Once all the effective techniques were identified by the trainees, they were told that the rest of the training sessions would involve a development and further testing of the techniques observed during the television segments. A major objective was to instill in the trainees the self-confidence to proceed with the process of creating their own role. The time should have been taken to guide them into their own formulation of what they considered effective.

The use of television, of course, involved risks. There was a danger that the trainees would be intimidated by the glaring eye of the camera and, as a result, any natural responses would be withheld. This was true in several instances, but essentially, the trainees enjoyed the experience, particularly after overcoming the anticipated fright during the first few minutes of taping. The immediacy and the truthfulness of the screen provided an excellent opportunity for the trainees to focus their attention directly on themselves. To be sure, all of the trainees had to overcome their very normal ego involvement as television performers, but they appeared to do quite well, as was evidenced by their perceptive comments on the screenings.[15]

---

15. If television had not been available, a tape recorder would have been used. Of course, the use of audio-visual equipment is not an absolute pre-condition to the experiment. If such equipment had not been available, the program planners would have staged the same role playing situation, but with the entire group watching each performance so that the benefit of collective observations would not be lost. The same fact situation could not be used, however, since those trainees who had been able to observe prior trainees handle the same case would be tempted to handle it in the same way.

Before the audio-visual experiment was undertaken, the program planners gave considerable thought to whether any written materials should be prepared for the trainees. There were at least two strong arguments against written materials. First, no one had any clear idea of what the materials should contain. The literature on the subject was almost non-existent.[16] Second, and more fundamentally, it was feared that if a written document had been prepared and distributed, the trainee might become dependent on it at the expense of drawing on his own ingenuity in defining his role. In spite of these arguments, however, the program planners prepared the *Procedure Manual and Training Materials for Forum Judges*.[17] They were excited about the potential of the audio-visual experiment, but were sufficiently unsure of its success to prompt them to put something in writing. Although the *Manual* was written at the time of the audio-visual experience, no one was certain at that time whether it would be used. The trainees were not told that it existed when they were asked to take part in the audio-visual experiment. After the experiment, the trainees were given the *Manual* and were asked to compare its contents with the approaches that they had used on television. In retrospect, it would have been more productive if the trainees had written their own *Manual* on the basis of their observations in the television sessions and in subsequent sessions.[18]

Armed with the audio-visual experience and the *Manual*, the program planners led the trainees into the remainder of the training program. It was a time for the planners to re-evaluate their role and to assess the extent to which the training program was achieving one of its primary goals: the development of the trainees' confidence both in themselves and in the Forum. It was clear that the program planners had biases as to what constituted good or poor Forum Judgeship, particularly after the audio-

Even with a varied fact situation, however, the trainees who took the role of the Forum Judge later in the session would have the tendency to borrow from the techniques used in the first few sequences.

16. *See* Ronayne, *Law School Training for Non-lawyer Judges*, 17 J. LEGAL ED. 197 (1964). On the subject of paraprofessional training in general, *see* W. Statsky and P. Lang, The Legal Paraprofessional As Advocate and Assistant: Roles, Training Concepts and Materials (published by the Center for Social Welfare Policy and Law, Columbia Law School, and also published in A Compilation of Materials for the Legal Assistant and the Lay Advocate (M. Ader, ed. 1971); Statsky, *The Education of Legal Paraprofessionals: Myths, Realities and Opportunities*, 24 VND. L. REV. 1083 (1971); Brown, *The Education of Legal Assistants, Technicians and Paraprofessionals*, 22 J. LEGAL ED. 94 (1969); Lee, *The Training of Nonprofessional Personnel*, 6 NURSING OUTLOOK 222 (1958) and Preliminary Report on a Survey of Paralegal Training in the United States, 1971 (University of Denver, College of Law).

17. W. Statsky, *supra* note 12.

18. The training program began on an open-ended basis since no one was sure how long the training would take. In fact, the program lasted approximately twelve weeks with the groups divided into two sessions, each meeting once a week for approximately two and half hours per session.

visual experiment. It would have been dishonest to pretend that such biases did not exist or that they would not be reflected in the way the planners would conduct the rest of the training sessions.

How could these biases be handled in a way consistent with the theme of community creation and ownership of the Forum? First, the planners had to recognize that they were influencing the structure of the Forum and that this could not be avoided. Second, they had to restrain themselves from injecting their own judgments as to what was or was not an effective technique for a Forum Judge. They did this by emphasizing the importance of flexibility: a Forum Judge should feel free to try any technique as long as he was flexible enough to try another technique, if necessary, to achieve the intended objective. Together, trainees and trainers would try to identify the techniques that were effective, but no Judge was forced to accept any technique that the group had defined as effective. If this process worked, it could not be said that the Forum Judge had been molded in the image of the planners' conception of a Forum Judge. This was the hope of the planners and the basis upon which they proceeded.

IV. DEFINITIONS

What were the definitions of Forum Judgeship that emerged from the group discussions of the techniques the trainees used in the audio-visual experience? The facts involved in the dispute between the young adult and the adult which every trainee had to deal with before the television camera were substantially those set out in the introduction to this article.[19] Gilbert Drinan, a young High School freshman, was stopped in the corridor by Mr. Huber, a teacher. When Mr. Huber questioned Gilbert about smoking pot, a struggle ensued resulting in a charge of assault by the teacher. Each trainee was asked to use whatever techniques he wanted to bring Gilbert and Mr. Huber together.

As the trainees watched each television taping, they were asked to engage in several levels of observation. First, and most importantly, was self-analysis. Each trainee was asked to analyze his own techniques. A second level was peer-analysis: what did the other trainees think about the tape? The third level of observation was instructor-analysis which was considerably deemphasized and used only when the individual trainee and his peers had come to an impasse in the discussion.

Everyone was asked to express his observations in terms of feelings as

---

19. *Supra* at 401. The only difference between the fact pattern described and that used in the television sequence was that in the latter, the incident took place in the school bathroom rather than in the corridor.

opposed to absolute judgments. In one of the screenings, for example, it was clear that the trainee was making little progress in reaching the young adult, Gilbert Drinan. Instead of telling this trainee that his approach was obviously wrong, the trainee was asked the following question: "How did you feel about that approach when you appeared to be having difficulty getting your point across to Gilbert?" The goal was to have the trainee identify the frustration that he felt rather than to recognize his error. A great deal can be said in favor of encouraging the trainee to define his frustration as precisely as possible. At the time of this definition, he is most receptive to considering and perhaps acting upon the suggestions offered from the group to overcome his frustrations.

What standard would be used in determining whether a particular technique used by a trainee was effective? It was clear to everyone that no one standard would cover every situation. The goal of the Forum was to be of genuine assistance to the young adult by bringing about a resolution of the conflict that existed between him and the adult (or between two young adults). Any technique that achieved this result was considered effective. Defining the usefulness of a technique in terms of its result had significant training implications. If the trainee realized there were no fool-proof techniques to be committed to memory, he would see that he must ultimately resort to his own resources in attacking the problem. The techniques that he used would have to grow out of the variables in every concrete situation that he considered as a Forum Judge.

Since effectiveness was to be measured in terms of results, there was no way of applying this standard during the training sessions since there were no real cases before the Forum. Role playing could only simulate the reactions of disputants to techniques used. Hence, the trainees had to define the effectiveness of a particular technique in terms of its *probable* rehabilitative impact on the parties. A sense of the probabilities came from the collective determinations by the trainees of the merits and demerits of each technique under discussion. In the final analysis, such determinations represented the "gut" reactions of the trainees. Some of the trainees did try to theorize a judgment on the effectiveness of a technique, but most of the judgments, and perhaps the best ones, were instinctive in origin.

Basically, two schools of thought on Forum Judgeship emerged from the group discussions of the techniques used by the trainees in the case of Gilbert Drinan. The following two segments from the screenings are representative of each view:

A

GILBERT:	I didn't hit him.
MR. HUBER:	That's not true. You ran away.
TRAINEE:	You must have felt guilty if you ran, Gilbert.

B

GILBERT: I don't smoke pot.

TRAINEE: I didn't say that you did. I want to ask you and Mr. Huber a question. What do you both think would be the best way for the two of you to begin communicating again?

One group of trainees, as represented by the trainee in sequence "A" above, tended to be very judgment-oriented. They took sides between the student and the teacher. When either the student or the teacher did something, the trainee did not hesitate to label it good or bad. A second group of trainees, as represented by sequence "B" above, took a very different approach. To the extent possible, they held back from expressing personal opinions and refused to take sides. These trainees pressured the disputants to come up with their own solution as to how the dispute could be resolved and their relationship restored. The two groups reflected a fundamental difference of opinion: should an intermediary project himself as an authoritative figure who is not afraid to tell the parties precisely what he feels, even if it involves taking sides, or should the intermediary deemphasize his own value judgments and concentrate on encouraging the disputants to see that they have the responsibility of resolving the dispute?

The group analysis of the two points of view was heated. About half of the trainees defined their role as mediators. They claimed that the participation of the Forum Judge should be limited to assisting the participants to achieve a level of communication that would enable them to solve their own problems. "If you come right out and tell them who's right and who's wrong," explained one trainee, "then all you will have achieved would be to emphasize and deepen the dispute between them. If you're so anxious to inject yourself into the dispute, you'll lose touch with them and you'll probably turn off the one you are saying was in the wrong." Many of the other trainees felt that the Forum Judge should play a more aggressive role. "When it's clear that someone has done something wrong, you'll lose everyone's respect if you don't say so," one trainee theorized. "In fact, it's impossible for a Forum Judge not to take sides in one way or another."

The proponents of mediation were the most articulate in describing the ways in which they felt that Gilbert and Mr. Huber could be brought together. During the audio-visual tapings, they emphasized the positive aspects of the Gilbert-Huber relationship and tried to get them to rebuild their relationship by locating possible areas of mutual agreement. For example, the mediators did the following:

1. Helped them to see and to admit the relative merits of the Forum as compared to a Family Court adjudication;

2. Guided their identification of the times earlier in their relationship when they *were* able to talk with each other;

3. Led them to agree that it was necessary to establish a relationship of trust, and a willingness to want to resolve their difficulties prior to coping with the specific incident;

4. Helped them decide the best way to determine what specifically happened and the best method for restoring their relationship;

5. Suggested the re-enactment of the specific incident with a *role-reversal* in order to gain a greater understanding of each other's position and point of view.

The two groups of trainees insisted on the efficacy of their respective points of view, but with coaching from the instructor, they were encouraged to consider the opposite viewpoint. The program planners clearly favored mediation as opposed to the more authoritarian approach. To the extent possible, however, they refrained from imposing this opinion on those trainees who disagreed. At this stage in the training, the instructor wanted to be sure that the trainees recognized the difference between the approaches. In subsequent training sessions there would be opportunities for each trainee to test *all* approaches. The key would be flexibility. Because there were no techniques or approaches that were absolutely acceptable, the Forum Judge had to be prepared to shift the focus of his approach and, if necessary, to adopt a totally different approach if he sensed that his initial efforts were not working.

V. Vehicles for Testing

In addition to audio-visual equipment, the program planners used three training mechanisms which were designed to provide an arena in which abstract notions of techniques and approaches could be tested: role playing, written plays and the recounting of personal experiences involving disputes between adults and young adults. The focus of these training devices was the development of ways for the trainee's individuality to be used in formulating his own style and definition of Forum Judgeship.

Role playing was the major mechanism for giving a trainee the chance to determine the probable impact of approaches that he had earlier identified as effective and to explore other approaches.[20] This device forced the trainee to develop his own style of Forum Judgeship. He was confronted with the immediate need to make a decision in a concrete setting. The

---

20. *See* ADULT EDUCATION ASSOCIATION OF THE U.S.A., HOW TO USE ROLE PLAYING AND OTHER TOOLS OF LEARNING 6 (1955). *See also* Day, Max and Robinson, *Training Aids Through Group Techniques,* 2 NURSING OUTLOOK 308 (1954).

anxiety generated from this need provided an excellent opportunity for the trainee to focus on the pros and cons of his action. Theoretically, he would be receptive to guidance from his peers and from the instructor because he would *feel* the need for assistance and relate the assistance directly to a visible situation.

Openness is the key to successful role playing if it is to be a genuinely explorative experience. A role player must be able to deal with his role from two points of view. First, he must be an advocate of a particular approach. He must determine what he hopes to accomplish and identify an approach designed to achieve his goal. Second, and most important, he must watch for signs of success and failure in his approach. He must have the flexibility to determine when and where he is unsuccessful and to restructure his efforts accordingly. The trainee is his own teacher while he is role playing because he is pressured into learning how to maneuver in and around a troublesome part of the role playing sequence.

The best role playing grew out of a dispute between two people or groups on a particular point. For example, during one of the sessions, Trainee X was explaining why he felt that the Forum Judges had to be careful not to antagonize the adult-complainant by being overly partial to the young adult in trouble. "Otherwise," according to this trainee, "the complainant could get right up and walk out on you and the case will be forced back into Family Court." Trainee Y, on the other hand, did not think it would be possible for a complainant, who had agreed to come to the Forum in the first place, to walk out unless someone physically attacked him. Instead of letting Trainee X respond abstractly to this comment by Trainee Y, the instructor asked Trainee X to play the role of a Forum Judge in such a way as to prove his point in front of Trainees A and B who would play the roles of a youngster and an adult respectively. Mr. X did so very convincingly. He almost totally antagonized B by talking to A in such a way as to convey the impression to B that X not only believed everything A was saying but that X was not even going to accord B the courtesy of being heard.

Role reversal was a significant part of a training process designed to achieve flexibility. In the situation involving Trainees X and Y, the position of X was acted out in order to convince a doubting Y. After this sequence, Y was asked to play the role of the Forum Judge in the case of A and B in such a way as to antagonize B, the adult. In effect, Y was asked to take a position as Forum Judge which he did not believe possible when he was simply verbalizing this position. In this way, Y was encouraged to adopt a multi-leveled perspective. The same result could have been achieved (the Forum Judge being able to understand the point of view of the adult and the youngster) by asking the trainee to be the Forum Judge and after about ten minutes, asking this same trainee to reverse his position and adopt the role of the adult or the child in the same case with another trainee taking the part of the Forum Judge.

It was difficult at times to determine when to stop a role playing sequence for purposes of discussion or for the structuring of a counter-role playing sequence. After about twenty minutes of role playing, it was not easy for the players to remember everything that was said during the earlier part of the sequence. If a tape recorder had not been used, some of the early comments of the participants might have been lost. One way to offset this difficulty and, more positively, to encourage the trainee to think in terms of alternative techniques while a particular technique is being tried was the use of a point system. Every observer is given the right to stop the role playing sequence by saying, "Point," at which time he gives his comment on what the Forum Judge has just done. The instructor must see to it that the comments are concise and to the point so that the Forum Judge can quickly respond and either adopt or reject the suggestion made by the observer. The danger of the point system is that everyone may be calling "Point" at each action by the Forum Judge, thereby impeding the flow of the unfolding of events. The instructor must be able to halt the point calling at any time and for any duration he deems appropriate.

Another training device used by the program planners was a series of short plays written by the instructor. They were basically morality plays and each one was representative of a particular dispute-resolving approach that the trainees had identified during the training sessions. The aim of the plays was to demonstrate that these approaches were often used in everyday situations. For example, one of the plays involved a grocery bill dispute which took place in a community grocery store. During these sessions, the trainees were asked to read, or to act out, the plays and to discuss them. The discussions were somewhat fruitful, but generally the plays were not sufficiently challenging. It would have been more effective to have had the trainees write the plays themselves. After they had identified a particular technique that they felt might be useful in the Forum, they should have been asked to write a short play showing how the same technique is often used in everyday experiences involving a dispute between two or more people.

In addition to role playing and written plays, the training sessions drew heavily on the personal experiences of the trainees. They were asked to relate their young adult relationships and confrontations with adults. The situations were varied: teacher-student and parent-child relationships, as well as more casual interactions between adults and youngsters, e.g., in department stores and on the streets. The trainees were asked to identify the confrontations in which a third party had intervened or tried to intervene in order to settle the dispute. The instructor asked the trainees to recall the techniques of conflict resolution that the third person had used and to discuss their effectiveness. Whenever a trainee described such a situation, he was always asked two questions: (1) what alternative methods could this third party have used to resolve the dispute, and (2) what did the trainee think about the use by the Forum Judge of the technique used by the third party?

VI. FACT-FINDING

Suppose that a child has been accused of stealing and categorically denies it, or suppose that a parent wants her child institutionalized because she claims that the child comes home late every night and the child denies it. How should the Forum handle this kind of a factual dispute? Again, two schools of thought emerged from the trainees during the discussion of these issues. One group of trainees maintained that every Forum should devote some of its attention to uncovering the facts. They felt that whenever necessary, witnesses should be called and written documents should be examined by the Forum Judges. Other trainees, however, felt that turning the Forum into an investigative tribunal would be a mistake. These trainees recognized the importance of knowing what the facts were before they could make intelligent determinations, but they felt that lengthy factual investigations could divert the Forum from its primary objective of reconciling troubled relationships.

The trainees and the program planners jointly arrived at a determinative question to be used in deciding when to attempt to resolve an issue of fact: would a resolution of the particular factual dispute contribute to the objective of reconciling the parties? The trainees had to realize that even if the Forum Judges were able establish the "real" facts, there might still remain a fundamental personality conflict or basic mistrust between the disputants. A statement, "I didn't do it," could be translated into a statement, "I don't like you," or "You don't respect me." If the Forum Judge could effectively establish a willingness on the part of the antagonists to restore their relationship, the major factual issues would be clarified.

VII. ON-THE-JOB TRAINING

There was little doubt that once the Forum Judges heard actual cases, they would be able to accelerate their training pace and place in focus the methods of conflict resolution which they had discussed during the training sessions. The program planners decided to provide the Judges every opportunity to explore their on-the-job training experiences. Forums were divided into five segments: the pre-hearing conference, the first part of the hearing, the recess conference, the remainder of the hearing, and the post-hearing conference. The conferences were designed to give the Forum Judges who were hearing a case opportunities to meet privately and evaluate the case before them that evening. For each Forum there were three Judges.

During the pre-hearing conference, the three Forum Judges met with the staff of the Neighborhood Youth Diversion Program who had been involved in the pending case. The general outline of the case would be discussed and the Forum Judges would map out preliminary strategies. After this conference, the actual Forum would begin. The Forum Judges would introduce themselves, explain the purpose of the Forum, and find out as much as they could about the problem by listening to the complainant and the young adult. Approximately halfway through the proceeding, the Forum Judges called a recess conference in which they privately evaluated what they had learned in the Forum and planned further strategy. After the recess, the hearing continued. The Forum Judges attempted to get the participants to agree to a plan for resolving their differences. If, for example, a youngster had broken a grocery store window, the store owner and the youngster might agree on a damage payment schedule. If a parent complained that her son constantly stayed out late, and this was established at the Forum, then the parent and child might agree on a time when the son would have to be home in the future. The Forum Judges might schedule a second Forum with the same participants in order to determine how successfully the participants had carried out their agreements. After the hearing was concluded, a private post-hearing conference was held. This was the final opportunity for the Forum Judges to exchange views on the effectiveness of their approaches and the manner in which they could improve in the future.

Adequate feedback from the resource-advocacy staff of the Neighborhood Youth Diversion Program is critical. The Forum Judges need to know what happens after a Forum is conducted. The program planners have discussed the possibility of inviting some of the youngsters whose cases had come before the Forum to become Forum Judges in future training cycles. An excellent opportunity would be provided for the pilot training group to obtain firsthand reactions to the Forum from participants-turned-colleagues. In addition, and perhaps much more importantly, the utilization of some Forum Judges who were approximately the same age as the youngster brought before the Forum could increase the identification level between this youngster and the Forum Judge panel.

VIII.   CONCLUSION: REHABILITATIVE ADJUDICATION

The agony of an experiment grows out of a tension between the will to give the imagination full reign and the fear of going too far. It was a tall order to construct the training program so that the trainees would be guided into the arena of rehabilitative adjudication in which every decision they made would have to contribute to the goal of restoring the relationship between the disputants, while at the same time diverting cases from the normal criminal justice system. Furthermore, the training program had to be structured so that the trainees would come to realize that the Forum was theirs because it could become, and had to become, a community undertaking. The fact that such a training program had never been tried before was an invitation to open it to any and every possibility to achieve these objectives. The fact that the Forum would be dealing with real people with intense problems was a mandate for caution.

There were no easy answers. The direction ultimately taken by the program planners was to focus on the development of the personalities that the trainees brought to the training program. It was felt that the imposition of rigorous parliamentary rules and regulations, even if they could have been devised or adapted from the normal criminal justice system, would hinder this development. First and foremost, the training had to take the shape of a process of self-investigation on the part of each trainee. The trainee was asked not only to identify what was good in himself but also to examine his approaches critically and constructively in light of the role playing experiences, the reactions of his peers and the guidance of the instructor.

When the trainee finally moved out of the hypothetical world of the training sessions and into the real world of the Forum, it would be important for him to feel alone. The staff of the program would not fail to support him once he became a Forum Judge. However, the Judge had to understand that he alone was responsible for resolving the dispute. In the final analysis, it was the innate talents of the Forum Judges that would determine the success or failure of the Forum. It was the task of the training program to identify these talents and to give them an arena for expression and testing.

7

THE APPLICABILITY OF THE FOURTH AMENDMENT EXCLUSIONARY RULE TO JUVENILES IN DELINQUENCY PROCEEDINGS

WILLIAM O. FLANNERY*

The Fourth Amendment's proscription of "unreasonable searches and seizures"[1] and its "correlative" remedy, the exclusionary rule,[2] have been extended to juvenile delinquency proceedings in a number of state juvenile court cases in the decade since the *Mapp v. Ohio*[3] decision.[4] It is the thesis of this article that this application should be held to be a constitutional requirement.[5]

Since the passage of Illinois' juvenile court statute in 1899,[6] the first such statute in the nation, the Supreme Court has delivered four opinions which have sought to determine the rights of juveniles in the juvenile courts.[7] In those four decisions, the Court has attempted to establish a

---

*Staff member, COLUMBIA HUMAN RIGHTS LAW REVIEW.

1. U.S. CONST. amend. IV:

  The right of the people to be secure in their persons, houses, papers, and effects, against unreasonable searches and seizures, shall not be violated, and no Warrants shall issue, but upon probable cause, supported by Oath or affirmation, and particularly describing the place to be searched, and the persons or things to be seized.

2. The Fourth Amendment exclusionary rule has been referred to as "the correlative duty of the government to the constitutional right of the individual to be secure from unreasonable searches and seizures." State v. Lowry, 95 N.J. Super. 307, 230 A.2d 907 (Super. Ct. 1967).

3. 367 U.S. 643 (1961). For a discussion of *Mapp*, see section 1 *infra*.

4. *See* note 166 *infra* and accompanying text.

5. In the three Supreme Court decisions to date which have considered the application of constitutional protections to the juvenile court process (*see* section 3 *infra*), the Court has limited its inquiry to whether the procedural right at issue should be applied to the adjudicative phase of a delinquency proceeding on a charge which would be considered criminal if the accused were an adult and which may result in institutionalization for the juvenile. *E.g.*, In re Gault, 387 U.S. 1, 12-13 (1967). The treatment in this article of the Fourth Amendment's applicability to the juvenile courts will be similarly limited, and the amendment's application to neglect and dependency proceedings will not be considered.

6. Juvenile Court Act, ILL. LAWS 1899, p. 131.

7. McKeiver v. Pennsylvania, 403 U.S. 528 (1971) (consolidated with In re Burrus *et al.* for the purpose of decision); In re Winship, 397 U.S. 358 (1970); In re Gault, 387 U.S. 1 (1967); Kent v. United States, 383 U.S. 541 (1966).

due process formulation which approaches the question of the selective application of the protections of the Bill of Rights to juveniles from two routes.[8] First, the Court has considered the historical origins of the procedural protection at issue and the relation the particular right bears to modern conceptions of due process.[9] Secondly, the Court has balanced the "necessity" of the constitutional right, as determined above in the first step, against the harm such application might cause to the salutary aspects of the juvenile court process.[10] The intent of this article is to analyze and evaluate the content and weight of individual elements of the balancing process likely to be used by the Supreme Court if and when it decides whether the exclusionary rule should be applied to the adjudicative phase of a delinquency proceeding.

The paper opens with a consideration of the Fourth Amendment and its exclusionary rule. Section 1 demonstrates the historical importance of the Fourth Amendment, and the continued expansion of interpretation that the Amendment has enjoyed at the hands of the Supreme Court.

Section 2 relates a brief history of the juvenile court movement: Part A outlines the theory and ideals of the juvenile court in its earlier years, and Part B indicates the problems that have hampered the successful implementation of the theory. Section 3 presents an analysis of the four Supreme Court decisions dealing with juvenile rights; more specifically, the section looks at the balancing process utilized by the Court as it established a due process standard for the juvenile courts. Finally, the concern in Section 4 is to determine the particular elements of the previously outlined balancing test that should be considered if the application of the exclusionary rule to the juvenile courts is litigated.

I. THE FOURTH AMENDMENT AND THE EXCLUSIONARY RULE

The stated thesis of this article is that the Fourth Amendment should be held applicable to juveniles, and that the protection of the Fourth Amendment's exclusionary rule should apply to juvenile court delinquency proceedings.[11] This suggested application of the Fourth Amendment is supported partially by a consideration of the history and reason behind the amendment, and further by an examination of the continued expansion of the amendment's protections in Supreme Court decisions.

---

8. For a discussion of "selective incorporation" and the relation between the Due Process Clause and the first eight amendments to the Constitution see note 152 infra.

9. See, e.g., McKeiver v. Pennsylvania, 403 U.S. 528 (1971); see also the discussion of this balancing process at section 4 infra.

10. Id.

11. See note 5 supra.

Although a search of pre-1789 sources reveals very little discussion directed to the Fourth Amendment,[12] its importance was never in doubt. Before the Revolution, revenue agents of the British made frequent use of *writs of assistance* which authorized the search and arrest of suspected smugglers who attempted to avoid the heavy duty on imports. These general writs, issued without names and accordingly without particularity or probable cause, were one of the direct causes of the ensuing revolution.[13]

In *Boyd v. United States*,[14] the first significant Fourth Amendment decision by the Supreme Court,[15] Justice Bradley, speaking for the Court, argued that a liberal construction of the Amendment was the only means

---

12. Justice Frankfurter in Harris v. United States, 331 U.S. 145 (1945) (dissenting opinion), traces the form of the Fourth Amendment back to the search and seizure provision of the first Massachusetts constitution:

> Every subject has a right to be secure from all unreasonable searches and seizures of his person, his houses, his papers and all his possessions. All warrants, therefore, are contrary to this right, if the cause or foundation of them be not previously supported by oath or affirmation, and if the order in the warrant to a civil officer, to make search in suspected places, or to arrest one or more suspected persons, or to seize their property, be not accompanied with a special designation of the persons or objects of search, arrest, or seizure; and no warrant ought to be issued but in cases, and with the formalities, prescribed by the laws.

Massachusetts Constitution (1780), Part the First, Art. XIV. For a general discussion of the pre-constitutional history of the Fourth Amendment, *see, e.g.,* Miller, Origins of the American Revolution (1943); Lasson, History and Development of the Fourth Amendment (1937); and Douglas, The Right of the People (1958).

13. Justice Bradley, speaking for the Court in Boyd v. United States, 116 U.S. 616, 620-21 (1886), stated:

> The practice had obtained in the colonies of issuing writs of assistance to the revenue officers, empowering them, in their discretion, to search suspected places for smuggled goods, which James Otis pronounced "the worst instrument of arbitrary power, the most destructive of English liberty and the fundamental principles of law, that ever was found in an English law book;" since they placed "the liberty of every man in the hands of every petty officer." This was in February, 1761, in Boston, and the famous debate in which it occurred was perhaps the most prominent event which inaugurated the resistance of the colonies to the oppressions of the mother country. "Then and there," said John Adams, "then and there was the first scene of the first act of opposition to the arbitrary claims of Great Britain. Then and there the child of Independence was born."

One writer has contended that the Fourth Amendment was the only procedural safeguard to grow "directly out of the events which immediately preceded the revolutionary struggle with England." Landynski, Search and Seizure and the Supreme Court 19 (1966).

14. 116 U.S. 616 (1866).

15. The Boyd decision has been called by the Supreme Court "the leading case" on the subject of search and seizure." Carroll v. United States, 267 U.S. 132, 147 (1925). Professor Landynski has noted that there are valid reasons why the *Boyd* decision, the first in depth statement by the Court on the subject of search and seizure, was to come over one hundred years after the adoption of the Fourth Amendment. Until the latter years of the eighteenth century "the criminal jurisdiction of the federal government was seldom exercised by Congress," and prior to 1891, the Court did not have jurisdiction to decide criminal cases on appeal. Landynski, *supra* note 13, at 49.

of protecting the privacy of citizens.[16] The first step in effectively providing that protection occurred in *Weeks v. United States*[17] when the Supreme Court explicitly held that evidence seized by federal officers in violation of the search and seizure provisions was to be excluded in federal criminal trials. The defendant, Weeks, was charged with using the mails to transport lottery tickets in violation of federal law. After a warrantless arrest, the police entered the defendant's room and seized letters and articles which were later used at trial. The major difficulty facing the Supreme Court was a long-standing common law rule supported by past decisions of the Court[18] that a trial court would not notice the manner in which otherwise competent evidence had been brought before its bench. That rule was distinguished, however, and the Court held that the evidence was unlawfully used at Weeks' trial. The amendment's protection was held to reach "all alike . . . and the duty of giving to it force and effect is obligatory upon all entrusted under our Federal system with the enforcement of the laws."[19]

Wolf v. Colorado[20] moved the Fourth Amendment a step closer to its present status. The defendant, a Denver obstetrician, was arrested, tried and convicted on charges of conspiracy to commit abortions.[21] The local

---

16. The Court's opinion stated:
   [Unconstitutional practices] can only be obviated by adhering to the rule that constitutional provisions for the security of persons and property should be liberally construed. A close and literal construction deprives them of half their efficacy and leads to gradual depreciation of the right, as if it consisted more in sound than in substance. It is the duty of the courts to be watchful for the constitutional rights of the citizens, and against any stealthful encroachments thereon.
116 U.S. at 635. The search and seizure issue was raised in *Boyd* when, at the trial, the judge ordered the defendants, George and Edward Boyd, to produce a document relating to the litigation. The Court faced two difficulties. First, there had been no search—only a court ordered production of the document; and secondly, the original proceeding dealt only with the forfeiture of property, and was ostensibly only a civil trial. The Court ruled that a proceeding to declare a forfeiture of property was criminal in "substance and effect" although "technically a civil proceeding." 116 U.S. at 633-34. The contention that there was no search was avoided by reading the Fourth and Fifth Amendments as supplementing each other. 116 U.S. at 629. This latter concept has since been discredited. *See, e.g.*, Hale v. Henkel, 201 U.S. 46 (1906).
   17. 232 U.S. 383 (1914).
   18. *E.g.*, Adams v. New York, 192 U.S. 585 (1904).
   19. 232 U.S. at 391-92. The Court's holding that the exclusionary rule was now applicable in the federal courts left several unanswered questions. There was no indication as to whether exclusion had constitutional status, nor did the Court's opinion consider the legality of "silver platter" practices whereby state officers would give illegally seized evidence to federal officers. The silver platter problems were to remain until Elkins v. United States, 364 U.S. 206 (1960), held the use of such evidence to be an unconstitutional practice; Jones v. United States, 362 U.S. 257 (1960), held unconstitutional the "reverse" silver platter situation in which evidence unlawfully seized by federal agents was made available for use in the state courts.
   20. 338 U.S. 25 (1949).
   21. Facts taken from the state court opinion, Wolf v. People, 117 Col. 259, 259-61, 187 P.2d 926, 926-28 (1948).

district attorney had been tipped that Wolf was performing illegal abortions and on the basis of this unverified information searched Wolf's office and seized the defendant's records for the years 1943-44. The warrantless search and seizure violated Colorado law.

The Court, in an opinion by Justice Frankfurter, ruled that although the protections of the Fourth Amendment were enforceable against the states through the Due Process Clause,[22] the Fourteenth Amendment did not require that evidence seized in violation of the Fourth Amendment be excluded by the state courts. The Court's decision to eschew the exclusionary rule was not based upon a lack of appreciation for the importance of the amendment; on the contrary, in an earlier opinion Justice Frankfurter had stated that "[the Fourth Amendment] is central to the enjoyment of the other guarantees of the Bill of Rights."[23] But the majority was particularly impressed by the fact that two-thirds of the states had not chosen to adopt an exclusionary rule in the wake of the *Weeks* decision.[24] The Court also determined to its satisfaction that other remedies utilized by the states to enforce the Fourth Amendment fully protected the right to privacy.[25] This decision was to last for twelve years.

The modern era of the Fourth Amendment began with *Mapp v. Ohio*.[26] Three Cleveland police officers went to the home of Dollree Mapp after receiving information that an individual wanted for questioning with regard to a recent bombing was hiding in the home. They had further information that policy materials were being kept in that same house. The defendant, living with her daughter on the top floor of a two story dwelling, refused to admit the officers when they sought entrance without a warrant. The group of officers broke through the defendant's door, entered her home, handcuffed her when she allegedly became belligerent, and searched the entire floor occupied by Mrs. Mapp and the basement of her building. During the warrantless search the officers discovered obscene materials which they seized, and which, ultimately, were presented in evidence at the defendant's trial. On appeal, the Ohio Supreme Court held that although the guilty verdict below had been based on the use of illegally seized evidence, exclusion of that evidence was not required as the evidence had not been taken "from defendant's person by the use of brutal or offensive physical force against defendant."[27]

---

22. The Court held that:
the security of one's privacy against arbitrary intrusion by the police [is] implicit [in] "the concept of ordered liberty" and as such enforceable against the states through the Due Process Clause.
338 U.S. at 27-29. For a discussion of the several due process incorporation theories, *see* note 152 *infra*.
23. Harris v. United States, 331 U.S. 145, 163 (1947) (dissenting opinion).
24. 338 U.S. at 29.
25. *Id.* at 30.
26. 367 U.S. 643 (1961).
27. Mapp v. Ohio, 170 Ohio St. 427, 431, 166 N.E.2d 387, 389-90 (1960).

The Supreme Court, in an opinion by Justice Clark, reversed and held that "all evidence obtained by searches and seizures in violation of the Constitution is by that same authority, inadmissible in a state court."[28] In granting the exclusionary rule the status of a constitutionally required remedy, the Court was forced to deal with the two contrary factual findings of the *Wolf* decision.[29] Whereas in *Wolf*, the Court had taken notice that two-thirds of the states had not adopted an exclusionary rule, in *Mapp* it was stated that "more than half of those [states] since passing on [the issue], by their own legislative or judicial decisions, had wholly or partially adopted or adhered to the *Weeks* rule [of exclusion]."[30] And what the Court considered more significant was the finding by the Supreme Court of California that other remedies had failed to protect the constitutional guarantee of the Fourth Amendment.[31]

Wolf had left to the states the opportunity to experiment with alternative remedies to the Fourth Amendment. The Court ruled that the experiment had failed and that the exclusionary rule was "the only effectively available way . . . to compel respect for the constitutional guarantee."[32] Without the exclusionary rule, the "assurance against unreasonable search and seizure . . . would be a 'form of words,' valueless and undeserving of mention in a perpetual charter of inestimable human liberties."[33]

The positive attributes the Court found contained in the exclusionary rule that justified its status as the "only effectively available remedy"[34] are especially relevant to this analysis. First, the Court noted that the exclusionary rule was a strong deterrent on unlawful police conduct—"the

---

28. 367 U.S. at 655.

29. The point of view from which the *Mapp* Court re-examined the *Wolf* holding is best indicated by looking to Justice Clark's suggestion in Irvine v. California, 347 U.S. 128 (1954) (concurring opinion), that he would overrule that part of *Wolf* which held that the exclusionary rule did not apply to the states, whenever a sufficient number of like-minded Justices came onto the Court. 347 U.S. at 139. Justice Harlan, dissenting in *Mapp*, contended that the Court, in fact, "reached out" to overrule *Wolf*. 367 U.S. at 672-75.

30. 367 U.S. at 651.

31. People v. Cahan, 44 Cal. 2d 434, 282 P.2d 905 (1955).

32. 367 U.S. at 656, *quoting from* Elkins v. United States, 364 U.S. 206, 217 (1960).

33. 367 U.S. at 655. As Justice Clark had promised, the Court overruled so much of *Wolf* as was inconsistent with its holding:

> Therefore, in extending the substantive protections of due process to all constitutionally unreasonable searches—state or federal—it was logically and constitutionally necessary that the exclusion doctrine—an essential part of the right to privacy—be also insisted upon as an essential ingredient of the right . . . recognized by the *Wolf* case.

367 U.S. at 655-56. The Court found the exclusionary rule to be "an essential part" of the Fourth and Fourteenth Amendments. 367 U.S. at 657. For a discussion of the "selective incorporation" due process theory followed by the Court in *Mapp*, *see* note 152 *infra*.

34. *See* note 32, *supra*, and accompanying text.

purpose of the exclusionary rule is to deter—to compel respect for the constitutional guaranty . . . by removing the incentive to disregard it."[35] Secondly, the imposition of the exclusionary rule achieved a logical harmony between the federal and state systems of criminal justice.[36] As an example of the previously unsatisfactory situation, the Court noted the possibility that a federal prosecutor and a state prosecutor might work across the street from one another, supposedly operating under the same Fourth Amendment prohibition. Yet one might be entitled to use illegally seized evidence, and the other not. The Court was concerned that the state, by allowing the use of the illegally seized evidence, encourages disobedience to the Constitution.[37] The compulsory application of the exclusionary rule removed this problem. And finally, the exclusionary rule fulfilled "the imperative of judicial integrity,"[38] i.e., the requirement that the judicial process not sully its hands by dealing with evidence illegally seized. Justice Holmes' reasoning in *Olmstead v. U.S.* was used to explain this concern:

> Our government is the potent, the omnipresent teacher.
> For good or for ill, it teaches the whole people by its example
> . . . . If the government becomes a lawbreaker, it breeds contempt for the law; it invites every man to become a law unto himself; it invites anarchy . . . .[39]

The Court found that the exclusionary rule, unlike the alternative remedies of civil damages or criminal statutes, was the only effective way to maintain judicial integrity.

In the past decade since the *Mapp* decision, the Court's Fourth Amendment rulings have primarily been concerned with refining the nature and number of the exceptions to the amendment's requirement that all searches and seizures be carried out under court approved warrants.[40]

---

35. 367 U.S. at 356, quoting from Elkins v. United States, 364 U.S. 206, 217 (1960). The Court found persuasive that the California Supreme Court in People v. Cahan, 44 Cal. 2d 434, 282 P.2d 905 (1955), had also reached this conclusion.

36. 367 U.S. at 657.

37. *Id.*

38. 367 U.S. at 659, quoting from Elkins v. United States, 364 U.S. 206, 222 (1960).

39. 367 U.S. at 659, quoting from Olmstead v. United States, 277 U.S. 438, 485 (1928) (Holmes, J. dissenting opinion).

40. *See, e.g.,* Chimel v. California, 395 U.S. 752 (1969). The Court has split in a number of cases in the past decade over the proper reading of the Fourth Amendment. The faction that has for the most part been in the majority argues that the Fourth is to be read as requiring warrants for all searches except in those carefully defined situations which have become recognized exceptions, for example, Warden v. Hayden, 387 U.S. 294 (1967) (hot pursuit); and Chimel v. California, 395 U.S. 752 (1969) (searches incident to arrest). Justice Stewart outlined this position in Vale v. Louisiana, 399 U.S. 30, 32 (1970):

However, one 1967 opinion, *Camara v. Municipal Court*,[41] is significant in that it explicitly expanded the Fourth Amendment's protection to encompass situations not directly related to criminal prosecutions. The appellant in *Camara* refused to permit a housing inspector from the San Francisco City Health Department to make a warrantless inspection of his residence. The resident was found guilty of violating a housing code provision which granted city employees the right to enter all premises in the city, upon a showing of credentials, at a reasonable time of the day for the purpose of inspecting the premises for code violations.[42]

Two previous Supreme Court decisions, affirming convictions under similar inspection statutes, had held that warrantless inspections touched only the "periphery" of the interests protected by the Fourth Amendment.[43] But the Court in *Camara* ruled that the inspections were "significant intrusions upon the interests protected by the Fourth Amendment."[44]

It is surely anomalous to say that the individual and his private property are fully protected by the Fourth Amendment only when the individual is suspected of criminal behavior.[45]

---

our past decisions make clear that only in a "few specifically established and well-delineated" situations . . . may a warrantless search . . . withstand constitutional scrutiny, even though the authorities had probable cause to conduct it. The burden rests on the State to show the existence of such an exceptional situation.

The opposing faction argues that the above approach is too strict a reading of the Fourth in that it excludes many situations in which reasonable searches should be held valid despite the lack of a warrant. As stated by Justice Black in Vale v. Louisiana, *id.* at 33 (dissenting opinion):

Searches, whether with or without a warrant, are to be judged by whether they are reasonable, and . . . common sense dictates that reasonableness varies with the circumstances of the search.

41. 387 U.S. 523 (1967). See v. Seattle, 387 U.S. 541 (1967), was decided the same day and held the *Camara* holding to be applicable to inspections of commercial premises.

42. SAN FRANCISCO HOUSING CODE §§ 503, 507. Section 503 granted authorized city employees the right to enter buildings for the purpose of inspection. Section 507 provided that anyone who interfered with an authorized inspection would be deemed guilty of a misdemeanor.

43. Ohio *ex rel.* Eaton v. Price, 364 U.S. 263 (1960); Frank v. Maryland, 359 U.S. 360 (1959).

44. 387 U.S. at 534.

45. *Id.* at 530. It is not entirely clear why the Court changed its mind. Justice White's opinion for the majority referred generally to the numerous decisions the Court had made since *Frank* that had "more fully defined the Fourth Amendment's effect on state and municipal action." *Id.* at 525. Also the opinion noted that in the eight years since the *Frank* holding, all governments had been making increased use of inspection ordinances to contain "urban blight," 387 U.S. at 525. There were further indications in the opinion that the Court was concerned with the security a warrant would offer to both inspectors and the public. When warrantless searches are made, there is a continuing danger to the inspector that the individual to be searched might suspect the agent of using a ruse to gain entrance in order to commit a crime, and make use of weapons to repel the intrusion.

The real difficulty the Court found, however, was not in overruling Frank v.

As will be described in the next section of this article, state courts had consistently rejected constitutional attacks on the juvenile court statutes in the first half of this century by designating juvenile delinquency hearings as civil proceedings.[46] *Camara* would seem to support the proposition that insofar as the Fourth Amendment is concerned, juveniles may not be deprived of its protection merely by characterizing the juvenile proceeding as civil rather than criminal.[47]

II. THE JUVENILE COURT PROCESS

For sixty-seven years after the establishment of the first juvenile court,[48] these courts, offering a "peculiar system [of justice] for juveniles, unknown to our law in any comparable context,"[49] were free to dispense this strange system of justice without check or guidance from the Supreme Court. In 1966 the Court found it necessary to concern itself with the rights of juveniles in these courts:

> There is evidence . . . that there may be grounds for concern that the child receives the worst of both worlds: that he gets neither the protections accorded to adults nor the solicitous care and regenerative treatment postulated for children [in the juvenile courts].[50]

A study of the history, theory and evolution of the juvenile courts will provide the background needed to properly evaluate the opinions of the four juvenile court cases decided by the Supreme Court to date.

A. History and Theory

The English common law accorded to juveniles charged with crimes relief from some of the harsh practices suffered by adult suspects: chil-

---

Maryland, but rather in determining the probable cause standard to apply when warrants are sought for routine housing inspections. The Court held that warrants could be used to cover "area" inspections so long as the decision as to when the right to privacy must yield to the needs of society is decided by a neutral magistrate and not by a city inspector or administrator. 387 U.S. at 529.

46. *See, e.g.,* Pee v. United States, 274 F.2d 556 (D.C. Cir. 1959). *See also* text accompanying notes 60-71 *infra.*

47. The support *Camara* offers for this proposition is somewhat weakened when it is recognized that the defendant in fact had been convicted in a criminal trial. However, as will be seen in section 3 *infra*, the Supreme Court, in its four decisions dealing with the rights of juveniles in the juvenile courts, has clearly discredited the argument that the juvenile delinquency adjudication is a civil proceeding. *See, e.g.,* Kent v. United States, 383 U.S. 541, 555 (1966).

48. The first juvenile court, located in Cook county, Illinois, was established on July 1, 1899. Mack, *The Juvenile Court,* 23 HARV. L. REV. 104, 107 (1909).

49. In re Gault, 387 U.S. 1, 17 (1967).

50. Kent v. United States, 383 U.S. 541, 556 (1966).

dren under the age of seven were held never to have the requisite intent to commit a crime; between the ages of seven and fourteen it was presumed that the child was incapable of criminal intent, but the presumption was rebuttable; youths over fourteen were treated as full adults in the eyes of the criminal courts.[51] These standards were carried over intact into American law.

In the first half of the nineteenth century, concern for children caught up in the criminal process resulted in movements to ameliorate the plight of youths convicted of crimes.[52] Attempting to segregate youthful offenders from the harmful influences of adult criminals, interested groups urged the establishment of separate correctional facilities for juvenile delinquents. The first such institution to meet this description, the New York House of Refuge, was organized in 1824 by private groups. In its early years the House of Refuge was privately funded, but public funding was later provided and the facility came to be widely copied by other communities.[53]

A significant step in the treatment of convicted juveniles was taken by Massachusetts in 1869. By statute, the State Board of Charities was authorized to have its agents appear at the trials of juveniles. The agent was to petition the court in appropriate cases (which cases were appropriate was not made clear) to release the child to the care of suitable foster parents, and the agent was to follow up this placement with periodic visits to the child.[54] The concept of a specialized probation service was utilized later by the founders of the juvenile court as an important part of the total process of rehabilitation established by juvenile court legislation.[55]

For years those concerned with the treatment of juvenile delinquents realized that not only was a criminal trial unduly harsh and shocking to the youth, but that the adjudicative phase of the judicial process could be an essential part of the child's rehabilitation.[56] Equally of concern to the

---

51. NATIONAL COUNCIL ON CRIME AND DELINQUENCY, GUIDES FOR JUVENILE COURT JUDGES 2 (1957). Professor Allen refers to a statement made by the English diarist, Charles Glenville, as he watched some boys about to be hung at the Tyburn Jail: "Never did I see boys cry so." ALLEN, THE BORDERLAND OF CRIMINAL JUSTICE 47 (1964).

52. For a description of the early history of the juvenile court movement, see, e.g., LOU, JUVENILE COURTS IN THE UNITED STATES 1-25 (1927); HURLEY, ORIGINS OF THE ILLINOIS JUVENILE COURT LAW, (3d ed., 1907); and TAPPAN, JUVENILE DE-LINQUENCY (1949).

53. FOLKS, THE CARE OF DESTITUTE, NEGLECTED, DELINQUENT CHILDREN 203 (1902).

54. A discussion of the Massachusetts statute, its background and related developments in that state, are discussed in SHELDON and ELEANOR GLUECK, ONE THOUSAND JUVENILE DELINQUENTS 9-12 (1934).

55. See, e.g., LOU, supra note 52.

56. See, e.g., Mack, The Juvenile Court, 23 HARV. L. REV. 104 (1909). The author viewed the adjudicative process as follows:
The judge on a bench, looking down upon a boy standing at the bar, can

reformers were the legal and social stigmas that attached to the individual for life as a result of such a criminal conviction, whether or not probation or other post-conviction care rehabilitated the child.[57] The crucial step was taken by the Illinois legislature in 1899, when the first state-wide juvenile court system was established.[58] Other statutes soon followed, patterned closely after the Illinois statute, and in the years since then, all states have adopted juvenile court acts.[59]

Parens patriae has been the justification and doctrine controlling these statutes.[60] A juvenile court under the *parens patriae* theory was not concerned with the guilt of the child.[61] The purpose of the specialized court was to bring an errant child under the paternal protection and instruction of the state.[62] With rehabilitation as its function, the hearing was deemed not to be a criminal trial, but rather the first step in the treatment process and a part of the therapy itself.[63]

The social and legal stigmas that usually attached to a criminal conviction were removed by several devices: the proceeding was characterized as civil;[64] the records of the hearing and the treatment were to be kept confidential;[65] the delinquency adjudication resulted in no legal disabilities beyond those essential to the rehabilitation;[66] and the disposition of the

---

never evoke a proper sympathetic spirit. Seated at a desk, with the child at his side, where he can on occasion put his arm around his shoulder and draw the lad to him, the judge, while losing none of his judicial dignity, will gain immensely in the effectiveness of his work.

Id. at 120.

57. *See* GLUECK, *supra* note 54.

58. Juvenile Court Act, ILL. LAWS 1899, p. 131.

59. *See, e.g.,* D.C. CODE, tit. 16, ch. 23 (Supp. V 1970); PA. STAT. ANN., tit. 11, § 261 (1965); Juvenile Court Act, ILL. REV. STATS. ch. 37, § 701-1 (1965); CALIFORNIA WELFARE AND INSTITUTIONS CODE § 500 (1961); CHILDREN'S CODE, WIS. STATS. ANN. tit. VII, ch. 48 (1956); JUVENILE DISTRICT COURT LAW, CODE OF VIRGINIA, tit. 16.1, ch. 8, § 16.1-139 (1972); ORE. REV. STATS., tit. 34, ch. 419, § 419.472 (1963); FAMILY COURT ACT, N.Y. LAWS 1962, ch. 686 (1962).

60. *Parens Patriae* is literally translated as "father of his country." BLACKS LAW DICTIONARY (4th ed. 1951). As originally applied in England, the doctrine of *parens patriae* was the justification for institutionalizing minors and the insane while denying to them the procedural rights normally granted to criminals. Paulsen, Kent v. United States, *The Constitutional Context of Juvenile Cases,* 1966 SUPP. CT. REV. 167, 173-74 (1966).

61. Guilt in its generic sense was relevant only for the matter of jurisdiction in delinquency proceedings. Judge Mack related the function of the court:

The problem for determination by the judge is not, has this boy or girl committed a specific wrong, but what is he, how has he become what he is, and what can best be done in his interest and in the interest of the state to save him from a downward career.

Mack, *supra,* note 56, at 119-20.

62. Welch, *Delinquency Proceeding—Fundamental Fairness for the Accused in a Quasi-Criminal Forum,* 50 MINN. L. REV. 653 (1966).

63. *See* Mack, *supra* note 56.

64. *See, e.g.,* Pee v. United States, 274 F.2d 556 (D.C. Cir. 1959).

65. *Id.*

66. *Id.*

child after a finding of delinquency was termed non-punitive.[67] The procedures the juvenile courts followed reflected the goals to be attained. As stated in the original Illinois act, "[t]he Court [was to] proceed to hear and dispose of the case in a summary manner."[68] The normal rules of evidence were set aside and the court was to consider in making a judgment not only the facts related to the alleged criminal infraction, but also reports as to the child's family and social environment and the observations of medical and psychological experts.[69]

What has been termed "the mutual compact theory of *parens patriae*"[70] resulted. In exchange for the removal of all stigmas normally associated with a finding of guilty, and in exchange for the care and treatment provided to the delinquent youth, the juvenile was denied the constitutional protections provided in a criminal court.[71] As will be described below, doubts were to arise as to whether society had kept its part of this bargain.

B. The Reality Intrudes

In the years immediately following the establishment of the juvenile courts, only mild criticism of this social experiment was generated. For the most part the objections focused on the scope of the courts' "arbitrary powers."[72] The juvenile court statutes easily withstood attack in the courts. Constitutional arguments based on equal protection and due process failed throughout.[73] One influential early decision by the Pennsylvania Supreme Court answered the alleged due process violation in a manner that was followed by the courts of many other states:

> The natural parent needs no process to temporarily deprive his child of his liberty by confining it to his home, to save it and to shield it from the consequences of persistence in a career of waywardness; nor is the state, when compelled, as parens patriae, to take the place of the father for the same purpose, re-

67. *Id.*

68. Juvenile Court Act, ILL. LAWS 1899, p. 137 § 5 (1899).

69. *See, e.g.,* Mack, *supra* note 56.

70. Ketcham, *The Unfulfilled Promise of the American Juvenile Court,* in JUSTICE FOR THE CHILD: THE JUVENILE COURT IN TRANSITION 25 (M. Rosenheim ed. 1962).

71. *Id.*

72. Lindsey, *The Juvenile Court Movement from a Lawyer's Standpoint,* 52 ANNALS OF THE AMERICAN ACADEMY OF POLITICAL AND SOCIAL SCIENCE 141 (1914). Mr. Lindsey expressed his fear that there was a danger to juveniles due to the absence in the juvenile court statutes "of any limitations on the arbitrary powers of the court." *Id.*

73. The highest appellate courts of over forty states were to hold their respective juvenile court statutes constitutional. The leading cases upholding the constitutionality of the acts have been collected in LOU, JUVENILE COURTS IN THE UNITED STATES 10, n.4 (1927), and Paulsen, *Fairness to the Juvenile Offender,* 51 MINN. L. REV. 549 (1957).

quired to adopt any process as a means of placing its hands upon the child to lead it into one of its courts . . . . [T]he court determines the [child's] salvation, and not its punishment.[74]

One early problem that plagued the juvenile court was the lack of sufficient funding to support the extensive services the juvenile court ideal required to properly fulfill its goals.[75] All juvenile court statutes not only established the courts themselves but the supplementary services necessary to make the court effective: there had to be intake services to house and care for children who for one reason or another could not be released immediately; personnel were needed to investigate and compile the information required to adjudicate and make a proper disposition of the child after state care was found to be necessary; and finally extensive probation services had to be established to continue the state's treatment of the child in an effective manner.[76] The original Illinois statute authorized the necessary probation staff but did not provide for the payment of salaries to this staff.[77] Few juvenile court systems were established in the early years that did provide sufficient funding to properly achieve their statutory goals.[78]

A second problem was the weak drafting of these statutes. Professor Clark has noted that broad gaps were left in all juvenile court statutes as to the precise place the courts occupied in their respective states' judicial systems.[79] More importantly, the statutes were unclear as to exactly when the juvenile came under the control of the juvenile court, and when jurisdiction over the juvenile might be waived in favor of the adult criminal courts.[80]

A third difficulty, related to the funding problem outlined above, involved the lack of knowledgeable, trained court personnel who were committed to, and familiar with the statutory ideals.[81]

Criticism, which began to increase as time passed, fell into two main categories: the first group of critics opposed the juvenile court concept

---

74. Commonwealth v. Fisher, 213 Pa. 48, 62 A. 198 (1905).
75. A general discussion of the problems of the juvenile court is found in Clark, Why Gault: *Juvenile Court Theory and Impact in Historical Perspective*, in GAULT: WHAT NOW FOR THE JUVENILE COURT 1 (V. Norden ed. 1968).
76. *See, e.g.*, Juvenile Court Act, ILL. REV. STATS. ch. 37, § 701-1 *et seq.* (1969).
77. Juvenile Court Act, ILL. LAWS 1899, p. 137. *See also* Rosenheim, *Perennial Problems in the Juvenile Court*, in JUSTICE FOR THE CHILD 9 (M. Rosenheim ed. 1962); Folks, *supra*, note 53, at 203.
78. *See, e.g.*, Rosenheim, *supra* note 77.
79. *See* Clark, *supra* note 75, at 9-11.
80. *Id.*
81. *Id.* Monrad Paulsen has noted another basic weakness of the movement: "The goals and purposes of the juvenile court have often been stated on too enthusiastic, almost romantic terms. Ideals have been set which are incapable of meaningful fulfillment." Paulsen, *The Juvenile Court and the Whole of the Law*, 11 WAYNE L. REV. 597, 611 (1965).

itself and wished the courts disbanded;[82] the second group saw the need for the courts but felt that the child should be granted more rights during the hearing.[83] Criticism soon followed from the judiciary. A California appeals court rejected the idea that an adjudication of delinquency was actually non-criminal: ". . . for all practical purposes, this is a legal fiction, presenting a challenge to credulity and doing violence to reason."[84]

A series of decisions by the federal courts in the District of Columbia in the 1950's were to provide the main judicial assault on juvenile court theory and practice prior to the recent Supreme Court decisions. In the first decision, *White v. Reid*,[85] a juvenile sought a writ of *habeas corpus* to gain relief from federal custody. He had been adjudged a delinquent by a District of Columbia juvenile court and had been sent for treatment to a federal correctional facility that housed adults convicted of crimes by regular criminal courts. The court in *White* held that under the Constitution and the District of Columbia juvenile court statute,[86] the youth could only be held for treatment in one of the correctional facilities created to deal with delinquent youth. In the course of its opinion the court considered the "mutual compact theory"[87] and indicated that unless the theory of *parens patriae* is carried out in practice, a delinquency adjudication by a juvenile court could not withstand an assault for violation of fundamental constitutional safeguards.

In re Poff,[88] a second decision by the same federal district court a year later, argued that the juvenile court acts were intended not to displace the usual constitutional rights granted to all accused of violating penal statutes, but rather to add to the juvenile's rights in consideration of his tender age. The petitioner, seeking *habeas corpus* relief from the district court, contended that a finding of delinquency by the juvenile court had been entered against him unlawfully because he had not been allowed the assistance of counsel. The district court held that Congress in creating the District of Columbia Juvenile Court Act intended to allow the juvenile those procedural rights that had existed prior to the establishment of the juvenile courts, and set aside the delinquency adjudication. The court summarized its opinion by questioning the notion that constitutional protections may be lost by designating a juvenile proceeding as civil:

Have we now progressed to a point where a child may be in-

---

82. *See, e.g.,* Olney, *The Juvenile Courts—Abolish Them,* 13 Cal. B.J. 1 (1938).
83. *See, e.g.,* Rappeport, *Juveniles Being Denied Basic Rights,* 1948 Harvard Law Record 3 (1948); Ellrod and Melaney, *Juvenile Justice, Treatment or Travesty?* 11 U. Pitt. L. Rev. 277 (1950).
84. In re Contreras, 109 Cal. App. 2d 787, 241 P.2d 631 (1952).
85. 126 F. Supp. 867 (D.D.C. 1954).
86. Juvenile Court Act of District of Columbia, D.C. Code § 11-901 *et seq.* (1938).
87. *See* Ketchum, *supra* note 70, and the accompanying text.
88. 135 F. Supp. 224 (D.D.C. 1955).

carcerated and deprived of his liberty during his minority by calling that which is a crime by some other name? . . . [T]he Federal Constitution, insofar as it is applicable, cannot be nullified by a mere nomenclature, the evil or the thing itself remaining the same.[89]

In *United States v. Dickerson*[90] Judge Holtzoff of the same federal district court dealt with another aspect of the "civil" proceeding theory—that constitutional protections were unnecessary to protect the juvenile because only non-punitive dispositions resulted from the juvenile court hearing. The petitioner sought to have a criminal indictment dismissed against him on the ground of double jeopardy. The youth had acknowledged his guilt before the juvenile court, and had been found to be within the court's jurisdiction. The judge, following the normal procedures, ordered the local juvenile agency to compile a study of the youth's background. After the social study was completed, the judge waived the jurisdiction of the juvenile court over the petitioner to the U.S. District Court and an indictment was returned. Judge Holtzoff held that jeopardy had attached in the juvenile court and no change of nomenclature could remove the due process rights due a suspect subject to a deprivation of liberty:

The test must be the nature and the essence of the proceedings rather than their title. If the result may be a loss of personal liberty, the constitutional safeguards apply.[91]

A final decision, by the Court of Appeals for the District of Columbia, *Pee v. United States*,[92] retrenched somewhat from the broad dicta of these three district court decisions. However, in so doing, *Pee* established a due process standard for determining which Bill of Rights protections are applicable to juveniles. This standard was to be followed by the Supreme Court eight years later in *In re Gault*.[93] Pee, whose case had been waived from juvenile court, had been convicted in U.S. District Court of robbery and assault with intent to commit rape. During the district court trial before a jury, the judge had imported a rule of evidence from the juvenile court, relating to the admissibility of confessions, which had harmed the defendant's case.[94] Judge Prettyman for the Court of Appeals held that the rule of

---

89. *Id.* at 226.

90. 168 F. Supp. 899 (D.D.C. 1958), *rev'd on other grounds*, 271 F.2d 487 (D.C. Cir. 1959).

91. *Id.* at 902; *accord*, dissent of Justice Musmanno in In re Holmes, 379 Pa. 599, 109 A.2d 523 (1954); and the dissenting opinion of Justice Crone in People v. Lewis, 206 N.Y. 171, 183 N.E. 353 (1932).

92. 274 F.2d 556 (D.C. Cir. 1959).

93. 387 U.S. 1 (1967).

94. The question at issue was whether the Mallory-McNabb rule was to be

evidence could not be imported to the district court criminal trial because the procedures of the juvenile court process, including the specialized rules of evidence, were not intended to serve as rules for juveniles *per se*, but as rules to be used only by the juvenile court by reason of its special function. Judge Prettyman, in conflict with the opinions of the *Poff* and *Dickerson* courts, stated that not all Bill of Rights protections were applicable to the juvenile court; he stated that the juvenile court proceedings were civil in nature, no conviction occurred, and the delinquent was not punished as a criminal. Because of the non-criminal nature of the juvenile court delinquency adjudication, the opinion argued that the procedural protections due a juvenile before the juvenile court were to be determined by a different standard than that used by the criminal courts:

> The constitutional safeguards vouchsafed a juvenile in such proceedings are determined from the requirements of *due process and fair treatment,* and not by the direct application of the clauses of the Constitution which in terms apply to criminal cases. [Emphasis added.][95]

The Supreme Court in its decisions that determined the rights of juveniles in the juvenile court, was to accept from *Pee* the "requirements of due process and fair treatment" as its standard. However, the court was to recognize also the concern of the federal district court in the opinions discussed prior to *Pee* that the ideals of the juvenile court theory were not being fully realized. This reality of performance was to affect the content of the *Pee* due process standard when the issues reappeared before the Court in the 1960's.

III. JUVENILE JUSTICE IN THE SUPREME COURT

With *Kent v. United States*[96] the Supreme Court handed down its first juvenile court decision 67 years after the establishment of the first of these specialized courts of justice.[97] In 1959 Morris Kent, Jr., the petitioner,

---

applied to the trial of the juveniles. Mallory v. United States, 354 U.S. 449 (1957); McNabb v. United States, 318 U.S. 332 (1943).

95. 274 F.2d at 559.

96. 383 U.S. 541 (1966).

97. Why the Court decided to act in 1966 was not stated, but the majority opinion by Justice Fortas noted that:

[s]tudies and critiques . . . raise serious questions as to whether [the] actual performance [of the juvenile courts] measures well enough against theoretical purpose to make tolerable the immunity of the process from the reach of constitutional guarantees applicable to adults.

383 U.S. at 555. It is likely also that the Court was concerned with the increasing numbers of juveniles that were coming into contact with the juvenile courts. A 1965

was apprehended at age 14 on charges of housebreaking and attempted purse-snatching and placed on probation by the District of Columbia Juvenile Court. Two years later Kent was taken into custody on suspicion of housebreaking, rape and robbery. Because of his age he was subject to the "exclusive jurisdiction" of the same juvenile court that directed his probation in 1959. For two days he was questioned by police, and during this investigation he confessed to the crimes charged and to other similar offenses. On the second day of questioning his mother retained counsel for the boy. The attorney went to talk to the Social Service Director of the juvenile court who told the attorney of the possibility that jurisdiction over Kent might be waived to the district court under D.C. CODE § 11-914 (1961).[98] Opposing the possible waiver, the attorney motioned the juvenile court for access to the petitioner's probation file, and the attorney sought a hearing regarding the possible waiver. To support his argument that the waiver should not be ordered, Kent's counsel offered to produce psychiatric testimony tending to show that Kent was suffering from a mental disorder, and he also offered to prove that rehabilitation would result from hospital treatment of the boy.

The waiver provision of the juvenile court statute stated that the juvenile court judge could waive the jurisdiction of the court only after a "full investigation."[99] There was no hearing, nor was the attorney given access to the social service records of the petitioner. Without talking to Kent, his mother, or his counsel, the judge waived jurisdiction to the criminal court by an order stating: "After full investigation, I do hereby waive [jurisdiction]."[100] An indictment was returned by a grand jury, and at trial Kent was found guilty on six counts of housebreaking and robbery.[101]

The Supreme Court reversed the conviction below by a vote of five to four.[102] The opinion by Justice Fortas began with an explanation of the

---

report by the Department of Health, Education and Welfare had estimated that 591,000 children were involved in juvenile court delinquency proceedings in 1964. U.S. DEPARTMENT OF HEALTH, EDUCATION AND WELFARE, CHILDREN'S BUREAU, JUVENILE COURT STATISTICS 1 (1965).

98. Now D.C. CODE, tit. 16, ch. 23, § 16-2307 (Supp. V 1970).

99. 383 U.S. at 546. It should be noted that under the rule of law at that time, as decided by the Court of Appeals for the District of Columbia in Wilhite v. United States, 281 F.2d 642 (D.C. Cir. 1960), a juvenile was not entitled to a hearing on the waiver issue. Wilhite had held the "full investigation" requirement of the District of Columbia Juvenile Court Act to mean only that a waiver decision must be based on information before the juvenile court sufficient to support a proper determination.

100. D.C. CODE § 11-914 (1961). The waiver section of the present D.C. CODE provides that before any waiver is made, a hearing shall be conducted to determine if reasonable prospects exist for rehabilitating the child before his majority. D.C. CODE, tit. 16, ch. 23, § 16-2307 (Supp. V 1970).

101. The Supreme Court's opinion stated that the trial court had found Kent innocent of the charges of rape by reason of insanity. 383 U.S. at 550 n.10.

102. The dissenting opinion written by Justice Stewart did not disagree with the rule of law established by the majority, but contended that subsequent decisions

theory underlying the juvenile court statute, outlining generally the doctrine of *parens patriae* and its objectives.[103] Justice Fortas next looked to the realities of the juvenile court process, and as indicated in the opening paragraph of section 2, questioned whether the juvenile court theory had worked.[104]

The maximum possible confinement that Kent would have been subject to after a finding of delinquency in the juvenile court was five years. He was sentenced to 30 to 90 years at his criminal court trial. This discrepancy convinced the Supreme Court that a waiver was a "critically important action determining vitally important statutory rights of juveniles."[105] The Court held that the critical significance of the waiver required the following: that the juvenile be offered counsel; that the attorney be granted access to all records and reports related to the child; that the waiver be preceded by a hearing; and that the judge give a statement of reasons for a waiver decision.[106] The opinion attempted to make clear that this holding was not based on constitutional requirements:

> The Juvenile Court Act and the decisions of the United States Court of Appeals for the District of Columbia provide an adequate basis for the decision of this case, and we go no further.[107]

But in the very next page of the opinion Justice Fortas stated that the holding flows from the statute when "read in the context of constitutional principles relating to due process and the assistance of counsel."[108] The decision may not have had its source in the Constitution but as Dean Paulsen has pointed out in his article discussing the *Kent* decision, it is unlikely that the waiver provisions of other juvenile court acts will ever be read differently by the Court.[109] The holding was one of statutory interpretation, but the reasoning was to provide the groundwork for the decision that followed the next year, *In re Gault*.[110]

---

by the Federal Court of Appeals for the District of Columbia had sufficiently overruled the *Wilhite* rule to require that the District Court conviction of Kent be vacated and the case remanded for reconsideration. 383 U.S. at 568.

103. *See* text accompanying notes 60-71, *supra.*

104. 383 U.S. at 556. The Court stated:
There is evidence . . . that there may be grounds for concern that the child receives neither the protections accorded to adults nor the solicitous care and regenerative treatment postulated for children.

105. *Id.*

106. *Id.* at 557.

107. *Id.* at 556. Monrad Paulsen points out that the Brief for Kent of Amicus Curiae at 7, urged the Court to use the *Kent* decision to define the constitutional standards applicable in the juvenile court. Paulsen, *supra* note 60, at 178.

108. 383 U.S. at 557.

109. Paulsen, *supra* note 60, at 179.

110. 387 U.S. 1 (1967).

Gerald Gault at age 15 was brought before an Arizona juvenile court on a complaint that he had made obscene telephone calls. An adjudication of delinquency was made by the juvenile court and he was committed to the State Industrial School for the remainder of his minority. *Habeas corpus* proceedings were brought in the Arizona state courts challenging the constitutionality of both the Arizona Juvenile Code and the procedures used in the juvenile court hearing. The Arizona Supreme Court dismissed the writ, finding the statute to be constitutional, and also holding that due process requirements were not offended by the procedures of the juvenile court.[111]

The Supreme Court, in an opinion written by Justice Fortas, the author of *Kent*, held that in the adjudicatory phase of delinquency proceedings before a juvenile court on charges that may result in incarceration, the juvenile is entitled to the following procedural rights: sufficient notice of the hearing and the charges against him;[112] notification of the right to counsel, and the fact that counsel would be appointed for the child if he or his parents could not afford one;[113] the privilege against self-incrimination and notice that the youth does not have to testify or make a statement;[114] and, absent a valid confession adequate to support a delinquency adjudication, a finding of delinquency must be based on the sworn testimony of witnesses available for confrontation and cross examination.[115] The Court did not pass on two of the claims urged by Gault—the right to a transcript or other record of the hearing, and the right to appeal from a delinquency adjudication.

The Court found the procedural rights it granted implicit in the notion of due process; however, it made clear that the Bill of Rights did not apply *in toto* to juveniles involved in a delinquency hearing:[116]

> We do not mean . . . to indicate that the hearing to be held must conform with all of the requirements of a criminal trial or even of the usual administrative hearing.[117]

Norman Dorsen and Daniel Reznick, the attorneys for the appellant Gault, were to state later: "The theoretical basis of *Gault* is far from evident."[118] Jus-

---

111. In re Gault, 99 Ariz. 181, 407 P.2d 760 (1965).

112. 383 U.S. at 13.

113. *Id.* at 41.

114. *Id.* at 55.

115. *Id.* at 56.

116. For a discussion of the relation between the Due Process Clause and the first eight amendments to the Constitution, *see* note 152 *infra.*

117. 387 U.S. at 30-31, quoting Kent v. United States, 383 U.S. 541, 562 (1966). *See* Pee v. United States, 274 F.2d 556, 559 (D.C. Cir. 1959).

118. Dorsen and Reznick, In re Gault *and the Future of Juvenile Law*, 1 FAM. L.Q. 1, 8 (1967). One student note contends that the *Gault* and *Kent* decisions presented the "paradox of broad dicta and narrow holdings, extending to juveniles every

tice Harlan complained in his separate opinion that the majority opinion failed to provide any functional guidelines for the place of due process in juvenile proceedings.[119] Dorsen and Reznick suggested that perhaps some guidance might be found in the theories rejected by the Court.[120]

The Court specifically rejected the argument that the *parens patriae* doctrine could provide the needed guidance. Justice Fortas felt that the appropriate role of *parens patriae* was in the disposition stage in shielding juveniles against such a prejudicial byproduct of the judicial process as the broadside disclosures of his contacts with juvenile authorities.[121] Rejected also was the *quid pro quo* notion that the juvenile traded away his constitutional rights in return for the state's treatment and rehabilitation. The Court reiterated its feelings expressed in *Kent* that society has not kept its side of that bargain.[122]

Justice Black, concurring and dissenting, urged as he had in past criminal decisions that the Fourteenth Amendment Due Process Clause specifically incorporates the first eight amendments of the Bill of Rights and applies them against the states.[123] Applying that theory to the case at hand, Justice Black contended, first, that the appellant was charged with a crime and that the Bill of Rights through the Due Process Clause enumerates the rights applicable to individuals charged with crimes, regardless of age or forum.[124] Black's second argument was based on the Equal Protection Clause: if Gault had been an adult he would be entitled to the usual due process guarantees; to deny him those protections because of his age was a denial of equal protection of the law.[125] The majority opinion did not agree with either of Justice Black's contentions.

Justice Harlan argued unsuccessfully in his concurring and dissenting opinion that those rights should be held applicable to juvenile courts that meet the test of "fundamental fairness."[126] The rights he felt applicable were not those transplanted from adult criminal trials, nor were they the rights derived from any of the specific provisions of the Bill of Rights; rather, the procedures that should be held applicable were those that, in the context of the needs of the juvenile court process, were required to grant the juvenile a fair hearing.[127]

---

right considered, yet failing to review the entire system." Note, *Juvenile Courts—Juveniles in Delinquency Proceedings Are not Constitutionally Entitled to the Right of Trial by Jury,* 70 Mich. L. Rev. 171, 177 (1971).

119. 383 U.S. at 67.

120. Dorsen and Reznick, *supra* note 118.

121. 383 U.S. at 24-25, 27.

122. *Id.* at 22-23. *See* text accompanying notes 70-71.

123. For a discussion of the "total incorporation" theory championed by Justice Black, *see* note 152 *infra.*

124. 383 U.S. at 61. *See* note 152 *infra.*

125. 383 U.S. at 61.

126. *Id.* at 74. For a discussion of the "fundamental fairness" theory of due process incorporation, *see* note 152 *infra.*

127. 383 U.S. at 74.

As prophesied by Monrad Paulsen [128] a year before the *Gault* decision, and as recognized by Gault's attorneys, Dorsen and Reznick,[129] the Court appeared to embark on the course of "selective incorporation" in determining which guarantees of the Bill of Rights were applicable to the juvenile courts.[130] The Court made clear, as stated earlier, that not all of the first eight amendments were to be applicable in the juvenile court hearing, ". . . but we do hold that the hearing must measure up to the essentials of 'due process and fair treatment.' "[131] What was meant by the "essentials of due process and fair treatment" was to be further clarified in the last two opinions of the Court.

In re Winship,[132] decided three years later, involved a youth who had been adjudged delinquent by a New York family court on the basis of a "preponderance of the evidence." The family court judge had rejected the contention of the juvenile's counsel that the proper standard of proof should be "beyond a reasonable doubt" as in criminal trials. The court relied on the fact that the preponderance standard was authorized by § 744(b) of the New York Family Court Act.[133] The New York Court of Appeals affirmed the decision.[134]

Justice Brennan's opinion for the Court asked whether ". . . 'proof beyond a reasonable doubt' is among the 'essentials of due process and fair treatment.' "[135] The Court made clear that the first step of its due process analysis was to determine the importance of the procedural protection at issue. The early portion of the opinion considered the "vital" role the "beyond a reasonable doubt" formulation has played in the "American scheme of criminal procedure."[136] The Court held that the reasonable doubt standard had constitutional status and was available to all who were charged with violating a penal statute whether the forum be a criminal or a juvenile court.[137]

In holding that this standard was constitutionally required as among "the essentials of due process and fair treatment," the Court for the first time explicitly indicated that a balancing process lay at the core of its

---

128. Paulsen, *supra* note 107, at 186.

129. Dorsen and Reznick, *supra* note 118, at 10.

130. For a discussion of the "selective incorporation" of the Due Process Clause, *see* note 152 *infra*.

131. 383 U.S. at 30-31, *quoting* Kent v. United States, 383 U.S. 541, 562 (1966).

132. 397 U.S. 358 (1970).

133. Section 744(b) provided that any determination at the conclusion of an adjudicatory hearing that the child committed an unlawful act "must be based on a preponderance of the evidence." Family Court Act, N.Y. LAWS 1962, ch. 686, § 744(b) (1962).

134. In re Winship, 24 N.Y.2d 196, 299 N.Y.S.2d 414, 247 N.E.2d 253 (1969).

135. 397 U.S. at 360. The "due process and fair treatment" formulation was borrowed from Pee v. United States, 274 F.2d 556, 559 (D.C. Cir. 1959).

136. 397 U.S. at 363.

137. *Id.* at 368.

due process standard. After Justice Brennan's opinion related the vital role of the "reasonable doubt" standard in modern jurisprudence, the Court went on to balance the need for the standard against the harm its use might cause to the beneficial aspects of the juvenile court process.[138]

The salutary elements of the juvenile court process singled out in the Court's opinion were as follows: 1) the non-criminal nature of the delinquency proceeding and the confidentiality which was to attach to all records of the juvenile's involvement with the law;[139] 2) the informality, flexibility and speed of the juvenile hearing;[140] 3) the opportunity for broad discretion in the prescription and use of treatment techniques;[141] 4) and finally, the distinctive pre-hearing intake procedures.[142]

The holding which resulted from this balancing was expressed as follows:

> We conclude . . . that the observance of the standard of proof beyond a reasonable doubt will not compel the states to abandon or displace any of the substantive benefits of the juvenile process.[143]

It was clear after *Winship* that a finding by the Court that a Bill of Rights provision was an important protection would not be enough to justify its application to juveniles if such a protection might cause substantial harm to the juvenile court process. This limitation was further amplified and defined by the last of the four Supreme Court juvenile decisions.

McKeiver v. Pennsylvania[144] and *In re Burrus*,[145] cases arising from the supreme courts of the states of Pennsylvania[146] and North Carolina[147] respectively, were decided together in 1971. The issue in *McKeiver* was whether a trial by jury was constitutionally required in the adjudicatory phase of a state juvenile court delinquency proceeding. Appellants in both cases were juveniles whose motions for jury trials had been rejected at their respective juvenile court hearings, and denied on appeals to their state appellate courts. The Court held that due process of law as applied to juveniles did not include the right to a jury trial,[148] and effectively ended predictions from some quarters that the Court was engaged in "an item by

---

138. *See* text accompanying notes 8-10 *supra*.
139. 397 U.S. at 366.
140. *Id.*
141. *Id.*
142. *Id.* at 366-67.
143. *Id.* at 367.
144. 403 U.S. 528 (1971), docket number 332.
145. *Id.*, docket number 128 [hereinafter referred to as *McKeiver*].
146. McKeiver Appeal, 438 Pa. 339, 265 A.2d 350 (1970).
147. In re Burrus, 275 N.C. 517, 169 S.E.2d 879 (1969).
148. *Id.* at 545-50.

item transplant of procedural safeguards from criminal trials to delinquency hearings."[149]

Justice Blackmun's opinion in *McKeiver*[150] causes some confusion. As emphasized above, the first three juvenile court decisions by the Supreme Court utilized the due process standard of "due process and fair treatment."[151] This standard "selectively incorporated"[152] those Bill of Rights

---

149. Note, *The Supreme Court, 1970 Term*, 85 Harv. L. Rev. 113 (1971); *see, e.g.,* Carr, *Juries for Juveniles: Solving the Problem*, 2 Loyola L.J. 1 (1971).

150. This opinion was joined by Chief Justice Burger, Justice Stewart, and Justice White. Justice White also filed a separate concurring opinion. Justice Brennan concurred with the decision so far as it was applicable to *McKeiver*, but dissented as to *Burrus*. Justice Harlan concurred in a separate opinion. Justices Douglas, Black and Marshall dissented in an opinion written by Justice Douglas.

151. *E.g.,* In re Winship, 397 U.S. 358, 360 (1970).

152. "Selective incorporation" is one of the three basic views of the relationship between the Bill of Rights and the Due Process Clause of the Fourteenth Amendment. In 1833, the Marshall Court held that the first ten Amendments limited only the powers of the federal government. Barron v. Baltimore, 7 Pet. 243 (1833). The enactment of the Fourteenth Amendment, however, provided the means for a greater federal control over the activities of the states. The relevant part of the Fourteenth Amendment provides that no state may "deprive any person of life, liberty or property without due process of law." The extent to which this clause serves as the vehicle for the application of the Bill of Rights to the states has been the subject of lengthy debates within the Supreme Court.

The first school of thought, the "fundamental rights interpretation," was for a number of years accepted by a majority of the Court. In Palko v. Connecticut, 302 U.S. 319 (1937), the majority held that the Due Process Clause applied against the states only those rights and procedures that were "implicit in the concept of ordered liberty."

The Bill of Rights as a unit was not to be applied to the states, nor were the guarantees of the first eight Amendments necessarily excluded. The "fundamental rights interpretation" argued that only those procedures, whether included in the Bill of Rights or not, that were needed to achieve fundamental fairness in the state criminal trial would be included within the purview of the Due Process Clause. *See also,* Adamson v. California, 332 U.S. 46 (1947).

The second major school, represented strongly by the late Justice Black, is the "total incorporation interpretation." The supporters of this view have contended that the Fourteenth Amendment incorporates the Bill of Rights, and only the Bill of Rights, and applies the Amendments, with their baggage of years of interpretations by the federal courts, directly against the states. This view has never gained the support of a majority of the Court, but it has been influential in fashioning the "selective incorporation interpretation" (discussed *infra*). An opinion outlining the tenets of total incorporation is found in Adamson v. California, *supra* (dissenting opinion by Black, J.).

The third major school, and the one that has seemingly gained a majority of the Court in the past decade, is the "selective incorporation interpretation." This doctrine agrees with the "fundamental rights interpretation" that the Due Process Clause encompasses all rights, whether or not in the Bill of Rights, that are "of the very essence of the scheme of ordered liberty." Cohen v. Hurley, 366 U.S. 117 (1961) (Brennan, J. dissenting). However, the selective incorporation view also argues that once it is decided that a particular right contained within the first eight Amendments is "fundamental," that right is wholly incorporated into the Fourteenth Amendment and is applied against the states in the same manner, and under the same standards, as it is applied to the federal government. A recent example of the use of selective incorporation may be found in Duncan v. Louisiana, 391 U.S. 145 (1968). *Duncan* also reviews the "incorporation" debate of the past decades, and

provisions into the juvenile court process that were found to be historically essential to a fair judicial hearing where liberty may be lost, but, nevertheless, subject to the caveat that those historically essential rights that threaten to substantially harm the juvenile court process would undergo very close scrutiny before they are held to apply to the court.[153] Justice Blackmun's opinion, however, did not use "due process and fair treatment." Instead, the Court presented the due process test in a different manner: "the applicable due process standard in juvenile proceedings is 'fundamental fairness,' as developed in *Gault* and *Winship*."[154] A "fundamental fairness" formulation had been offered unsuccessfully by Justice Harlan in his minority opinion in *Gault*.[155] The reappearance of that phrase in *McKeiver* raises the following question: either the due process standard had indeed been changed by the Court in *McKeiver*, or the second part of the Court's formulation quoted above—". . . as developed in *Gault* and *Winship*,"[156]— indicates that despite the changed wording, and despite the historical significance that lies behind the "fundamental fairness" wording,[157] this different due process formulation was to be understood as if to read "essential to due process and fair treatment." Until the Court provides elucidation this confusion will remain.

The helpful portion of *McKeiver* lies in the criteria the Court used in finding the historical importance of the jury right to be offset by the potential harm the procedure might cause to the juvenile court. The majority in *Winship* had tested the proposed standard of proof against three general criteria—the harm threatened to the non-criminal procedures of the juvenile court;[158] the harm threatened to the speed, informality and flexibility of the hearing process itself;[159] and the possible damage that might result to the specialized pre-judicial and dispositional treatment stages of the process.[160] *McKeiver* offered four criteria of a somewhat different nature by which the effect on the juvenile courts of a right to jury trial might be measured: first, the Court looked to the possibility that the jury right might

cites those guarantees of the Bill of Rights that have been applied to the states prior to 1968. *Id.* at nn.3-9 (1968).

For a discussion of this subject, *see, e.g.*, Fairman, *Does the Fourteenth Amendment Incorporate the Bill of Rights? The Original Understanding*, 2 STAN. L. REV. 5 (1949); Morrison, *Does the Fourteenth Amendment Incorporate the Bill of Rights? The Judicial Interpretation*, 2 STAN. L. REV. 140 (1949); BLACK, *Due Process of Law*, in A CONSTITUTIONAL FAITH 23 (1968).

153. *See* In re Winship, 397 U.S. 358, 367 (1970); *see also* text accompanying notes 136-43 *supra*; text accompanying notes 7-10 *supra*.

154. 403 U.S. at 543.

155. 387 U.S. at 30-31, 74. For a discussion of the "fundamental fairness" interpretation of the Due Process Clause, *see* note 152 *supra*.

156. 403 U.S. at 543.

157. *See* note 152 *supra*.

158. 397 U.S. at 366.

159. *Id.*

160. *Id.* at 366-67.

turn the juvenile hearing into an adversarial proceeding which would effectively end the hopes of the juvenile court ideal;[161] secondly, the opinion questioned whether the jury would help remedy the defects of the juvenile process;[162] thirdly, it was emphasized that a procedure would not be welcomed that removed the ability of the states to experiment with its adjudicatory process to better achieve its ends;[163] and finally, the Court considered the delay and formality that a jury would entail.[164]

The *McKeiver* criteria, as compared to the *Winship* tests, more effectively cover the real harm that may result to the juvenile court process from the application of a Bill of Rights provision. The juvenile court ideal emphasizes at the core of its theory the desirability of dealing with a child who is suspected of criminal activities by procedures that are designed to not only judge but also rehabilitate the child.[165] *McKeiver* recognizes that what limited success there has been in attaining the goals of the juvenile court ideal has been due both to the flexibility and informality of the hearing, and to the availability of varied pre-adjudicative and post-adjudicative treatments designed to individually care for the delinquent. The criteria utilized by the Court also recognizes that to the extent that the theory could be maintained, it should be; and too, that to the extent that the defects could be remedied, they ought to be. Such a formulation appears to be properly concerned for the juvenile courts' continued existence, and at the same time suitably broad to allow for the adaptation of those constitutional provisions necessary to grant juveniles a fair hearing. Section 4 will attempt to demonstrate that the Fourth Amendment exclusionary rule would survive the criteria of *McKeiver* and also meet as a prerequisite whatever due process standard was established by that same decision.

IV. THE JUVENILE COURTS AND THE EXCLUSIONARY RULE

Courts and commentators who have considered the question of whether the Fourth Amendment exclusionary rule should be or will be held applicable to juvenile court proceedings have answered in the affirmative. Approximately one dozen state court decisions dealing with the Fourth Amendment and the juvenile courts have been reported in the decade since

161. 403 U.S. at 545.
162. *Id.* at 547.
163. *Id.*
164. *Id.* at 550. One author has suggested that the balance should be among three factors: 1) will the proposed right further the "fairness of the system"; 2) will it further the administrative and economic fairness of the juvenile system; and 3) will it promote the juvenile court's role as a rehabilitative agency. Note, *A Balancing Approach to the Grant of Procedural Rights in the Juvenile Court,* 64 Nw. U.L. Rev. 87, 95 (1969).
165. *See* Section 2 *supra.*

Mapp.[166] Although the quality of legal reasoning offered in the opinions has fluctuated between one-sentence holdings and more thorough attempts to treat the issue involved, it should be noted that all of the decisions have either explicitly or implicitly held that the Fourth Amendment is applicable to juveniles.[167] Legal writers who have considered the issue have also supported the Amendment's application in this context.[168]

The virtually unanimous support from these sources which this proposition receives, however, has not gone far to settle the issue. Judge Orman Ketchum, a distinguished scholar of the juvenile court, has stated that:

> policemen have . . . scoffed at the thought that *Mapp v. Ohio* and the Fourth Amendment are matters with which they should be concerned when frisking, or searching juveniles and when seizing evidence to be used in juvenile court.[169]

166. In re Robert T. 8 Cal. App. 3d, 990 88 Cal. Rptr. 37 (Ct. of App., 1st Dist. 1970); In re R. 60 Misc. 2d 355, 303 N.Y.S. 2d 406 (Fam. Ct., N.Y.C. 1969); State in Interest of L.B., 99 N.J. Super. 589, 240 A.2d 709 (Juv. and Dom. Rel. Ct., Union Co. 1968); In re Marsh, 40 Ill. 2d 53, 237 N.E.2d 529 (Super. Ct. Ill. 1968); Matter of Two Brothers, 95 Wash. Law Rptr. 113 (D.D.C. 1967); State v. Lowry, 95 N.J. Super. 307, 230 A.2d 907 (1967); Urbasek v. State, 76 Ill. App. 2d 375, 222 N.E.2d 233 (App. Ct. 1st Dist. 1966); In re Williams, 49 Misc.2d 154, 267 N.Y.S.2d 91 (Fam. Ct., Ulster Co. 1966); In re Lang, 44 Misc.2d 900, 255 N.Y.S.2d 987 (Fam. Ct., N.Y.C. 1965); In re Ronny, 40 Misc.2d 164, 242 N.Y.S.2d 844 (Fam. Ct., Queens Co. 1963). The limited number of reported decisions dealing with the question at hand reflect generally the very small number of cases that are appealed from the juvenile courts. In some jurisdictions this can be explained partially by the absence of a right of direct appeal and the fact that no transcripts may be kept of the delinquency hearing. But an article by the Attorney General of California notes that in California where some right of appeal has always been granted, and where transcriptions are now routinely made, from January 1, 1967, to January 1, 1968, only 14 appeals from juvenile court decisions were filed or requested. Only three related appellate cases which tested other provisions of the juvenile court statute were decided that same year. Lynch, *Review of Juvenile Court Proceedings Under* Gault, in GAULT: WHAT NOW FOR THE JUVENILE COURT 157, 170 (V. Norden, ed. 1968).

167. Cases cited note 166 *supra*.

168. Only two articles, both student comments, have studied in any detail the relation of the Fourth Amendment to the juvenile courts: Comment, *Juvenile Rights Under the Fourth Amendment*, 11 J. FAM. LAW 753 (1972); Comment, *Application of the Rules Against Search and Seizure to Juvenile Delinquency Proceedings*, 16 BUFF. L. REV. 462 (1967). For the most part, commentators have discussed the applicability of the exclusionary rule only as that issue has been considered relevant to the larger question of whether constitutional rights generally are applicable to the juvenile court process. See, e.g., Ferster and Courtless, *The Beginning of Juvenile Justice, Police Practices, and the Juvenile Offender*, 22 VAND. L. REV. 567 (1969); Note, *Standards of Proof and Admissibility in Juvenile Court Proceedings*, 54 MINN. L. REV. 362 (1969); George, *Gault-Notice and Fair Hearing*, in GAULT: WHAT NOW FOR THE JUVENILE COURT 1 (V. Norden ed. 1968); Foster, *Notice and "Fair Procedure": Revolution or Simple Revision?*, in Norden, *id.* at 51; Dorsen and Reznick, *In re Gault and the Future of Juvenile Law*, 1 FAM. L.Q. 1 (1967); Paulsen, *Kent v. United States: The Constitutional Context of Juvenile Cases*, 1966 SUP. CT. REV. 167 (1966); Quick, *Constitutional Rights in the Juvenile Court*, 12 HOW. L.J. 76 (1966). See also COUNCIL OF JUDGES OF THE NATIONAL COUNCIL ON CRIME AND DELINQUENCY, MODEL RULES FOR JUVENILE COURTS RULE 44 (1969).

169. Ketcham, *Guidelines from Gault: Revolutionary Requirements and Reap-*

The differing views with respect to the Fourth Amendment rights of juveniles, and the importance of the question, are strong reasons for the Supreme Court to decide this issue. To determine the manner in which the Court will act, however, demands an accurate reading of the due process standard that the Court has utilized in its four previous juvenile court cases.

The Supreme Court has made it clear, as indicated in Section 3, that not all of the provisions of the Bill of Rights would be held to apply to the juvenile court.[170] In *Gault* the procedures the Court held to be constitutionally required in a delinquency proceeding were those that were among the "essentials of due process and fair treatment." The *Winship* decision gave some content to that phrase. The Court undertook to balance the benefits the "reasonable doubt" standard of proof would offer against the harm its application would cause to the juvenile court process.

McKeiver v. Pennsylvania held that the "applicable due process standard in juvenile proceedings is 'fundamental fairness,' as developed in *Gault* and *Winship*." It was stated in Section 3 of this paper that it is not clear to what extent that formulation modified the due process standard of the previous two decisions. The balancing process used by the Court in *Winship* was continued, however, and the *McKeiver* majority found that the value of the jury right was offset by the harm the jury would cause to the juvenile court. The intention of this section is to demonstrate that the application of the Fourth Amendment exclusionary rule to juveniles would meet the balancing criteria established by the Court, regardless of which due process formulation is applied.

As outlined in section 3, *supra*, *McKeiver* set out the following criteria by which to evaluate the harm that might be done to the juvenile court process by a proposed procedural protection:

1. Will the proposed provision turn the hearing into an adversarial proceeding which would effectively end the hopes of the juvenile court ideal?

2. Will the proposed provision help to remedy the defects of the juvenile process, or, more positively, will it help the juvenile courts to function more effectively?

3. Will the ability of the states to experiment with the adjudicatory phase of the hearing in order to better achieve its goals be compromised?

4. Will the delay and informality of the proceedings be threatened by the provision in question?

---

praisal, 53 VAND. L. REV. 1700, 1715 (1967). *But cf.*, the legal department of the New York City Police Department states that full *Mapp* requirements are met in the handling of juveniles in New York City. Telephone conversation with unidentified New York City Police Department attorney (Feb. 22, 1972).

170. In re Gault, 387 U.S. 1 (1967):

We do not mean . . . to indicate that the hearing to be held must conform with all of the requirements of a criminal trial or even of the usual administrative hearing . . . .

Id. at 30-31.

Before an attempt is made to apply the criteria above to the exclusionary rule, it should be recognized that the exclusion of evidence seized in violation of the Fourth Amendment from delinquency hearings raises a difficult conceptual problem. To the extent that the juvenile court process is successful in treating youths in need of society's help, is the exclusion of probative evidence to be welcomed when it operates to prevent the child's treatment? Although this issue is examined in more detail later in this section, it is introduced at this point to demonstrate that the following question, along with the four listed above, is likely to be asked by the Court if and when it examines the relationship between the exclusionary rule and the juvenile courts:

5. Will the loss to the juvenile court of otherwise probative evidence do irreparable harm to the ability of the juvenile court to properly attain its goals?

The exclusionary rule does not threaten to turn the juvenile hearing into more of an adversarial process or to delay or make more formal the present hearing. The first *McKeiver* criterion was specifically directed towards the obvious consequences of a jury trial—the precise application of rules of evidence; the increased formality of the proceeding; the greater reliance on oratory by the attorneys; and the psychological manipulations used in choosing a jury and feeding it facts. The fourth criterion of *McKeiver* was directed to the same end as the first—to maintain the informal non-oppressive nature of the proceeding. The Court clearly felt that much of the present value of the juvenile court hearing lay in its ability to make the child aware that the state was not confronting or punishing him, but attempting to treat him in a fair manner. As the formality of the process increases, the more the hearing becomes a full blown trial. The exclusionary rule would not affect the present temper of the juvenile court hearing. That which was illegally seized would be suppressed in a pre-adjudicative evidentiary hearing. The juvenile court hearing would continue as it is with the exception that the judge would be unable to consider the information previously suppressed when it came time to determine whether the youth had in fact done the act of which he is accused.[171]

The jury proposal failed the second criterion because the Court found that the jury would not remedy the defects that had developed in the juvenile court process, nor would it add in a positive way to the effectiveness

---

171. The distinction posited between the adjudicatory and pre-adjudicative stages of the juvenile proceeding may not be realistic. Where personnel and facilities are limited, the trier of fact may also sit at the evidentiary hearing, and because no jury is involved in the juvenile hearing, the possibility of bias on the part of the judge who has seen the "excluded" evidence will be difficult to prevent. One writer has suggested using court administrators to sit at the preliminary hearing. Note, *Extending Constitutional Rights to Juveniles—Gault in Indiana*, 43 IND. L.J. 661 (1968). For a discussion of this issue, *see* State v. Lowry, 95 N.J. Super. 307, 230 A.2d 907 (Super. Ct. 1967).

of the court. The *McKeiver* opinion did not state what precise defects the Court had in mind. The first opinion in this area, *Kent v. United States*, however, did list some problems of the juvenile court:

> There is much evidence that some juvenile courts . . . lack the personnel, facilities, and techniques to perform adequately as representatives of the state in a *parens patriae* capacity, at least with respect to children charged with a law violation.[172]

The use of the exclusionary rule would admittedly not help relieve these problems, if those were the problems which *McKeiver* had in mind. But it is clear that the application of the reasonable doubt standard of proof in *Winship* was expected to go no further as a solution.

Although extending the exclusionary rule will not provide the necessary personnel and facilities, it does improve the juvenile court process in another manner. Inherent in society's concern for the juvenile accused of a violation of a criminal statute is the notion that the misdeed, if it occurred, was not caused by an irreversible "bad streak" in the youth. It is correctible and the theory of juvenile justice places the juvenile court in an extremely important position as one of the first points of contact between the child and the state.[173] The judge, representing the state at this crucial point in the juvenile process, must not only decide how to treat the child, but he must also take maximum care to ensure that the procedure of the court is directed towards demonstrating to the youth that "fair play" is being done.[174] When evidence that has been taken from a youth in a manner that would be unconstitutional if he were an adult is used against him in the juvenile court, "fair play" is not being accorded and there is the danger that the child will leave the juvenile court without the proper respect for the law's process:

> Since family court judges must be fact finders as well as law interpreters, we would do well to stand solidly in behalf of children before us, to avoid contamination of the fact sources and to see to it that we brook no shabby practices in fact gathering which do not comport with fair play. We must not only be fair; we must convince the child before us that the state is firm but fair and that the judge, a parent image, is careful to ensure those civilized standards of conduct toward the child, which we expect of the child toward organized society.[175]

---

172. 383 U.S. 541, 555-56 (1966).
173. *See* text accompanying note 63 *supra*.
174. *Id.*
175. In re Ronny, 40 Misc. 2d 164, 180-81, 242 N.Y.S.2d 844, 860-61 (Fam. Ct., Queens Co. 1967).

The freedom of the states to experiment with the juvenile hearing procedures, the third criterion of *McKeiver*, would not be hampered by the application of the exclusionary rule. The Court felt in *McKeiver* that a jury would severely lock-in the number of alternatives available to the states in their attempt to provide a hearing designed to both adjudicate and treat the child. The exclusionary rule has no direct effect on the procedures used at the juvenile delinquency hearing. The status of questioned evidence is determined at a pre-adjudicatory evidentiary hearing.[176]

The potential loss of information available to the juvenile court to determine delinquency presents the most difficult problem for analysis. The goal of the juvenile court theory is to treat and rehabilitate the erring youth and any procedure, whether denominated "constitutional" or not, cannot be totally welcomed if it operates to free a child who is truly in need of care. Neither the child's nor society's interests are properly protected. If the exclusionary rule is held to be applicable to juvenile court proceedings, there will be instances when the state will be forced to return the child to his or her home without aid because the piece of evidence vital to proving his or her delinquency is the product of an illegal search and seizure.

A further consideration enters into the picture when the total juvenile justice process is examined. Only a small part of the information that comes before the juvenile court is directed to the question of whether the youth committed the delinquent act. Both before and after the adjudicatory stage, other agencies involved in the juvenile court process investigate the child's background, his home and social environment, and his school records. This information is compiled in a social service report that is used by the court to determine how to properly treat a juvenile who had been adjudged a delinquent. Since the goal of the process is to effectively rehabilitate the child, it can be seriously questioned whether, and to what extent, information gained as a result of a Fourth Amendment violation should be withheld not only from consideration by the court when making an adjudication, but withheld from the judge when he attempts to fashion the proper treatment for the delinquent youth. Theoretically, the most distinctive and beneficial part of the juvenile court process is its specialized treatment program. The delinquency adjudication is one part of this treatment, but the real value of the juvenile court process, and ultimately its success, lies in its ability to fashion a variety of rehabilitation programs adaptable to the individual needs of the juvenile. Presumably the Supreme Court will not want to damage this portion of the juvenile process. However, the Court could grant the protection of the exclusionary rule to the juvenile without harming the treatment phase by limiting the rule's applicability to the adjudicatory portion of the process.

This would not be a unique act by the Court. In *Gault* and *Winship*

---

176. *See* note 171 *supra.*

the Court specifically stated that the procedural protections they granted were to apply only to the adjudicatory phase of a delinquency proceeding.[177] This distinction between the adjudicatory and treatment phases of the juvenile court process, particularly with respect to the Fourth Amendment, has been specifically adopted by a few states in recent years.[178] One representative provision is section 704-6 of the Illinois Juvenile Court Act which provides that in the adjudicatory hearing to determine if the youth has committed a delinquent act, the "standard of proof and the rules of evidence in the nature of criminal proceedings in this state are applicable."[179] Section 705-1 then states that once the child has been ruled to be a delinquent, the court shall hear "[a]ll evidence helpful in determining [the proper disposition of the child]."[180]

The distinction made between the treatment and the adjudicatory phases by the Illinois statute attempts to resolve the conflicts between society's desire to help the youth and its need to provide him with due process protections when the help is ineffective or unavailable. It is a forceful argument that the rehabilitation of the child should come before all other considerations. However, as discussed in section 3 *supra*, the Supreme Court in *Kent* found that the juvenile court had failed to fulfill its promise. And because the juvenile system continued to function improperly,[181] *Gault* and *Winship* held that youths appearing in juvenile courts must be granted at least some of the protections propounded in the

---

177. See note 5 *supra*.
178. See note 179 *infra*, and accompanying text.
179. Illinois Juvenile Court Act, ILL. REV. STATS. § 704-6 (1969):
At the adjudicatory hearing, the court shall first consider only the question whether the minor is a person described in Section 2-1 [Section 2-1 generally grants jurisdiction to the juvenile court over children who are delinquent, otherwise in need of supervision, neglected, or dependents]. The standard of proof and the rules of evidence in the nature of criminal proceedings in this state are applicable to Section 2-2 [Section 2-2 grants jurisdiction to the court over children who have violated penal laws].
See, e.g., CALIFORNIA WELFARE AND INSTITUTIONS CODE § 701 (1971). But see ALASKA STAT. § 47.010-.070 (1970); Mo. REV. STAT. § 211.171 (1970). These latter states have diluted the Fourth Amendment rights of juveniles.
180. Illinois Juvenile Court Act, ILL. REV. STATS, § 705-1 (1969) provides, *inter alia:*
(1) After adjudging the minor a ward of the court, the court shall hear evidence on the question of the proper disposition best serving the interests of the minor and the public. All evidence helpful in determining this question, including oral and written reports, may be admitted and may be relied upon to the extent of its probative value, even though not competent for the purposes of the adjudicative hearing.
181. A study by the President's Crime Commission in 1967 estimated that one out of every six youths would be brought before a juvenile court on delinquency charges before their eighteenth birthday. But what was more important, the Commission concluded that the more a youth was handled by the juvenile courts and the treatment system, the more likely he was to be convicted of a crime as an adult. PRESIDENT'S COMMISSION ON LAW ENFORCEMENT AND ADMINISTRATION OF JUSTICE, THE CHALLENGE OF CRIME IN A FREE SOCIETY 5, 46 (1967).

Bill of Rights. When rehabilitation is not provided, other considerations, especially constitutional ones, should control.

The second point to consider when the rehabilitative ideal of the juvenile court is raised as an objection to the use of the exclusionary rule, is the manner in which the Fourth Amendment exclusionary rule has been treated by the Supreme Court. Justice Cardozo in 1926 questioned whether the "criminal is to go free because the constable has blundered,"[182] a refrain that has been reiterated against the use of the exclusionary rule ever since. Notwithstanding that hazard, the Court has consistently held since *Mapp* that the value to society of the constitutional right protected by the exclusionary rule far outweighs the harm caused by the release of an occasional criminal. In light of the juvenile court's failure to provide effective rehabilitation for the child, the policies underlying the Fourth Amendment similarly outweigh the competing policy of rehabilitation.

The more telling argument for the application of the exclusionary rule, however, comes directly from the *Mapp* decision. As described in Section 2 above, the Court in *Mapp* held exclusion to be a constitutionally required remedy partially because it had been demonstrated that it was the only effective way to deter the police from disregarding the commands of the Fourth Amendment. If the exclusionary rule is to successfully deter police misconduct, exclusion ought to be uniformly and assiduously supported by the courts. Once apparently arbitrary exceptions, such as for age, are made to the coverage of the exclusionary rule, then not only are the police likely to skeptically view the reasoning of the courts, but also in street situations when the age of the suspect is not readily ascertainable, the police skepticism may be translated into violations of the Fourth Amendment rights of suspects who appear younger than their calendar age. The harm to the effectiveness of the exclusionary rule that would be done by holding juveniles not to be entitled to its protection has been suggested by Professor Quick:

Can a police officer be told, in effect, that when he is conducting an investigation concerning a child under 17, there is no practical restraint as to the manner in which he may acquire evidence. But when the suspect is 17 years or older, then he must tread constitutional paths lest his zealousness destroy the case.[183]

V. CONCLUSION

The problems discussed in the preceding Section lie at the heart of the balancing process that is likely to be used by the Supreme Court if and

---

182. People v. Defore, 242 N.Y. 13, 16 (1926).
183. Quick, *supra* note 168, at 97.

when it decides whether or not due process demands the application of the exclusionary rule. It should matter little whether the Court embodies the substance of this holding under the rubric of "due process and fair treatment" or "fundamental fairness."

The particular elements of the balancing formula are readily summarized. On the one side will lie 1) the historical significance and broad scope of the Amendment's protection as outlined in numerous Supreme Court decisions, and 2) the favorable results that the exclusionary rule enjoys when measured against the five post-*McKeiver* criteria. On the opposing side of the balance lies the potentially irreparable harm that may be done to the juvenile and the juvenile court process when probative evidence is unavailable to the court when it decides whether a youth may be treated. An examination of the juvenile system leads to the conclusion that the balance should be struck in favor of applying the exclusionary rule to the juvenile court.[184]

---

184. A final question not considered in the text colors the analysis of the entire article—the future of the exclusionary rule as a constitutionally required doctrine. In recent years the exclusionary rule has come under heavy criticism from commentators, the American Law Institute, and the present Chief Justice of the Supreme Court. A study of the exclusionary rule was made by Dallin Oaks in which he suggested that the "assumed" deterrent value of the rule has never been adequately demonstrated or disproved, and pointed out that because of *Mapp* all comparative statistics were 10 years old and no new figures can be obtained. Oaks, *Studying the Exclusionary Rule in Search and Seizure*, 37 U. CHI. L. REV. 665 (1970). For other articles critical of the exclusionary rule, *see, e.g.,* Hufstedler, *Directions and Misdirections of Constitutional Right of Privacy*, 26 RECORD 546 (1971); Wingo, *Growing Disillusionment with the Exclusionary Rule*, 25 Sw. L.J. 573 (1971).

The conceptual bases of the exclusionary rule have been recently questioned by Chief Justice Burger in his dissenting opinion in Bivens v. Six Unknown Named Agents of Federal Bureau of Narcotics, 403 U.S. 388, 411 (1971). The Chief Justice suggested that while the exclusionary rule must be kept until a workable alternative was available, such an alternative should come from Congress in the form of an "administrative or quasi-judicial agency" which could provide compensation or restitution that would be available to those who suffered from an illegal search and seizure. *Id.* at 422. The American Law Institute proposed that the exclusionary rule be maintained but its application allowed only in cases where the illegality was "palpably wrong." AMERICAN LAW INSTITUTE, MODEL CODE OF PRE-ARRAIGNMENT PROCEDURE §§ 8.02(2), (3), pp. 23-24 (text, draft no. 4 1971).

Given the attacks upon the exclusionary rule, and given also the present makeup of the Supreme Court, while the exclusionary rule may not be thrown out in the near future, it is possible that the Court may begin either to limit the scope of the rule's protection or to freeze the exclusion doctrine in its present posture. Either situation may mean that the juvenile courts will remain free of the exclusionary rule's strictures.

For a summary of sources dealing with alternative remedies to Fourth Amendment violations, *see* Comment, *Police Use of Remote Camera Systems for Surveillance of Public Streets*, 4 COLUM. HUMAN RIGHTS L. REV. 143, 172 n.165 (1972).

8

Case Note:
IN THE MATTER OF ELLA B.— A TEST FOR THE RIGHT TO ASSIGNED COUNSEL IN FAMILY COURT CASES

VIRGINIA S. CARSON*

In the Matter of Ella B., an opinion by the New York Court of Appeals reviewing a decision of the Westchester County Family Court, focused on the right to counsel of an indigent parent in a child neglect proceeding. The parent's successful appeal affirmed the provisions of the Family Court Act Section 343(a),[1] allowing attorneys for parents, and guaranteed the right to representation for indigent parents to be provided by existing legal services organizations or by private attorneys appointed by the Court.[2] In so holding, this opinion marked a firm step in the trend toward extension of legal protections to participants in juvenile cases. The Court found that child neglect hearings may pose serious threats to parents including loss of the child's society, a probationary period of supervision of the child while in the home, a civil commitment of the parent to a mental health facility for thirty days, or even criminal proceedings for child abuse.[3] Because these sanctions were available against the parent and because the state government played an adversary role against the parent, the Court of Appeals held that Mrs. B. was entitled to assigned counsel and to notice of that right.[4]

The case arose from an alleged incident of June 21, 1969 in which the respondent Jeri B. left the child alone, strapped in her crib from 1:00 to 4:00 A.M. A male adult entered the house, took the child, allegedly assaulted her, and left her near the Westchester County Airport.[5] The Westchester Commissioner of Social Services then instituted proceedings to have

---

*Staff member, COLUMBIA HUMAN RIGHTS LAW REVIEW.

1. NEW YORK FAMILY COURT ACT § 343(a) (McKinney 1962):
The Court shall advise the parent or other person legally responsible for the child's care of a right to be represented by Counsel of his own choosing and to have an adjournment to send for counsel and consult with him. The Court shall also inform the parent or other person legally responsible for the child's care of the child's right to be represented by a law guardian under part four of Article 2 of this act.

2. In the Matter of Ella B., 30 N.Y.2d 352 (1972).

3. 30 N.Y.2d at 356, *citing* FAMILY COURT ACT §§ 1014, 1052, 1055, and NEW YORK PENAL LAW § 260.10.

4. 30 N.Y.2d at 357.

5. Brief for County Attorney at 1, In the Matter of Ella B., 30 N.Y.2d 352.

Ella B. declared a neglected child and placed in his custody. At the hearing in Westchester Family Court, the judge advised Mrs. B. of her right to be represented if she chose to obtain an attorney at her own expense. He also instructed her that she could waive her right to an attorney and admit or deny the facts in the petition.[6] The judge said, "Do you want an attorney?" and Mrs. B. replied, "No." He asked, "Do you admit the facts in the petition?" Mrs. B. replied, "Yes, I do." In short order, Ella B. was found to be a neglected child and placed in plaintiff's custody. The judge also ordered an inquiry into the welfare of a younger child in the home.[7] The Legal Aid Society of Westchester County appealed to the Appellate Division on behalf of Mrs. B., but the Family Court order was affirmed. Legal Aid petitioned the Family Court for termination of the child's placement with the County, but that motion was denied. This appeal to the Court of Appeals from the initial determination of neglect followed immediately after the placement termination hearings.[8]

Before the Court of Appeals the Commissioner of Social Services, represented by the County Attorney, argued three main points: 1) that the Family Court procedure provided sufficiently for the representation of parents; 2) that historically the constitutional right to assigned counsel applied only to criminal defendants; and 3) that the imposition of a right to assigned counsel would create an intolerable burden on the state's resources. The County Attorney maintained that the judge in his opening statement advised Mrs. B. of her right to counsel under Section 343(a) of the Family Court Act.[9] He asserted that only if the parent signifies her lack of financial resources is the Court under a duty to advise her of the availability of free counsel. Moreover, the County Attorney maintained that the right to counsel is mandatory only in criminal cases. In support of this contention, he cited *In the Matter of Bido*,[10] in which the Appellate Division declared that the Family Court had no obligation to advise a respondent in a paternity suit of his right to counsel or to assign counsel to him because of the civil nature of the action. Finally, the County Attorney noted that Mrs. B. had, in fact, obtained counsel from the Legal Aid Society. He emphasized that the Legal Aid lawyer had appealed to the Appellate Division, moved in the Family Court for a termination of the child's placement with the County, and asked for an injunction against the Commissioner's placement from the Federal District Court. Not only were all these actions unsuccessful, but in none of them did Mrs. B. bring forth any testimony to refute or contradict the facts alleged in spite of her oppor-

6. Record at 4, 5.
7. *Id.* at 5.
8. County Attorney's brief at 2.
9. *Id.* at 3.
10. In the Matter of Bido, 36 A.D.2d 537, 318 N.Y.S.2d 547 (1971).

tunity to do so.[11] The County Attorney thus concluded that the appeal to the Court of Appeals was unnecessary in view of the previous legal failures to win reversal of the Family Court order.

The brief submitted by the New York Attorney General's office as Amicus Curiae took no position on the specific case, but rather expressed concern over the "preservation of the unique and protective character of Family Court dispositions" and the burdens on the state if a right to appointed counsel for the parent were established in child neglect cases.[12] The Attorney General pointed to the analogous cases of *In re Robinson*[13] and *In re Cager*,[14] from California and Maryland respectively, which held that there existed no right to counsel at public expense in child neglect cases. The state relied on the benevolent purpose of the proceedings, as well as the absence of detention or incarceration of the parent, to distinguish neglect proceedings from criminal proceedings and those few civil cases in which appointment of a lawyer is considered mandatory. He noted, as an example, that deportation proceedings, which carry a serious civil sanction, have no provision for free counsel for indigent defendants.[15] Finally, the Attorney General's brief urged that referrals to established legal services programs fulfill the requirement of a right to free counsel, so that appointment of private counsel by the Court would be an unnecessary expense. OEO legal service groups have expertise in this area, but the brief noted that MFY Legal Services, Inc. claimed that it cannot represent clients where the state is constitutionally required to furnish attorneys.[16] Thus the state estimated that court appointment of private attorneys in these cases would add an estimated $228,000 to the state court costs.[17] For these reasons, the Attorney General advocated a finding that existing Family Court practices were sufficient to meet constitutional standards.

The Legal Aid Society argued for appellant Mrs. B. that the Family Court Act Section 343(a) and the judge's recitation of counsel rights to Mrs. B. under that section violated the due process clause of the Fourteenth

---

11. County Attorney's brief at 5.

12. Brief of the Attorney General of the State of New York as Amicus Curiae at 2.

13. In re Robinson, 8 Cal. App. 3d 783, 87 Cal. Rptr. 678 (1970). The California Appeals Court said, "We view a proceeding to adjudicate the dependency status of a child as a true civil cause comparable in essentials to a child custody controversy between parents." 87 Cal. Rptr. at 680.

14. The Maryland Supreme Court agreed in Cager, 251 Md. 423, 248 A.2d 384 (1968). "The mothers were given full notice of the actions the State's Attorney took and the ends he sought and were given full opportunity to be heard by the Court." 248 A.2d at 391.

15. Attorney General's brief at 4.

16. Attorney General's brief at 5. MFY, a large New York City poverty program, based this decision on a recommendation in the OEO guidelines for legal services and stated their intentions in an affirmation filed in Aido Soto v. Hyman Gamso, pending in the Appellate Division, First Department.

17. Attorney General's brief at 6.

Amendment because neither mentioned a right to assigned counsel. The brief contended that a fundamental right was involved, that the sanctions against the parent were quite serious, that the parent was faced by an adversary with extensive resources, and that the issues were complex and confusing to a lay person. These factors combined to deny this indigent parent her right to be heard effectively, which is the essence of the due process safeguard first outlined in *Powell v. Alabama*.[18] The brief elongated this argument first by reference to *Meyer v. Nebraska*[19] and *May v. Anderson*,[20] in which the Supreme Court recognized the fundamental nature of a parent's rights in regard to her children. Next, the brief asserted that the loss of a child's society, the possibility of permanent termination of parental custody, the emotional turmoil for the child, the direct effect of a child neglect proceeding on other children in the home, and the possibility of criminal prosecution all testify to the coercive nature of these proceedings against the parent.[21] Legal counsel was essential to Mrs. B's defense aginst these sanctions, and to the protection of her rights to the other child in the home.

The Legal Aid Society emphasized further the complexity of the legal issues which confront a parent in child neglect proceedings and the consequent necessity of legal counsel to protect the parent's rights. The state can bring to the case the county attorney, a law guardian for the child, medical and other expert witnesses, and various social caseworkers.[22] Moreover the Court is called upon to render a decision on the fact of neglect and a disposition of the child after weighing vague evidence on the deficiency of the home, the influence on the child, the medical testimony of abuse, the conclusions of the caseworkers, and the potential for future harm or rehabilitation if the child is left with the parent. A lay parent, often awed or intimidated by the proceedings, can hardly conduct an effective cross-examination of the state's witnesses or utilize the discovery procedures available. Moreover the focus of this delicate determination is on the parent's behavior. Therefore, Legal Aid argued, an attorney is essential to presentation of the parent's defense and fair interpretation of the evi-

18. Legal Aid brief at i, ii. Powell v. Alabama, 387 U.S. 45 (1932), reversed the rape conviction of a young black man because the hurried, makeshift attempts to provide counsel for him effectively denied him the right to be heard and to present his defense.

19. In Meyer v. Nebraska, 262 U.S. 390 (1923), a statute which prohibited the teaching of German in high schools was struck down as an unconstitutional invasion of parents' rights to direct the education of their children.

20. May v. Anderson, 345 U.S. 528 (1953), was an appeal by a mother from an unfavorable child custody award, in which the Court declared, "Rights far more precious to appellant than property rights will be cut off if she is bound by the Wisconsin award of custody." 345 US at 533.

21. Legal Aid brief at 15.

22. *Id.* at 16.

dence.[23] In this particular case, the brief pointed out, no evidence was introduced to support the facts alleged or to prove that the child's removal from the home was necessary. For all these reasons, the Legal Aid Society asserted that the essence of due process, the right to be heard effectively, demanded that Mrs. B. be represented by court appointed counsel notwithstanding the nominally civil nature of the child neglect proceeding.[24]

As an additional ground for relief, Legal Aid alleged that the current statutory scheme violated the equal protection clause of the Fourteenth Amendment. The Supreme Court held in *Harper v. Virginia Board of Elections*[25] that a fundamental right, in that case the right to vote, cannot depend on wealth. Family Court Act § 343(a) providing for counsel for parents at their own expense, clearly discriminated against a poor parent in a proceeding involving "fundamental" rights to her children. The brief conceded that the state is not obligated to provide every possible legal service to the indigent parents, but it insisted that an exclusion from legal representation solely on the basis of wealth is not the kind of rational distinction among its citizens allowed under the Fourteenth Amendment.[26] The command that the states afford all citizens the equal protection of the laws then, it was argued, compels the state to arrange for legal counsel for all parents if some parents were so privileged.

Finally, Mrs. B. claimed that she had not made a valid waiver of her right to counsel at the initial hearing because she had not been advised that the state would provide her with an attorney. In *Johnson v. Zerbst*,[27] the Supreme Court declared that courts should "indulge every reasonable presumption against waiver" of constitutional rights. Certainly this parent, faced with cou. plex issues and proceedings and told that she would have to find her own attorney, cannot be deemed to have made a knowing waiver of that right. Moreover, the brief asserted, the state recognized that parents need legal counsel in these cases when it enacted the counsel provisions of § 343(a). If indigent parents are not provided with counsel, then the state's announced intentions towards parents are frustrated.[28] Indeed, Mrs. B's appearance here was in form only, since she was unable to comprehend the possibility that the child would be taken from her

---

23. *Id.* at 24.
24. *Id.* at 43.
25. *Id.* at 45.
26. *Id.* at 55.
27. Johnson v. Zerbst, 304 U.S. 458 (1938), concerned an alleged waiver of the right to counsel by two defendants in a counterfeiting case. The Supreme Court declared, "It is the duty of a federal court in the trial of a criminal case to protect the right of the accused to counsel, and, if he has no counsel, to determine whether he has intelligently and competently waived that right." 304 U.S. at 465.
28. Legal Aid brief at 57.

or to present her side of the story.[29] The Legal Aid Society urged that a finding that Mrs. B. had waived her right to an attorney would violate both the Constitution and the state's statutory purposes.

Legal Aid filed a supplemental brief in which they cited two recent cases that reinforced the main brief's principal argument.[30] *Stanley v. Illinois*[31] affirmed a parent's fundamental rights in his children, and *Cleaver v. Wilcox*[32] rendered a declaratory judgment that indigent parents in child neglect proceedings be afforded counsel by the state of California. In *Stanley*, a father challenged the state's statutory presumption against awarding him custody of his illegitimate children. The Supreme Court held that such a broad presumption discriminated against those individual fathers who do provide an adequate home for their children, thus depriving them of fundamental rights to their children without a hearing as to their fitness as a parent. *Cleaver v. Wilcox* was a class action brought by an indigent parent to obtain appointed legal counsel in child neglect cases. Attorneys for plaintiff presented substantially the same arguments on due process and equal protection grounds as those the Legal Aid Society prepared for Mrs. B. Accordingly, the California District Court found that the civil nature of her action was no bar to a Constitutional safeguard of right to counsel where fundamental rights were involved.

The Court of Appeals opinion in *Ella* by Chief Judge Fuld began with a description of the summary proceedings in the Family Court and the subsequent procedural history of the case. Judge Fuld quickly determined that, given the fundamental rights involved, the Fourteenth Amendment due process clause required the right to assigned counsel.[33] He cited *Stanley v. Illinois, Cleaver v. Wilcox, supra,* and *Boddie v. Connecticut,*[34] in support of his conclusion on the mandates of the due process clause. In view of the statutory provisions for attorneys for parents who can afford one, Judge Fuld found equal protection grounds as well for providing indigent parents with legal counsel.[35] The state had argued as a supplemental ground for denying relief, that Mrs. B. had waived her right to an attorney when she answered negatively the Judge's questions on that point. The Court of Appeals noted that the Judge preceded his question, "Do you want an attorney?" with the statement that if she desired a lawyer, she must find one and pay for his services herself. Since Mrs. B. was

---

29. *Id.* at 59.
30. Supplemental Brief for Mrs. B. at 2.
31. Stanley v. Illinois, 405 U.S. 645. (1972).
32. Cleaver v. Wilcox, — F. Supp. —, 40 U.S.L.W. 2658 (April 11, 1972).
33. 30 N.Y.2d at 356.
34. Boddie v. Connecticut, 401 U.S. 371 (1971) involved a challenge to the statutory court fees which blocked access to the civil courts for indigent citizens. The Supreme Court held that Connecticut's refusal to waive these high fees denied due process of law to low income citizens.
35. 30 N.Y.2d at 357.

not advised that free counsel was available, her waiver of counsel was not based on an intelligent understanding of the legal issues involved, but rather on her immediate financial situation.[36] For that reason, the Court of Appeals held her nominal waiver invalid and insisted that the right to counsel included the right to be advised of free legal representation if financially warranted. The Court disposed of the case by remitting it to the Family Court for rehearing of both the fact finding and the child's placement. The order appealed from (the Appellate Division's affirmance of the initial Family Court determination) was affirmed as modified with the understanding that Mrs. B. would be represented in the next hearing.[37]

This short opinion by Chief Judge Fuld is swift and conclusive as to the case at hand but silent on the constitutionality of the statute or a specific rule for later cases. There seems to be no doubt that Judge Fuld intends for the Family Court to provide counsel for indigent parents in neglect cases. Perhaps his silence is designed to allow the widest latitude for administrative rules. The Family Courts are not unaware of the problems of the parents in these cases. On the contrary, Florence M. Kelley, Administrative Judge of the Family Court of the State of New York, submitted an affidavit along with the Attorney General's brief, which set out the existing practice of the Family Court when faced with indigent parents. She said that

the Family Court will advise the parent that he may obtain the free services of an attorney from a legal services agency, whose address is provided by the Court. On occasion, when the legal services agencies have had insufficient personnel to handle the cases at that time, referral to a Bar Association panel of attorneys has been utilized.[38]

Judge Kelley also mentioned that adjournments are granted so that the parent may obtain legal counsel. Although the Attorney General and the Family Court seemed to be aware of the problems facing indigent parents and stated that they are willing to direct such parents to free legal services, a survey by the COLUMBIA JOURNAL OF LAW AND SOCIAL PROBLEMS showed that in 1969-70, 76% of respondents in child neglect proceedings were not represented at any stage.[39] Not surprisingly, 79.5% of these adjudications resulted in neglect findings. Mrs. B.'s brief cited this study and noted that neglect cases constituted only 6,000 cases a year as opposed to

36. 30 N.Y.2d at 358.
37. *Id.*
38. Affidavit of Florence M. Kelley, submitted with the Attorney General's brief.
39. Note, *Representation in Child Neglect Cases: Are Parents Neglected?* 4 COLUMBIA JOURNAL OF LAW AND SOCIAL PROBLEMS 230, 236-37 (1968).

24,000 delinquency proceedings and 35,000 support cases.[40] Indeed, the Attorney General welcomes legal representation from Federally funded legal programs; he pleads only that the state not be compelled to shoulder the entire expense.[41] From the tone of the opinion, it seems likely that the procedure outlined by Judge Kelley will suffice as long as Family Court judges endeavor conscientiously to see that indigent parents understand their full rights and the opportunities for obtaining free counsel.

In the Matter of Ella B. deals with a problem that the entire judiciary seems well aware of: the burdens imposed on a lay person caught up in our legal system. The Family Court judges responding to the Columbia Journal survey reported many difficulties in fulfilling their judicial duties and in protecting the rights of parents appearing *pro se*, some with severe language barriers.[42] The Supreme Court of the United States demonstrated continued concern over legal representation for the indigent in a unanimous 1972 decision, *Argersinger v. Hamlin*,[43] which extended the right to assigned counsel to any offense for which a person might be imprisoned. The protection of assigned counsel is also gaining headway in the more serious civil cases. The Legal Aid brief notes that the right to counsel has been extended in cases involving commitment to a mental institution,[44] in welfare benefits termination proceedings,[45] in Family Court probation hearings,[46] and to children facing confinement for treatment rather than punishment.[47]

The Attorney General's reservations, however, are not without merit. The expense involved in extending legal services to just 6,000 child neglect cases could cost over $200,000.[48] The legal aid services are already overburdened, and the bar association volunteer arrangement described in the Columbia Journal survey is completely inadequate for the overflow.[49] Moreover, as Justice Powell points out in his concurring opinion in *Argersinger*, extending legal services to thousands of cases would cause "intolerable delays in an already overburdened system."[50] One can imagine increasing disputes over eligibility under OEO income limits, over quality of counsel and resources available for defense, and the exaggeration of existing problems of the distribution of lawyers in many parts of the country. Surely the line must be drawn somewhere between traffic violations and criminal

40. Legal Aid brief at 53.
41. Attorney General's brief at 4.
42. Note, *supra* note 39, at 247.
43. Argersinger v. Hamlin, 407 U.S. 25 (1972).
44. People *ex rel.* Rogers v. Stanley, 17 N.Y.2d 256 (1966).
45. Goldberg v. Kelly, 397 U.S. 254 (1970).
46. People *ex rel.* Decker v. Martin, 57 Misc.2d 57 (S. Ct. Onondaga Co. 1968).
47. *In re* Gault, 387 U.S. 1 (1967).
48. Attorney General's brief at 6.
49. Note, *supra* note 39, at 239.
50. Argersinger v. Hamlin, 407 U.S. at 58.

offenses, yet the history of the Sixth Amendment gives us no guidance for dealing with cases on the civil side.

Justice Powell suggests the fundamental fairness test often articulated by Justice Harlan and a case-by-case approach in determining the limits of the right to assigned counsel. "Fundamental fairness" and the "benevolent role of the state" have always been hallmarks of the juvenile legal system, yet these general purposes have failed to result in adequate safeguards for citizens caught up in the juvenile process. Certainly, more specific tests are needed to determine when the Constitutional safeguards articulated for criminal proceedings should be invoked for any or all participants in juvenile cases. Perhaps a better guide for the Family Courts would be a factor alluded to in *Cleaver v. Wilcox, supra*, and in *Ella B.*: the fact that the state is an adversary in child neglect cases. In many civil cases, as in the paternity suit involved in *Bido, supra*, the state is merely an arbitrator between two private parties. In other juvenile proceedings, though acting in the child's welfare, the state enters the case as a party and employs its full resources in support of its contentions. Here the citizen without representation is at a greater disadvantage than he would be if his adversary were a citizen of more modest means and lacked the persuasive tone of authority of the state welfare agencies. The defendant in a juvenile suit brought by the state is also faced with a wider variety of sanctions than the money damages most often awarded in private suits. Here as elsewhere when the state is an adversary, some fundamental right of citizenship is usually at stake: juvenile commitment for treatment, civil commitment of adults, loss of a child's society and others. Defendants in actions brought by the state have a strong claim to public resources for legal counsel, similar to criminal defendants. The state adversary test, though still in the formative stage, is an intelligible and workable guide for Family Court judges. For these reasons, *In the Matter of Ella B.* will contribute a firm step toward a juvenile legal process which protects individual citizens and society at large.

9 | JUVENILE POLICE RECORD KEEPING

EDWARD R. SPALTY*

I. INTRODUCTION

Records are likely to be accorded legitimacy and authority lacking in more informal types of communication.[1] Written records require special attention. It is the thesis of this article that juvenile police records[2] are not currently given proper treatment or attention and that, as a result of the inconspicuous nature of the record-keeping process, statutory assurances[3] of confidentiality are illusory.

Throughout the country juvenile courts have substantially the same control over youths who have been accused of criminal offenses as they have over those youths accused of offenses that would not be crimes if committed by an adult. Both classes of youths are committed by the same procedures to the same institutions for the same length of time.[4] Adult records are partially protected by constitutional guarantees. To a certain extent, juvenile court records are beginning to be protected.[5] The protections sought to be applied to court records can and should be applied to the analogous area of police records.[6] The United States Supreme Court, however, has not yet addressed its attention to either juvenile police or court records. Because

---

*Staff member, COLUMBIA HUMAN RIGHTS LAW REVIEW.

1. ON RECORD: FILES AND DOSSIERS IN AMERICAN LIFE 5 (S. Wheeler ed. 1969).

2. Although this article will focus on juvenile police records, an analogous problem exists in the area of juvenile court records where, despite statutes promising confidentiality in the interest of protecting the youth, juvenile courts and police departments permit nearly all governmental agencies to inspect court records. KETCHAM & PAULSEN, JUVENILE COURTS, CASES AND MATERIALS 412 (1967); but see note 6 infra.

3. See notes 42-47 infra and accompanying text.

4. Dembitz, Book Review, 23 RECORD OF N.Y.C.B.A. 669, 673 (1968).

5. Several states have enacted sealing and expungement statutes for court records. For a 1969 list, see Ferster & Courtless, The Beginning of Juvenile Justice, Police Practices and the Juvenile Offender, 22 VAND. L. REV. 567, 605 n.206 [hereinafter cited as Ferster & Courtless].

6. It seems both fairer and easier to control access to the youth's record by controlling the formation of the record. Additional problems arise after there has been a public hearing. It is ironic that the often advanced rationale for expanding police record-keeping is to avoid the creation of possibly harmful court records. Note, Juvenile Delinquents: The Police, State Court and Juvenile Justice, 79 HARV. L. REV. 775, 784 (1966) [hereinafter cited as Harvard Note].

the recognition of the juvenile as a full citizen within the meaning of the Constitution does not appear imminent, interim protections are suggested.[7]

Since the inception of separate treatment for juvenile records[8] it has been recognized that a record "severely limits the juvenile offender's career opportunities and often hinders rehabilitation."[9] While the problem of stigmatization[10] may be inherent in record-making and record-keeping, until it is proven that records do not protect the interests of both the juvenile and society, the solution seems to be in minimizing the possibility of harm to the juvenile that can arise from record-keeping. This article questions whether records, as maintained, are necessary,[11] and discusses the law and practice concerning juvenile record-keeping.[12] In conclusion, proposals are made in an effort to prevent injustice to the juvenile.[13]

7. Recent developments indicate a slowed trend toward recognition of the juvenile as a citizen for constitutional purposes. Three Supreme Court cases trace this trend. In re Gault, 387 U.S. 1 (1967), affords juveniles some of the same due process rights as adults in regard to the adjudicatory stage of the juvenile process where commitment to a state institution is probable. In re Winship, 397 U.S. 358 (1970), requires the standard of proof in a juvenile proceeding to be "beyond a reasonable doubt." The trend was temporarily halted by the failure of the Court to recognize a right to jury trial in juvenile court. McKeiver v. Pennsylvania, 403 U.S. 528 (1971). See also United States v. Costanzo, 395 U.S. 441, cert. denied, 398 U.S. 883 (1968) (jury trial).

8. See, e.g., N.Y. FAM. CT. ACT § 784 (McKinney 1963).

9. Harvard Note, supra note 6, at 784.

10. For a discussion of the stigmatizing effects of a juvenile record, see generally J. Coffee, Privacy Versus Parens Patriae: The Role of Police Records in the Sentencing and Surveillance of Juveniles, 57 CORNELL L. REV. 571, 592-94 (1972) [hereinafter cited as Coffee]; Stapleton, A Social Scientist's View of Gault, 1 YALE REV. OF L. & SOC. ACTION 72, 74 (1970). Stapleton feels that the Court's reliance on the assumption that the juvenile court experience is a stigmatizing one "is based more on common sense than hard fact." Coffee would agree that it is premature to consider this point conclusively proven.

11. In defense of the proposition that records need not be made, it is noteworthy that in England no record is made of informal cautioning of juveniles. Somerville, A Study of the Preventive Aspect of Police Work with Juveniles, 1969 CRIM. L. REV. 407, 408. Informal cautioning is made for a non-indictable type of offense. A formal written caution might also be appropriate. The use of informal cautioning is fairly extensive and "without it, the task of enforcing the law might become heavy-handed and inflexible." In England when a decision is made not to prosecute, a formal written or verbal caution is used. Oral cautions are used mostly in connection with first offenders who have admitted responsibility for a minor indictable offense. The caution by letter is used for non-indictable offenses. Records are kept of the formal cautions. Id. at 409-14. There is, however, considerable variation in use and practice among police forces.

It is the absence of method or policy together with conflicting police attitudes which are behind the inconsistent application of the formal caution.

Id. at 479.

12. One article states that it is not the making of the record that is questioned, but its maintenance and accessibility. Ferster and Courtless, supra note 5, at 602; but see O'CONNOR & WATSON, JUVENILE DELINQUENCY AND YOUTH CRIME: THE POLICE ROLE (1964).

13. Although New York practice and law are emphasized the guidelines are intended to be broad enough to be applied generally. For a brief description of Toronto practice see note 18, infra.

A. What Records Are Kept?

Generally, a juvenile police record card contains spaces for various personal identification items, a description of the incident, the date of the occurrence, and the disposition of the incident.[14] The cards are kept separate from adult records until the individual passes the juvenile age limit[15] at which time the cards are transferred to an overage file where they are used by police for reference purposes. In some cases, the cards are destroyed.[16]

Large metropolitan police departments generally maintain a number of different juvenile files, all accessed by various forms of index card systems. These files include complaint reports, field contact reports, investigation reports, family interview reports, custody and arrest reports, and records of referrals to juvenile court or social service agencies.[17] In New York City, for example, these records are retained on one of two forms: the Y.D.-1 card[18]

---

14. In New York, however, "[o]nce the Y.D.-1 cards have been filed with the Youth Records Section of the Central Records Division, they are not further modified." *Special Comm. on the Y.D.-1 System of the Criminal Justice Coordinating Council, Staff Report: Juvenile Record-Keeping in New York City* 61 (K. McMahon & N. Dubler eds. 1971) [hereinafter cited as *CJCC Report*]. As a consequence many Y.D.-1's contain no indication of final disposition. See text accompanying notes 18-22, *infra*, for a description of the Y.D.-1 system.

15. In New York, the Y.D.-1 cards are generally issued to youths between the ages of seven and sixteen. They may however be issued to individuals of any age less than twenty-one. The age seven limit seems to be one of practice rather than law. *CJCC Report, id.* at 21 N.Y. FAM. CT. ACT § 712 restricts a juvenile delinquency charge to those between ages seven and sixteen thus conforming to the Y.D.-1 practice.

16. *E.g.*, where the youth has committed only one offense and has been promised that his record will be destroyed. *Harvard Note, supra* note 6, at 784-85. In at least one jurisdiction, destruction of records normally occurs after a waiting period. *CJCC Report, supra* note 14, at 79 n.49 (Philadelphia (3 years)); *see also* U.S. DEPT. OF HEALTH, EDUCATION AND WELFARE, FAMILY AND JUVENILE COURT ACTS § 48 (1969) (proposed 2 year waiting period); 54 MINN. L. REV. 433, 448 (3 year recommendation); *cf.* CALIF. WELF. & INST. CODE § 781 (1972) (5 years before sealing).

17. Lemert, *Records in the Juvenile Court*, in ON RECORD, *supra* note 1, at 361.

18. An excellent description of the Y.D.-1 system appears in *Coffee, supra* note 10, at 573-74, 578-89. *See also CJCC Report, supra* note 14, at 25 *and* Appendix B, Exhibit VII. The New York City Transit Authority and Housing Authority issue Y.D.-1's as well as the Police Department. The Transit Authority issues cards liberally while the Housing Authority issues cards only sparingly. *CJCC Report, id.*, at 20, 25, 29-32. A brief description of Toronto practice as outlined in Gandy, *The Exercise of Discretion by the Police as a Decision-Making Process in the Disposition of Juvenile Offenders*, 8 OSGOODE HALL L.J. 229 (1970), is relevant to our Y.D.-1 card discussion. The counterpart of the Y.D.-1 in Toronto is the Juvenile Contact Card. The Toronto Police Department's rules and regulations indicate that Juvenile Contact Cards are intended to aid police in crime prevention by deterring juveniles from violating the law and provide information for investigation purposes. The Toronto Youth Bureau has, unlike the New York Youth Aid Division, developed guidelines giving more emphasis to the child protection function of the police in their use of records. "The result was a difference in perception between the Youth Bureau officers and the other officers of what they should seek to achieve through the use of the cards."

and the "incident" report (called the "arrest report" by police).[19] Incident reports are generally made out when the offense alleged would have been a Penal Code violation, and Y.D.-1 forms are issued when the offense was for lesser conduct.[20] All incidents except "aided" cases—those that are referred to a Youth Aid Division where youth and parents are interviewed and counseled[21]—are filed on index cards at the Youth Records Section, as are disposition reports[22] from the courts.

B. Why Are Records Kept?

Police records are considered a necessity for several well-defined police operations.[23] They are kept for: (1) use by police officers, the juvenile court and other interested governmental agencies for informational purposes;[24] (2) planning control and prevention of juvenile crime; (3) internal administrative control through evaluation of policies, procedures and individual officer performances; and (4) in-service training programs with respect to juveniles.[25] Police records also serve to support the *parens patriae* rationale. It is thought that an understanding of the juvenile's total personality and social background are relevant to his rehabilitation.[26] Accordingly excessive record-keeping occurs.[27]

---

19. Interview with Sgt. Robert Paganelli, Supervisor, Youth Records Section, New York City Police Department, in New York City, Feb. 22, 1972.

20. *Id.*

21. These offenses are generally in a middle range between those referred to court and those in which the youth is released outright after apprehension. *Id.*

22. The only dispositions entered on the forms are from the courts and "the courts feel [the Youth Records Section] shouldn't even get dispositions." *Id.* When it is considered that there are seven dispositional alternatives available to the police: (1) release, (2) release accompanied by an official report describing the encounter with the juvenile, (3) an official "reprimand" with release to parent or guardian, (4) referral to other agencies when it is believed that some rehabilitative program should be set up after more investigation, (5) voluntary police supervision used when it is felt that an officer and parent can assist a child cooperatively, (6) referral to the juvenile court without detention, (7) referral to the juvenile court with detention; Piliavin & Briar, *Police Encounters with Juveniles*, 70 AM. J. SOCIOL. 206 (1964); it seems that some record should be made of these dispositions.

23. KENNY & PURSUIT, POLICE WORK WITH JUVENILES, ch. VIII (1965), *cited in* ON RECORD, *supra* note 1, at 361.

24. One of the most frequent uses of records is to check addresses and other personal information. Interview with Sgt. Paganelli, *supra* note 19.

25. *See* note 19, *supra*.

26. ON RECORD, *supra* note 1, at 11. Most states try to implement the policy of a therapeutic system of juvenile justice in their legislation. For example, most jurisdictions use the phrase "taking into custody" instead of "arrest" so that juveniles will be able to respond in good faith that they have not been arrested when they are asked that question on school, military, employment and other forms. To date this protection has proved useless as the drafters of the forms have taken to rephrasing their question: "Have you ever been taken into custody?" and "Have you ever appeared in court?" *Harvard Note*, *supra* note 6, at 800. A bill to eliminate this form of questioning has been proposed in New York. S.I. 135 *cited in Weisberg, infra* note 77. Recently a popu-

II. STATEMENT OF THE PROBLEM

A. *Safeguards Missing*

As will be discussed below, formation of juvenile records is uncontrolled by statute. The making of records involves the threshold problem of police discretion. When do the police decide that certain behavior deserves recordation? Nearly one-half of 1969's Y.D.-1 cards were "issued for behavior which, exercising discretion differently, might not have been administratively acted upon."[28] Arbitrary use of police discretion and lack of periodic review of the files can lead to unintended injustice. For example, the sheer weight of a file can compel referral of the juvenile to court regardless of the nature of the entries.[29] The police, as decision-makers, rely

---

lar radio show in New York City called for legislation prohibiting the question "Have you ever been arrested?" on job applications:

> Sure we have a crime problem. But simply being arrested is no crime
> —and the State Legislature ought to make sure everybody knows it. Radio
> editorial by R. Peter Strauss, President, WMCA, Dial-log, Radio 57, February 21-22, 1972.

As it is commonly accepted that our system of justice brings only a small percentage of those who commit crimes to trial, there is a presumption that a person is arrested only for good cause. It is this presumption that is responsible for the contrived presence of the arrest question on applications despite the fact that it has little relationship to the guilt of the arrested person. *Cf.* Gregory v. Litton Systems, Inc., 316 F. Supp. 401 (C.D. Cal. 1970), where the use of arrest records in personnel recruitment was considered a violation of Title VII of the CIVIL RIGHTS ACT (42 U.S.C. § 2000e (1970)). (For a discussion of *Gregory, see* Note, *Arrests as a Racially Discriminatory Employment Criterion*, 6 HARV. CIV. RIGHTS—CIV. LIB. L. REV. 165 (1970)).

Police claims to *in loco parentis* authority are extremely tenuous. The source of their claim arises from the logical dilemma that children are a part of society and the police must protect both children and society. To protect the children they must protect them from themselves. In the somewhat analogous area of school *in loco parentis* authority there is a statutory base. Furthermore there is an implication that the parent confers responsibility by sending his children to school. *See* FLOWERS & BOLMEIER, THE LAW OF PUPIL CONTROL (1964). The police do not have a statutory grant of power.

27. An indication of the magnitude of record-making for offenses that would not be crimes if committed by adults is shown by recent statistics. In New York 53,681 Y.D.-1 cards were issued for this purpose in 1969. Annual Report 1969, Youth Aid Division, Police Department, City of New York, at p. 1. Nationally, FBI reports indicate that 1,092,981 juveniles were taken into custody (includes "arrests") in 1967. J. HOOVER, CRIME IN THE UNITED STATES 38 n.16 (1968). No conclusion as to the usefulness of records in police decision-making can be drawn but discretion is exercised over a broad range.

> . . . [w]hile those [officers] who had a social service outlook (bringing assistance to juveniles who needed it) were generally more tolerant . . . .
> [one officer] described the function of the cards solely as making a record for future punitive action—they were "nails in the coffin." *CJCC Report, supra* note 14, at 28.

For issuing a Y.D.-1: *Id.* at 27-32; for referring to court: *id.* at 41.

28. *CJCC Report, supra* note 14, at 41.

29. *See Coffee, supra* note 10, at 587 n.53, for a discussion of the so-called

upon the easy standard of the frequency of the involvement of the juvenile in delinquency. Of the four criteria that are normally employed by the police in making decisions regarding disposition of a juvenile case, frequency of involvement is the one which written records most easily distort. The other major criteria are: (1) severity of the delinquent act; (2) community attitudes toward the delinquency problem; and (3) the demeanor of the juvenile in the police-juvenile interactional setting.[30]

The compilation of a record for a non-criminal offense leads to several problems. Police will often make a record of non-criminal activity on the basis of an unsubstantiated phone call.[31] Injustice often results when a record is maintained without the subject's knowledge of its existence or opportunity to review it and is then used by a court or potential employer. Even if a challenge of the record is allowed at a hearing or by the employer, the facts of the incident will often be beyond the individual's present knowledge and therefore he may no longer be able to refute an untrue accusation.

Administrative indifference and human error are commonplace record-keeping problems. Problems arise in coding the offense to simplify handling of the data. The offense is reduced to a legal conclusion, often vague and non-specific. Further, the amount of misclassification is overwhelming. A study by the Mayor's Criminal Justice Coordinating Council produced evidence that levels of error and ambiguity in Y.D.-1 record-keeping are very high. Twenty-five percent of the Y.D.-1 cards issued for disorderly conduct and forty-four percent of those for "harassment, unclassified" were considered

"accordian" file. When the police determine that it is in the juvenile's best interest to be referred to court because of a rapidly increasing file he is referred on the next offense regardless of its nature. In New York, it was determined that there was a one hundred percent correlation between four or more Y.D.-1 cards and court referral. *CJCC Report, supra* note 14, at 30; *see also id.* at 45.

30. *Ferster & Courtless, supra* note 5, at 577, *citing* A. CICOUREL, THE SOCIAL ORGANIZATION OF JUVENILE JUSTICE (1963); H. GOLDMAN, THE DIFFERENTIAL SELECTION OF JUVENILE OFFENDERS FOR COURT APPEARANCE (1963); P. LICHTENBERG, POLICE HANDLING OF JUVENILES (Office of Juvenile Delinquency and Youth Development, U.S. Dept. of Health, Education & Welfare, 1966); PILIAVIN & BRIAR, *supra* note 22; Terry, *The Screening of Juvenile Offenders*, 58 J. CRIM. L. C. & P. S. 173 (1967); C. WERTHMAN & I. PILIAVIN, GANG MEMBERS AND THE POLICE (undated, but internal evidence suggests publication between 1964 and 1966); Wilson, *The Police and the Delinquent in Two Cities*, in CONTROLLING DELINQUENTS 9 (S. Wheeler ed. 1968); *Harvard Note, supra* note 6.

This article is primarily concerned with the frequency criterion. Terry, *id.* at 180, has called that criterion the most important and most frequently employed after seriousness of the offense. This criterion is unevenly applied because there generally is no standard used to determine when the juvenile will be referred to court. A. CICOUREL, *id.* at 223; *Ferster & Courtless, id.* at 578; interview with Sgt. Paganelli, *supra* note 19; *contra, CJCC Report, supra* note 14, at 30 n.25.

31. *See, e.g., CJCC Report, supra* note 14, at 28. In Cuevas v. Leary, *infra* note 89, such an allegation was conceded. In *In re* Gault, *infra* note 47, the accusor did not even appear at the hearing.

by the Criminal Justice Coordinating Council to be improperly classified.[32] Without adequate notice and proper review such mistakes go undetected. As the file ages, inaccuracies become more difficult to refute. The proposals suggested in this article primarily seek to minimize the harm that results from inaccurate record-keeping.

B. *Harms Resulting From Current Practice.*

Unfortunately, under current practice the state has not achieved its aim of securing treatment, and, if necessary, adjudication of appropriate juveniles without simultaneously seriously hindering their chances for social and economic success. A juvenile proceeding attaches a stigma very similar to that produced by criminal proceedings—only the juvenile does not have the Constitutional protections afforded the accused criminal.

A few examples of situations where records have been made and kept but have served no useful purpose should indicate in broad perspective the nature of the problem.

1. By police

A fourteen-year-old boy kissed his thirteen-year-old girl friend in public and was written up by a police officer for child molesting.[33] Similarly shocking was the record of burglary attached to an eleven-year-old who stole a package of bologna after he had run away from home.[34] While these cases are extreme examples, even the common entry of assault or truancy establishes a presumption of guilt that highly prejudices the juvenile's future opportunities.

The injury that a police record may cause has been fully documented.[35]

---

32. *Coffee, supra* note 10, at 583-85; *CJCC Report, supra* note 14, at 8-16, 20, 41. In only sixty percent of the Y.D.-1 forms was the specific statement of misconduct clear. *CJCC Report, id.* at 59.

33. A. Gough, *The Expungement of Adjudication Records of Juvenile and Adult Offenders: A Problem of Status,* 1966 WASH. U.L.Q. 147, 173.

34. *Id.* For use of a fourteen-year-old record, see Adler v. Lang, 21 App. Div. 2d 107, 248 N.Y.S.2d 549 (1st Dept. 1964).

35. Seventy-five percent of employment agencies in New York City and ninety percent of private employers will not accept an applicant with an arrest record. E. SPARER, EMPLOYABILITY AND THE JUVENILE "ARREST" RECORD 5 (1966), *cited in Coffee, supra* note 10, at 591 n.73, Hess & LaPoole, *Abuse of Record of Arrest Not Leading to Conviction,* 13 CRIME & DELIN. 494, 495 (1967), Comment, *Arrest Records as a Racially Discriminating Employment Criterion,* see *supra* note 26, at 174; *see also* REPORT OF THE PRESIDENT'S COMM'N ON LAW ENFORCEMENT AND ADMIN. OF JUSTICE, *The Challenge of Crime in a Free Society* 75 (1967) [hereinafter cited as *The Challenge of Crime in a Free Society*]. The potential impact of being mislabeled a criminal is examined in Schwartz & Sholnick, *Two Studies of Legal Stigma,* 10 SOCIAL PROB. 133-42 (1962) concluding that a criminal charge alone is a bar to employment. The injury that a police record engenders has been fully documented:

In most states police keep a complete file of requests for information about juvenile records.[36] Police departments regularly receive requests from the FBI and other law enforcement agencies, the Armed Forces, social service agencies, and public and private employers.[37] Although most police departments generally comply,[38] disclosure practices seem to vary widely. In some areas[39] employers have been regularly informed of the juvenile's record; while in other areas only other law enforcement agencies have been allowed access.[40]

Henry v. Looney, *infra* note 84, at 851 ("too thoroughly documented to necessitate detailed discussion"); Menard v. Mitchell, 430 F.2d 486, 490 (D.C. Cir. 1970) (mere fact of arrest limits opportunities for schooling, employment, professional licenses); Matter of Smith, *infra* note 81 (opportunities are narrowed); Wheeler v. Goodman, 306 F. Supp. 58 (W.D.N.C. 1969) (same); Morrow v. District of Columbia, 417 F.2d 728, 731 (D.C. Cir. 1969) (summarizing extensive study of hardship of arrest records in securing employment); REPORT OF THE CALIF. ASSEMBLY INTERIM COMM. ON CRIM. PROCEDURE 68 (1961); *cf.* United States v. Kalish, 271 F. Supp. 968, 970 (D.P.R. 1967) (violates right of privacy, unwarranted attack on character; not a juvenile).

> [E]xperience has shown that in too many instances such knowledge [of the juvenile's record] results in rejection or other damaging treatment of the juvenile, increasing the chances of future delinquent acts. *The Challenge of Crime in a Free Society, id.* at 87.

36. *In re* Gault, *infra* note 47, at 24. In New York City police personnel must sign a log when they check a file. Their immediate supervisor is notified that they have checked the records. Records are, however, given in response to telephone requests by officers on a return call basis. If an officer calls and says that there is an investigation and he would like certain information he will be called back at his precinct but there is no verification that there is indeed an investigation. Interview with Sgt. Paganelli, *supra* note 19.

37. *Harvard Note, supra* note 6, at 785-87, *cited in Gault, infra* note 47, at 24; *contra*, Interview with Sgt. Paganelli, *supra* note 19, who when asked if the Youth Records Section would give out records to the Army responded: "Never had a request."

38. *In re* Gault, 387 U.S. 1, 24 (1967).

39. *E.g.*, Wisconsin Rapids, Wisconsin. *Harvard Note, supra* note 6, at 785 n.36 (1966).

40. *E.g.*, Tucson, Arizona, *id.* at n.37. In New York, prior to the stipulations agreed upon in Cuevas v. Leary, *see* note 89 *infra* and accompanying text, access was available to: (1) the New York City Police and Housing and Transit Authority Police Departments to provide background information about prospective employees and to assist in determining what disposition should be made of a Y.D.-1 complaint; (2) other police departments and state and federal law enforcement agencies; (3) the United States Armed Forces although only the Air Force Office of Special Investigation requests Y.D.-1 information and then only for their criminal and personal security investigation; (4) the District Attorney's office, although only Queens County made use of their access; (5) the Youth Council Bureau which uses access for the purpose of attempting to understand the juvenile's difficulties and to limit the time spent in investigation; (6) the Civilian Complaint Review Board which uses the information for investigatory and factual purposes; (7) the Waterfront Commission which uses the material for employment background of applicants less than 21; (8) the New York City Corporation Counsel which generally does not exercise its access power; (9) the Department of Probation which makes recommendations concerning disposition at intake level of Family Court, prepares presentence reports, and supervises persons in

Another serious problem for the youth with a police record is that it renders him the subject of police suspicion in the event of neighborhood illegality.[41] Once an individual is labelled a trouble-maker he is watched more closely and will be picked up sooner and on less substantial grounds than someone without a record.[42] The police act out their self-fulfilling prophesies when they focus their attention on ghetto areas. At least one police source states that the police concentrate on the ghettos because they feel poverty contributes to delinquency.[43] However, since almost all children go through periods of delinquent acting-out,[44] these activities will be recorded. The greater the volume of records, the more the police focus their attention.

One of the most subtle record problems is the use of police records to justify decisions already made. Selective reference to a large record can support a decision and justify it.[45]

---

probation—they use the information for background and for checking records city-wide as they have no central filing system; (10) the Board of Education uses the information to supplement their truancy reports; (11) other groups that have authorized access from the Youth Records Section include the Fire Department, the Port of New York Authority, and "welfare agencies concerned with the welfare of the youth." Dissemination occurs throughout the record-making and keeping process. Formal dissemination also occurs from the Youth Aid Division to welfare agencies. *CJCC Report, supra* note 14, at 43-54. Pursuant to the temporary stipulation in *Cuevas* it was agreed that the Police Department would not divulge contents of Y.D.-1 records to the Office of Probation, the Youth Council Bureau, the Department of Social Services or School Board officials, other than the Bureau of Attendance. *Id.* at 2. A final stipulation has been agreed upon. It is not clear that the temporary stipulation was followed, however. Note 95, *infra.* Reading from a dissemination list the Supervisor of the Youth Records Section stated that probation officers, the District Attorney's office, the Fire Department, the Criminal Courts (incident reports only), and the Vocational Advisory Service, among others which he chose not to reveal, had access to the records but access is denied the FBI, other police departments, state and private agencies, and the Army. Most requests are from the New York City Police Department. Interview with Sgt. Paganelli, *supra* note 19.

41. The problem of police surveillance is discussed in Lemert, *Records in the Juvenile Court*, ON RECORD, *supra* note 1, at 380-81. The "not uncommon" police practice of "rousting" brings to mind Claude Rains' famous line in the motion picture "Casablanca": "Round up the usual suspects." Rousting is used both to obtain leads to solve crimes and to harass persons not welcome in a community. Either use would be difficult to justify on a sociological or psychological basis if the police took *parens patriae* seriously, but in any event the instant use seems to lack constitutional support.

42. *In re* Smith, *infra* note 81, at 622; *see* E. ERIKSON, CHILDHOOD AND SOCIETY 249 (1st ed. 1950).

43. INTRODUCTION AND HISTORY OF POLICE WORK WITH CHILDREN AND YOUTH 10 (mimeo, undated, internal evidence suggests after 1967). "Certainly, poverty contributes to delinquency. There are, without question, social disabilities of underprivileged neighborhoods which variously influence the normal development of young people."

44. D. MATZA, DELINQUENCY AND DRIFT 21-27 (1964); letter from Charles W. Lidz, a psychiatrist, to N.Y. Times, Oct. 2, 1970, at 36 (late city ed.).

45. ON RECORD, *supra* note 1, at 13.

2. By the courts

If the police decide to refer a juvenile, the court will have access to his records. Because the records are (1) kept in unofficial form, (2) frequently the result of unsubstantiated reports and (3) at most, are an accusation of guilt with no rebuttal by the accused; they would seem to be hearsay evidence and their uncorroborated and unverified use in the juvenile court proceeding at the disposition stage would violate due process standards.[46]

In the most prominent juvenile rights case, *In re Gault*,[47] one factor against Gerald Gault in the juvenile court was that the judge remembered a referral made on the youth that he had stolen a baseball glove and lied to the Police Department about it. Because of the lack of material evidence there was "no accusation" and consequently, no hearing; yet the judge used this incident as an input in his decision against the youth.[48]

3. By employers and general private sector evaluators

In most jurisdictions prominent private employers, among others, can ascertain whether a juvenile has a police record.[49] Even if this information

---

46. *Cf.* N.Y. FAM. CT. ACT § 745 (McKinney 1963) (allowing material and relevant evidence at dispositional hearing); OHIO REV. CODE § 2151.358 (1971) (*contra* as to sentencing); *contra*, UNIF. JUVENILE CT. ACT 29(d); NAT'L CONFERENCE OF COMM'RS ON UNIF. STATE LAW, HANDBOOK 267 (1968). Argument has been made that the juvenile record should be admissible to rebut testimony tending to establish the nonexistent good character of the defendant. *Character Evidence and the Juvenile Record*, 20 CLEVE. STATE L. REV. 86 (1971). Juvenile police records consisting of arrests and other non-dispositional entries are recognized as misleading, unreliable and damaging. ABA PROJECT ON MINIMUM STANDARDS FOR CRIMINAL JUSTICE, STANDARDS RELATING TO PROBATION 2.3, at 37 (Tent. draft 1970); *see generally Coffee, supra* note 10, at 609; *see also* note 103 *infra.*

47. 387 U.S. 1 (1967). Gerald Gault, age 15, allegedly made lewd remarks by telephone to a neighbor. He was found delinquent by an Arizona juvenile court and committed for the remainder of his minority unless sooner discharged by due process of law. The due process violations found by the United States Supreme Court in reversing the Arizona Supreme Court's affirmance of the juvenile court decision were legion. He had been taken into custody without notice to his parents, the charges were not specifically delineated, he was not advised of his constitutional rights, a questionable confession was elicited, an adequate record was not kept of his hearing, and he did not have an opportunity to cross-examine and confront the witness testifying to his alleged act. The Supreme Court held only that the Fourteenth Amendment's Due Process Clause applies to juveniles in state court proceedings in an adjudication of delinquency in all cases which "may result in commitment to an institution in which the juvenile's freedom is curtailed."

48. *Id.* at 9.

49. KETCHAM & PAULSEN, *supra* note 2, at 412; REPORT OF THE COMMITTEE TO INVESTIGATE THE EFFECT OF POLICE ARREST RECORDS ON EMPLOYMENT OPPORTUNITIES IN THE DISTRICT OF COLUMBIA (1967) (unpublished report ordered by the D.C. Bd. of Comm'rs) (stating that 3500 arrest records are released each week for use by persons other than law enforcement officials and that influential employers may obtain information in areas with similar police guidelines as D.C. notwithstanding legal or policy prohibitions), *cited and discussed in* 6 HARV. CIV. RTS.-CIV. LIB. L. REV. *supra* note

cannot be obtained directly from the police, private employers word their application forms in such a way as to produce information concerning juvenile arrests.[50] The employers obviously do not solicit this information in the juvenile's interest but to assist them in deciding whether or not to hire the applicant. The danger is that the employers will not consider that an arrest may be indicative of nothing more than that a person was suspected of committing an offense.[51] In the juvenile context the police record might show only that an officer disapproved of the conduct of the youth at one moment in time.

III. THE PRESENT STATE OF THE LAW

At this point it is appropriate to consider what the law is concerning access to and use of juvenile police records.[52] Emphasis is placed on New

26, at 174. For the proposition that records are readily available to third persons despite their purported confidentiality as a ground in holding that a juvenile delinquency proceeding does not become moot after the juvenile's release and loss of jurisdiction of the court, see In re E.J., 2 CCH Pov. L. REP. ¶ 11,773 (1970) (Alaska Sup. Ct.). Matter of Smith, infra note 81, at 620:

> With respect to private employers, there is reason to doubt that the prohibition on access to police arrest records is rigidly enforced. See Matter of Campbell v. Adams, 206 Misc. 673, 674, 133 N.Y.S.2d 876, 877 (Sup. Ct. Queens Co. 1954).

As to the theoretical privacy of police records, see Sears, Roebuck & Co. v. Hoyt, 202 Misc. 43, 48, 107 N.Y.S.2d 765, 771 (Sup. Ct. Jefferson Co. 1951); Hale v. New York City, 251 App. Div. 826, 296 N.Y.S. 443 (2d Dept. 1937), N.Y.C. Charter § 1114. Furthermore, arrest records can be obtained on a waiver of confidentiality from the job applicant. Cf. Matter of Smith, id., Judge Dembitz states that it was so well-known in New York City that private investigators could secure police arrest records, that she took judicial notice of that circumstance.

50. See note 26, supra.

51. Schware v. Board of Bar Examiners, 353 U.S. 232, 241 (1957) (mere fact that a man has been arrrested has little, if any, probative value in showing that he has engaged in any misconduct), Matter of Smith, infra note 81, at 621, People v. Razezica, 206 N.Y. 249, 273, 99 N.E. 557, 565 (1912); President's Comm'n on Law Enforc. and Admin. of Justice, TASK FORCE REPORT: JUVENILE DELINQ. AND YOUTH CRIME 54 (1967); cf. Gregory v. Litton Systems, Inc., 316 F. Supp. 401 (C.D. Cal. 1970), where a private employer was enjoined from soliciting, obtaining or considering arrest records in recruiting personnel. Gregory had been arrested fourteen times. There had been no convictions. He was offered a job but the offer was later withdrawn pursuant to a company policy that no one arrested "on a number of occasions" would be employed. The court found for Gregory, reasoning that the disproportionate number of arrests experienced by Negroes made the use of these records by the private employer a violation of Title VII of the Civil Rights Act (42 U.S.C. § 2000e (1970)). See generally 6 HARV. CIV. RTS.-CIV. LIB. L. REV. 165 supra note 26; see also Hearings on Dissemination of Criminal Records, Before the Interim Comm. on General Research, Senate Comm. on the Judiciary, Oct. 22, 1970; A. Gough, supra note 92; 1966 WASH. U.L.Q. at 155-56, 169-70, supra note 33; also cf. WIGMORE, EVIDENCE § 980a. Arrest, by itself, is not considered competent evidence to prove a person did certain prohibited acts.

52. The law of the fifty states, the District of Columbia and Puerto Rico was

York law. New York's statute is one of the most protective of the juvenile's rights. Further, considerably more case law has developed under New York law than under other equally protective statutes.[53]

A. Federal Law

Twenty-six states have no police records statute.[54] In these states accessibility to the records is unclear. One commentator suggests that the records are presumably public and access to them is therefore open to the public.[55] Generally, any document considered a public record is subject to inspection.[56] Whether or not a record is strictly public to which all persons have access regardless of motive, depends, in the absence of statute, on the nature and purpose of the record, and possibly, on custom and usage.[57]

Twenty-four states have juvenile record statutes.[58] All these statutes require that juvenile records be separated from adult records.[59] In only one

examined. Neither the District of Columbia nor Puerto Rico have a juvenile police records statute so all references below will be to the law of the states. Additionally, English, Welsh and Canadian practice have been surveyed.

53. See note 62, infra.

54. Alabama, Arizona, Arkansas, California, Delaware, Louisiana, Maine, Massachusetts, Michigan, Mississippi, Montana, Nebraska, Nevada, New Hampshire, New Jersey, New Mexico, North Carolina, Ohio, Oregon, Pennsylvania, Rhode Island, Tennessee, Texas, Utah, Washington, and West Virginia.

55. Ferster & Courtless, supra note 5, at 604. Although New York has one of the most restrictive police record statutes the CJCC Report, supra note 14, at 42, indicates that as

. . . the law is presently understood, Y.D.-1 cards are considered "public records" and thus are never destroyed.

56. Cf. U.S.C. § 552 (1970); Kavanaugh v. Henderson, 350 Mo. 968, 973, 169 S.W.2d 389, 392 (1943).

57. People v. Harnett, 131 Misc. 75, 226 N.Y.S. 338, aff'd 224 App. Div. 127, 230 N.Y.S. 28, aff'd 249 N.Y. 606, 164 N.E. 602 (1928).

58. ALASKA STAT. § 47.10.090 (Supp. 1971); COLO. REV. STAT. ANN. § 22-2-2(5) (Supp. 1967); REV. GEN. STAT. CONN. § 17-57a (Supp. 1969); FLA. STAT. ANN. § 39.03(6)(a) (Supp. 1972); GA. CODE ANN. § 24A-3502 (1971); HAWAII REV. STAT. § 571-84 (1968); IDAHO CODE ANN. § 16-1811(7) (Supp. 1971); ILL. STAT. ANN. ch. 37, §§ 702-8(3), 703-2(2) (Smith-Hurd Supp. 1972); ANN. IND. STAT. § 9-3115 (Burns Supp. 1971); IOWA CODE ANN. § 232.56 (1969); KAN. STAT. ANN. § 38-815(g) (Supp. 1970); KY. REV. STAT. ANN. § 208.340 (1971); ANN. CODE MD., art. 26, § 70.23 (Supp. 1971); MINN. STAT. ANN. § 260.161, subd. 3 (1971); ANN. MO. STAT. § 211.321(2) (Vernon Supp. 1972); N.Y. FAM. CT. ACT § 784 (McKinney 1963); N.D. UNIFORM JUV. CT. ACT § 27-20-52 (Supp. 1971); OKLA. STAT. ANN., tit. 10, § 1127(a) (Supp. 1972); S.C. CODE §§ 15-1281.20(6), 15-1291.18(6), 15-1301.18(6), 15-1311.18(6) and 15-1321.31(6) (1962) (Counties at Greenville, Greenwood, Lancaster, Lexington and Orangeburg, respectively); S.D. COMP. LAWS § 26-8-19.5 (Supp. 1971); VT. STAT. ANN., tit. 33, § 663 (Supp. 1972); VA. CODE ANN., § 16.1-163 (1960); WISC. STAT. ANN. § 48.26 (Supp. 1972); WYO. STAT. ANN. § 14-115.42 (Supp. 1971).

59. Indiana does not make this provision but its statute is not directed to protection of police records from public inspection but rather the obligation of the police department to provide probation officers with records upon request. The Indiana statute is only marginally a police records statute as that term is used in this article.

state are these juvenile records a matter of public record.[60] Fifteen states require that a court order be obtained before inspection of the records is allowed.[61] Seven states absolutely restrict inspection of juvenile police records to certain statutorily specified persons who have a direct interest in the child's welfare or to those who have obtained a court order.[62] Another state does not address itself to the access of the records but requires that police records must be made available to probation officers upon their request.[63] Even in those states that have a police records statute, the courts are seldom given a standard for determining whether or not to grant a disclosure order.[64]

In recent years there has been no clear trend in legislation although there is slight movement toward limiting the availability of police records to non-court and non-law enforcement personnel seeking access without a court order.[65] In the last three years, four states that had no juvenile police record statute have passed one.[66] Each is different: Maryland prohibits inspection without a court order; Connecticut prohibits disclosure to non-court or non-law enforcement personnel without court order; North Dakota indicates that the records are not public but allows certain statutory exceptions; and Indiana makes no reference to public access to juvenile police records. At the same time in Wyoming a statute that stated that records were not

---

60. Iowa, *supra* note 58.

61. Alaska, Hawaii, Kansas, Maryland, Missouri and Wisconsin, *supra* note 58, prohibit "inspection" except by court order. Colorado, Connecticut, Illinois, Minnesota, Oklahoma, South Dakota, Virginia, and Wyoming, *supra* note 58, prohibit "public" disclosure or "public" inspection except by court order. Florida, *supra* note 58, provides that the records shall not be public but allows a judge to open the police records of any child over fourteen adjudicated a delinquent to inspection by anyone.

62. Georgia, Idaho, Kentucky, New York, South Carolina and Vermont, *supra* note 58.

63. Indiana, *supra* note 58.

64. At a minimum the statute should specify "in the interests of the child" as is done in VT. STAT. ANN., tit. 33, § 663(a) (Supp. 1972).

65. *Compare* notes 42-47 *supra* with 22 VAND. L. REV. at 604 n.199, 605 n.202; *but see* Speca and White, *Variations and Trends in Proposed Legislation on Juvenile Courts*, 40 U.M.K.C.L. REV. 129 (Winter 1971-72) [hereinafter cited as *Legislative Trends*]. *Legislative Trends* anticipates a trend toward a breakdown in privacy controls dealing with inspection of juvenile records. *Id.* at 160. They reach their conclusion by analyzing proposed legislation nationwide in the recent past. *See, e.g.,* Ill. S.B. 432, 76th G.A. (1969); Conn. B. 1397 (1971); Kan. H.B. 1990 (1968); Kan. S.B. 111 (1971); Mo. H.B. 231 (1969) (tending toward increased access) *and* Ga H.B. 1030 (1970); Ga. S.B. 105 (1971); S.D.H.B. 554, 43d Sess. (1968); Conn. B. 6752 (1971) (increasing judge's discretion in allowing access); *but see* Wis. A.B. 856 (1969) (prohibiting disclosure to anyone). While they are correct that the proposed bills might indeed indicate a trend they do not consider whether the bills have been enacted or evaluate what support they received. Without some indication of legislative response to the bills their analysis of a trend is highly suspect and the value of the article considerably diminished. In so much as the bills do represent a manifestation of current thought and a necessary prelude to the reform of the law they are offered here to indicate proposals that have already been made.

66. Connecticut, Indiana, Maryland, and North Dakota, *supra* note 58.

public was repealed and in its place a statute prohibiting public disclosure except by court order was added.

Further, as will be shown by the dearth of litigation as compared to the volume of record-keeping, these statutes provide little protection in their executory[67] form. The reported cases, while generally favorable to the juvenile do not delineate the magnitude of the problem. Often the juvenile is unaware that he has a record and even if he is aware that he has such a record he does not know or care that it can be corrected.[68] Even if it can be expunged he may not know how to proceed to have it expunged or does not have the time or money to expunge it.[69]

B. *New York State Law*

New York's Family Court Act § 784, entitled "Use of Police Records," reads as follows:

> All police records relating to the arrest and disposition of any person under this article shall be kept in files separate and apart from the arrests of adults and shall be withheld from public inspection, but such records shall be open to inspection upon good cause shown by the parent, guardian, next friend or attorney of that person upon the written order of a judge of the family court in the county in which the order was made or, if the person is subsequently convicted of a crime, of a judge of the court in which he was convicted.[70]

---

67. The author uses "executory" to apply to that situation where the protection of the statute operates effectively only upon request. The burden is on the youth to show good cause or to bring an action for expungement. A self-executory statute would be one whose protections operated without a special application by the youth.

68. Legislators have not frequently considered this problem. Cal. S.B. 1530 (1971) provided that minors be given notice that their records could be sealed. The more common proposed solution has been to permit a court to act *sua sponte. See, e.g.*, Ind. P. J. P. C. § 31(a) (1970); Ariz. H.B. 1, 29th Leg. (1970); Iowa H. File 619 (1971); *see also* Hawaii H.B. 515, 6th Leg. (1971) (allowing governor or attorney general to demand any or all juvenile records collected and sealed).

69. Little encouragement or assistance would seem to be available to persons who telephone for accurate information from the New York City Family Court. On October 16, 1972 the author called the Clerk's Office and asked: "How frequently are juvenile records expunged in circumstances not resulting in a published decision?" The individual who answered the telephone responded: "I don't think they are expunged." Later questioning of a high-level administrator who prefers to remain anonymous produced the answer: "It doesn't happen very often." While the Family Court publishes monthly statistics concerning their activities, the frequency of expungement without reported opinion is not available. It is a safe assumption that it is infrequent.

70. (McKinney 1963). Unfortunately, the protections of this statute are often ignored. Kentucky and Wisconsin expressly allow schools, hospitals, churches, social and welfare agencies, juvenile courts and law enforcement agencies access to police records and other states, specifically New York, allow "many private employers, state and city employment agencies, housing authorities and others" to inspect these records despite the statutory protections described. *Ferster & Courtless, supra* note 5 at 605.

As the decisions described below indicate this law has been enforced when a suit is brought.[71] The problem is that few cases are brought.[72] In so far as attempts have been made to use § 784 to gain expungement orders, these attempts have been largely successful although only recently was it settled that New York's Family Court had enough control over police records to order expungement.[73] The statute addresses itself to access but its use as an expungement vehicle and the legal response to problems of record creation and expungement are of primary concern in this article.

In New York the remedies available to the juvenile seeking to protect himself from improper formation and use of his police records are severely limited. The range of remedies stretches from normal enforcement of the present statutory formulation, presumably by injunction, to destruction or expungement of the record. In theory expungement is destruction.[74] In practice expungement is the elimination of the offending entry; sometimes by merely placing a piece of tape over it.[75] Destruction is the elimination of the entire record. Whatever dissemination has occurred prior to the actual expungement or destruction is difficult to correct. Traces of the record can return to haunt the youth.[76]

In *Weisberg v. Police Department of Village of Lynbrook*,[77] the juvenile sought the destruction of a Lynbrook Police Department arrest card alleging that the record would harm him professionally. The arrest occurred when the plaintiff, a diabetic, tried to take something sweet to eat from a grocery store while he was in a diabetic seizure. The charge was later withdrawn. The court, per Judge Bernard Meyer, held that state courts lack the inherent power to order a police record sealed or otherwise withheld from public knowledge. He distinguished between police records and the court's own records, which could be sealed. In dicta, Judge Meyer suggested that a legislative remedy was needed because the *destruction* of "public" records is a matter to be regulated by statute.

---

71. *E.g.*, Adler v. Lang, 21 App. Div. 2d 107, 248 N.Y.S.2d 549 (1964).

72. Those cases discussed *infra* represent the bulk of the reported cases in New York.

73. *See* discussion accompanying notes 81-83 *infra*.

74. BLACK'S LAW DICTIONARY 693 (Rev. 4th ed. 1968). The words "erasure", "annulment", and "sealing" are often used interchangeably to mean expungement and will be so used in this article. *Legislative Trends* defines expungement as placing the records under the utmost confidentiality and stringently controlling access to them. They distinguish it from destruction in that records pass out of existence altogether when destroyed. *Legislative Trends, supra* note 65, at 162.

75. For an article generally critical of expungement *see* Kogan & Loughery, *Sealing and Expungement of Criminal Records—the Big Lie*, 61 J. CRIM. L.C. & P.S. 378 (1970).

76. *Id.*; Donner, *The Theory and Practice of American Political Surveillance*, monograph reprinted from THE NEW YORK REVIEW OF BOOKS 27 (April 22, 1971). Only a few bills consider what happens to the records after they are sealed. *See, Legislative Trends, supra* note 65, at 167-68.

77. 46 Misc. 2d 846, 260 N.Y.S.2d 554 (Sup. Ct. Nassau Co. 1965).

In *Statman v. Kelly*,[78] another jurisdictional decision, the petitioners were college students who had been arrested by New York City police at the 1964 World's Fair while engaged in a peaceful picket of an exhibit. When arrested they slumped to the floor and refused to submit voluntarily. Consequently, they were charged with trespassing on private property, disorderly conduct and resisting arrest. The charges were dropped two months later. Immediately thereafter, a motion to expunge the entries of arrests and charges was made and denied. The petitioners argued that the arrests were illegal and unless the court and police arrest records were expunged the permanency of the records would cause petitioners to suffer unjustly. The court granted the defendant's motion to dismiss, holding that petitioners were not entitled to expungement in the instant proceeding. Citing New York Family Court Act § 784 as evidence that orderly government requires police records to be maintained, the court viewed the legislative history of expungement bills in New York and found no legislative intent to expunge records.[79] As in *Weisberg*, the court's holding was grounded on a purported lack of subject matter jurisdiction.[80]

In 1970 Judge Nanette Dembitz found jurisdiction to provide for the expungement of police *arrest* records in *In re Smith*.[81] In *Smith* a fourteen-

---

78. 47 Misc. 2d 294, 262 N.Y.S.2d 799 (Sup. Ct. N.Y. Co. 1965).

79. 47 Misc. 2d at 297, 262 N.Y.S.2d at 802.

80. Although the state courts were not yet ready to formulate remedies without statutory guidance they were willing to correct their own misuse of arrest records when directly presented with the question. People v. Rehm, 24 App. Div. 2d 517, 261 N.Y.S.2d 808 (2d Dept. 1965), *remanded* 52 Misc. 2d 853, 276 N.Y.S.2d 751 (Kings Co. 1966) (police record had been admitted as evidence on cross-examination; court found that such use violated a promise of confidentiality made to defendant in preparing the records and was contrary to the prohibitions of N.Y. FAM. CT. ACT § 784). *Cf.* Adler v. Lang, where the court had overturned a decision by the New York Civil Service Commission to turn down an engineer's job application because of a twelve-year-old juvenile arrest record. 21 App. Div. 2d 107, 248 N.Y.S.2d 549 (1st Dept. 1964). *Adler* was an easy case because the Commission was not entitled to access to the records much less to make decisions based upon them. For another attempt by the New York Civil Service Commission to disqualify applicants on the basis of arrest records *see* Cuccio v. Dept. of Personnel—Civil Service Commission, 40 Misc. 2d 345, 243 N.Y.S.2d 220 (Sup. Ct. 1963); *cf.* Anonymous v. New York City Transit Authority, 4 App. Div. 2d 953, 167 N.Y.S.2d 715 (2d Dept. 1957), *aff'd* 7 N.Y.S.2d 659, 163 N.E.2d 144, 194 N.Y.S.2d 39 (1959).

81. 63 Misc. 2d 198, 310 N.Y.S.2d 617 (Fam. Ct. N.Y. Co. 1970) (Dembitz, J.). Three years earlier the Supreme Court of New York County had applied the protection of § 784 to a police report (as opposed to an arrest record or an incident report). Public Service Mut. Ins. Co. v. Nassau Co. Fire Marshall, 55 Misc. 2d 951, 287 N.Y.S.2d 104 (Sup. Ct. N.Y. Co. 1967) (*per curiam*). Read with *In re* Smith, *Public Service* lends support to a claim of state court jurisdiction to expunge all police records.

Public Service was decided on a motion for an order to compel the Fire Marshall of Nassau County to give the insurance company who paid the damages for a fire set by the youths, the names and last known addresses of the youths. The Fire Marshall had cited § 784 and refused to give the insurance company the information which had appeared in a report from the Nassau County Police Department to the Fire Commissioner. The court denied the motion because the insurance company did not come within the statutory exceptions to § 784.

year-old and a fifteen-year-old were taken into custody during a demonstration. The charge would have been unlawful assembly if committed by an adult. Charges were dropped when the state did not have enough evidence to make out a *prima facie* case. The instant decision was on a motion for an order directing expungement of the court and police arrest records. Judge Dembitz held that the juveniles were entitled to have their names expunged from court and police records even though they did not prove present injury. She pointed out the possibility of employer access to records, the handicap such access would impose upon the juveniles, and the lack of a justification for keeping the records. The Family Court found that it had the power to order expungement of police arrest records as "implicit in the authority granted it in § 784 of the Family Court Act."[82] The power to order expungement was to be considered ancillary to the court's broad powers in dealing with youth. Considering the wide discretion and powers of the Family Court, Judge Dembitz found concurrent authority with courts of general equitable jurisdiction to direct a change in police records.[83]

The *Smith* decision was followed in *Henry v. Looney*.[84] Petitioner in *Henry*, aged fifteen, and two companions were arrested and charged with attempted burglary. An officer suspected misconduct when he saw the boys looking through the window of a friend's house. The charge was later withdrawn and the court record sealed. The action in *Henry* was brought to have the police records destroyed after the police refused to do so. The question Judge Sol Wachtler posed was:

> [W]hether a court may relieve a party of the practical stigma of a criminal arrest record. Theoretically the problem should not exist, for an arrest in and of itself, lawful or otherwise, is legally and logically probative of nothing regarding the character and background of the person arrested. As a practical matter, however, an arrest record may stigmatize and impede its victim throughout his lifetime.[85]

While *Henry* is noteworthy in that it found jurisdiction to expunge police arrest records, it is an open question whether the court in *Henry* would expunge in a case where there is *any* circumstantial evidence prejudicial to the petitioner. The court concluded that the records had no value

82. Matter of Public Service Ins. Co., 63 Misc. 2d at 204 *citing*, People v. Rhem, *supra* note 80; 310 N.Y.S.2d at 624, *compare* Murphy v. City of New York, 273 App. Div. 492, 78 N.Y.S.2d 191 (1st Dept. 1948). And *see* Matter of Chin, 41 Misc. 2d 641, 650, 246 N.Y.S.2d 306, 316 (Sup. Ct. Westchester Co. 1963) as to the Family Court's implied powers.

83. While the specific records in this case were arrest or incident reports, Judge Dembitz's view of the broad powers of the Family Court would seem to extend to the power to expunge Y.D.-1 forms.

84. 65 Misc. 2d 759, 317 N.Y.S.2d 848 (Sup. Ct. Nassau Co. 1971) *(Mem.)* (Wachtler, J.).

85. 65 Misc. 2d at 760, 317 N.Y.S.2d at 849.

to society and could be expunged under the authority of *Smith*. The court opposed self-executing expungement preferring to evaluate each case as it arises because "[c]onvictions frequently fail for reasons other than a defendant's innocence,"[86] and there is a public need to keep records.[87]

Whether or not an arrest record will be expunged depends upon the facts and circumstances of the particular case. It is unclear whether the court can expunge the record of non-criminal conduct; that is, Y.D.-1 cards and incident reports.[88] Section 784 provides protections to those records that relate "to the arrest and disposition" of the juvenile. Implied expungement power under § 784 might not extend to Y.D.-1 cards (or incident reports) unless they relate "to the arrest and disposition" of the juvenile. An argument can be made that there is an obvious relationship between Y.D.-1 cards (or incident reports) and arrest and disposition. If enough reports are filed their cumulative effect could lead to the juvenile's eventual arrest and, if used by the court or probation officer or in making out a pre-sentence report, they could affect the disposition of the case.

Because of the greater ease in establishing a class action and for forum shopping reasons, the lawsuit of *Cuevas v. Leary*[89] challenging the constitutionality of the New York City Police Youth Division record-keeping procedures was brought in *federal* court.[90] On different facts expungement orders had previously been made in at least two federal district court cases.[91]

Cuevas alleged that the Police Department was in violation of the Fifth and Fourteenth Amendments[92] in that Y.D.-1 cards were issued solely upon suspicion of misconduct. The *Cuevas* complaint further charged that when disseminated, Y.D.-1 cards can create an invasion of privacy. Furthermore, the plaintiffs alleged that the files were preserved for a period of time in excess of any compelling state interest.[93] Indeed, this author's investigations suggest that the records were kept indefinitely.

As a result of the *Cuevas* complaint the Police Department agreed, as

---

86. *Id.* at 762, 317 N.Y.S.2d at 852.

87. *Id.* However, these records can be kept without identification of the juvenile.

88. Few state legislatures have considered this problem. *Cf. Legislative Trends supra* note 65, at 163; *but see* Conn. H.B. 8510 (1969), Conn. B. 6370 (1971), Iowa S. File 1107 (1970), N.Y.A.B. 832 (1971).

89. 70 Civ. 2017 (S.D.N.Y., filed May 13, 1970).

90. Letter from John C. Coffee, co-counsel in Cuevas v. Leary and author of *Privacy Versus* Parens Patriae, *supra* note 10 to Edward R. Spalty, February 8, 1973. A federal forum was also desirable because of uncertainty whether ancillary jurisdiction over Y.D.-1 cards existed in state courts under § 784. Furthermore, § 784 does not apply to the use of misleading records in sentencing, which was the principal target of *Cuevas. Id.*

91. Gomez v. Wilson, 323 F. Supp. 87 (D.D.C. 1971) (where police officer intruded on plaintiff's Fourth Amendment rights); Wheeler v. Goodman, 306 F. Supp. 58 (W.D.N.C. 1969) *vacated and remanded on other grounds*, 401 U.S. 987 (1971) (extreme police misconduct); Morrow v. District of Columbia, *supra* note 35.

92. Jurisdiction was also based on the First, Fourth, Sixth and Ninth Amendments.

93. Complaint in Cuevas v. Leary, *supra* note 89, at 1-2.

of August 1, 1970, not to allow access to Y.D.-1 cards to anyone but school attendance officials until at least June 1, 1971.[94] The temporary stipulation of the court prohibited the dissemination of juvenile records to other government agencies, including the Probation Department and the New York City courts, which had previously used such records in the formulation of pre-sentence and probationary reports.[95] The parties agreed to evaluate the alternatives to be proposed by the Mayor's Criminal Justice Coordinating Council (CJCC) after the CJCC had made an extensive study of police record-keeping in New York City.[96] Acting, in part, on the study's recommendation the parties agreed to a permanent stipulation requiring the destruction of all Y.D.-1 reports when the juvenile reaches age 17. The stipulation also limits access to the records, while they exist, to police investigating crimes, welfare officials attempting to aid or rehabilitate the juvenile, and scholars studying juvenile problems.[97] Destruction of the records has begun. Although it is too soon to evaluate the impact of the stipulations this development may well be important as a model for other jurisdictions and as "an indicator that representatives of poverty interests can accept a practice with unpleasant aspects" if they believe that the police are acting in good faith.[98]

Reported case law seems to indicate that the problems of who shall have access to juvenile police records and who shall be entitled to expungement are infrequently litigated.[99] When a suit is brought, New York's Family Court Act § 784 has been read in the juvenile's favor. However, in none of these cases was there a critical public need for the records. When it is apparent that a juvenile will be injured by later reference to his arrest record, expungement may be ordered but the burden rests with the juvenile to bring and prove his case. Considering the consequences of inaccurate and unnecessary record-keeping, the low volume of case law speaks loudly. The poor, upon whom much of the police's attention is focused and whose ac-

---

94. N.Y. Times, Aug. 9, 1970, at 34, col. 1 (late city ed.). A similar suit brought in New Jersey alleging that the maintenance of such records denied the juvenile equal protection and due process failed. Dugan v. Police Department, City of Camden, 112 N.J. Super. 482, 271 A.2d 727 (1970).

95. *Coffee, supra* note 10, at 572 n.4. The *CJCC Report, supra* note 14, at 40 expresses the opinion that the practice appears to have ended. As recently as Feb. 22, 1972, however the Police Records Section was still informed that they were authorized to release records to the probation department. Interview with Sgt. Paganelli, *supra* note 19. The author reported this inconsistency to Deputy Commissioner Ward's office, Police Department, City of New York, on Mar. 9, 1972.

96. N.Y. Times, *supra* note 94. For the results of the CJCC's work, *see CJCC Report, supra* note 14.

97. Stipulation in Cuevas v. Leary, 70 Civ. 2017 (signed by Brieant, J. on June 28, 1972); 6 CLEARINGHOUSE REV. 283 (Aug.-Sep. 1972).

98. Interview with Oscar Chase, Professor, Brooklyn Law School, Co-counsel, Cuevas v. Leary, in New York City, Oct. 20, 1972.

99. *See* note 69, *supra.*

tivities contribute to the bulk of these records,[100] do not have the time or money to go to court to clear their records. It is doubtful that they are aware that they can. Often, because of lack of notice, they do not even know that they have a record. The *Cuevas* stipulation is a step in the right direction; however, a comprehensive statutory response is clearly more desirable.

IV. Proposals

A. *Statutory*

1. Expungement and destruction

It is proposed that juveniles will be adequately protected under a statute that automatically expunges juvenile police records. Without an automatic, self-executory statute, only those with sufficient interest, knowledge or money are fully assured of statutory protection. The following proposal is made in recognition of the need for the existence of certain types of juvenile police records where such records indicate a history of criminal or unstable psychological behavior. All records kept on conduct that would not be criminal if committed by an adult should be destroyed or expunged when the subject approaches the end of his teens.[101] For our purposes, age sixteen or some time thereabout is appropriate. Primary considerations in setting the expungement age are the state's definition of a juvenile, the incidence of recorded juvenile behavior at the subject age, and the need to expunge the record before harm is done to the youth's educational and employment opportunities. Records kept on criminal-type behavior should be reviewed when the individual reaches age sixteen and those without a felony conviction or clear evidence of a psychological problem should be destroyed or expunged. Those records with such blemishes should be retained for a waiting period (for our purposes, two years) and then destroyed or expunged if no judicial action is pending against the individual at that time. If the individual is accused of further criminal activity during the waiting period (between ages sixteen and eighteen) that conduct will be part of his adult record and protected, to some extent, by due process guarantees —the juvenile record can, however, be used at his trial for sentencing pur-

---

100. INTRODUCTION AND HISTORY OF POLICE WORK WITH CHILDREN AND YOUTH, *supra* note 43, at 10.

101. The *CJCC Report, supra* note 14, at 71, recommends that access to Y.D.-1 cards should be severely curtailed and all Y.D.-1 cards should be discarded when the juvenile reaches age 16.

While the use of relatively inaccurate information may be permissible in a system that offers only assistance, it is intolerable in one that imposes serious sanctions, or desires important benefits. *Id.* at 72.

The final stipulation in *Cuevas* is in accord. *See* text accompanying note 97, *supra*.

poses. If he is accused of no criminal offense during the waiting period he will have no record at the end of the period (age eighteen).[102]

2. Access and dissemination

Under current law police records are generally either a matter of public record or require that a court order be obtained by those people who have an interest in the subject if they want access to his records. The latter formulation is preferable. Any use of the records other than by social agencies acting in the juvenile's interest, or by the police for one of several clearly defined police purposes should raise a presumption of improper use that can be rebutted only by a very strong showing, such as, proof that a court order granting access was issued.[103] Illegal use of police records should carry criminal penalties and the police department responsible for the access or dissemination should be liable to injunction and perhaps damages.

A court order should only be granted on a good cause basis for the benefit of the youth. In practical effect the burden is currently on the youth to show that the records have been illegally used. Instead the burden should be on those who use the records to prove that they had judicially sanctioned use or custody of the records. Cases will not clog the courts because all that is necessary here is a simple showing that the requisite court order

102. See note 88, *supra* for legislative consideration of expungement in recent years. Usually a certain age must be attained before an expungement petition is entertained. Twenty-one is most common. *Legislative Trends, supra* note 65, at 166. *E.g.,* Ariz. H.B. 1, 29th Leg. (1970); Nev. S.B. 32 (1971); *but see* Mo. H. B. 227, 75th G.A. (1969) (17 years old); Cal. A.B. 468 (1971) (18 years old); *cf. Cuevas* stipulation (destruction at 17 years old). State legislators have also considered it appropriate for there to be a waiting period after the termination of the juvenile court's jurisdiction before an expungement order will be entertained. Two years: Ga. S.B. 105 (1971); Ill. H.B. 810, 77th G.A. (1971); N.M.H.B. 125, 1st Sess. (1969); Tex. 2-1721; Cal. A.B. 468 (1971); *accord* U.J.C.A. § 57(a)(1); *but see* Nev. S.B. 32 (1971); Cal. A.B. 1530 (1971) (5 years); Cal. A.B. 914 (1971), Hawaii H.B. 515, 6th Leg. (1971), COLO. NEW CHILDREN'S CODE as amended through 1971 (termination of court's jurisdiction); Wyo. S.B. 77, 41st Sess. (1971) (1 year). Usually the juvenile must not have been involved in questionable conduct from the date the subject record was created to the date of the expungement petition. *E.g.,* N.M.H.B. 125, 1st Sess. (1969); COLO. NEW CHILDREN'S CODE as amended through 1971; *accord* U.J.C.A. § 57(a)(2); *but see* Wis. A.B. 831 (1969) (3 years).

103. The statement is often made that the record of past convictions or unfavorable dispositions should be available to the judge for sentencing purposes. *E.g.,* J. MAQUIRE, J. WEINSTEIN, J. CHADBOURN & J. MANSFIELD, CASES AND MATERIALS ON EVIDENCE 29 n.9 (1965). Even in sentencing however the use of the juvenile police record is questionable as hearsay and is subject to abuse. ABA PROJECT ON MINIMUM STANDARDS FOR CRIMINAL JUSTICE, STANDARDS RELATING TO PROBATION, 2.3 at 37 (Tent. draft 1970), *supra* note 46. *E.g.,* Townsend v. Burke, 334 U.S. 736 (1948) (the sentencing judge read the arrest reports into the record stating they represented convictions); United States v. Weston, 448 F.2d 626, 631-33 (9th Cir. 1971). While traditional theory dictates that the judge is in a position to aid the child and with more information can better perform his task, the records have proven themselves to be so unreliable or speculative that they should not be available for any determination in which the juvenile could suffer loss of significant benefits. *See* OFFICE OF PROBATION FOR THE COURTS OF NEW YORK CITY DIRECTIVE, CF 30-14 (Revised), Draft II, June 14, 1972.

was obtained. The records would still be available for statistical purposes but only as long as the subjects could not be personally identified.

B. *Administrative*

In the absence of statutory change, juveniles can still receive some protection under the current statutes if these statutes are properly administered. It is the responsibility of the police, in their role as the creator and maintainer of the juvenile records, to provide adequate safeguards. At a minimum these safeguards should include periodic review of the records for accuracy[104] and adequate notice to the juvenile concerned that a record has been created.[105]

The records should *always* indicate the disposition of the case and allow the subject an opportunity to explain the circumstances that led to the entry.[106] Of course, such opportunity is dependent upon notice having been given to the juvenile[107] and his parents at the time of or soon after the making of the record. A periodic review would probably increase expenditures by the police department. Aside from their duty to protect the youth, the police department will probably receive dividends from this review in the form of increased public confidence in police record-keeping.[108] Furthermore, the police will benefit directly as their own information will be more accurate and they will thus be better able to perform their duties.

The integrity of the record-keeping system can be further buttressed by instituting the following procedures: (1) prohibit the juvenile or his parents from consenting to access to his record[109] by individuals other than the juvenile or his representative; (2) designate a professional to be responsible for record maintenance and access on a full-time basis and educate the staff at the record center about maintenance and access policies, especially with regard to the juvenile and their parents' privacy rights;[110] (3) maintain strict physical security at the record center;[111] (4) revise police

---

104. *Cf.* GUIDELINES FOR THE COLLECTION, MAINTENANCE & DISSEMINATION OF PUPIL RECORDS: REPORT OF A CONFERENCE ON THE ETHICAL & LEGAL ASPECTS OF SCHOOL RECORD KEEPING 23 (Russell Sage 1970) [hereinafter cited as *Guidelines*]. *See also Minutes of Due Process Committee, ACLU,* Oct. 18, 1960, *cited at* Policy #202, *Arrest Records, The Policy Guide of the American Civil Liberties Union* (rev. Oct., 1967) [hereinafter cited as *Minutes of Due Process Committee*].

105. In New York no such review presently exists, interview with Sgt. Paganelli, *supra* note 19, and at the time of *Cuevas* no such notice was issued.

106. *Cf. Minutes of Due Process Committee* on Mar. 10, 1965, *supra* note 104.

107. *CJCC Report, supra* note 14, at 69.

108. *Cf. Guidelines, supra* note 104, at 31.

109. *CJCC Report, supra* note 14, at 79.

110. *Cf. Guidelines, supra* note 104, at 23; *Minutes of Due Process Committee* on Mar. 10, 1965, *supra* note 104.

111. *Id.*

forms, where appropriate, to provide for efficient expunction and offense recordation.[112]

Accessibility should be more clearly defined. While employers have some right to be informed concerning the past conduct of an applicant, the extent of disclosure should be quite limited. A heavy burden of proof must be overcome before any disclosure is made to the employer and even then disclosure should be limited to information pertinent to the nature of the job sought.[113] The courts should have access for sentencing; as should the social agencies to which the youth is referred.[114] Access should be limited within the police department to those who work with the administration of juvenile records[115] and then only upon a showing of valid police purpose. Thus a balance must be maintained between the employer's and the juvenile's interests and the police function of investigation and prevention in the area of crime detection.[116] The juvenile's interest should predominate.

The youth should have access to his own record,[117] except those parts of the youth's record that are inappropriate for him to see such as letters of reference or psychologist's reports. No state with a police records statute makes such a provision. In several states the child is provided access through his lawyer or representative, be he parent or the fictive next friend. Personal access by the juvenile provides the child the opportunity to review his file to assure himself that the records are accurate. As the police generally do not review their files periodically, the child's or his representative's self-interest would, in part, perform this function. Because of the special relationship between an individual and his file, inspection should be allowed for any purpose, even mere curiosity.

C. Conclusion

Every state should enact a comprehensive juvenile police records stat-

---

112. *E.g.*, the space on the Y.D.-1 form for dispositions is too small. *CJCC Report*, *supra* note 14, at 59 *and* Appendix VII. A small space discourages the detailed description of facts and circumstances often necessary for a meaningful record. Additionally, a new form—perforated between the identifying material and the offense so that the identifying data can be easily torn off and discarded after a disposition is made favorable to the youth—would be advisable as it would aid expungement.

113. *Cf. Minutes of the Due Process Committee* on Sep. 23, 1963, *supra* note 104.

114. *CJCC Report, supra* note 14, at 74. For conditions necessary for release of this information see *id*.

115. *Id*. at 72.

116. *Cf. Minutes of the Due Process Committee* on Sep. 23, 1963, *supra* note 104.

117. *Cf.* N.Y. Times, Oct. 20, 1972, at 42, col. 1 (city ed.) (recommending laws be devised to give any individual the right of access to computerized databank files, and the right to challenge effectively any recorded information felt to be erroneous, irrelevant or of a particularly confidential nature) *citing* WESTIN & BAKER, DATABANKS IN A FREE SOCIETY (1972); N.Y. Times, Feb. 29, 1972, at 1, col. 6 (city ed.) (parents may see school records); *Minutes of the Due Process Committee* on Mar. 10, 1965, *supra* note 104.

ute which provides for automatic expungement and requires that a court order be obtained by any prospective user of the records unless they meet the exceptions enumerated above. Such a statute should be strictly enforced. Moreover, the administrative integrity of the record-keeping system should be enhanced by implementing the safeguards discussed in this article. Implementation of the statutory and administrative proposals will require substantial modification of the practice in most jurisdictions. Whatever the inconvenience or expense, it is necessary and justifiable as a service to the community.

10 | APPELLATE REVIE FOR JUVENILES: A "Right" to a Transcript

JONATHAN I. MARK*

The Supreme Court has never held that states must afford citizens the right of appellate review as an element of due process.[1] Yet, every state has undertaken to provide procedures for appellate review for adults and juveniles. Whereas every state makes provision to stenographically or electronically record adult trials to create a transcript as a basis for appellate review, fourteen states[2] and one territory that have specific juvenile appeals statutes maintain a statutory silence as to whether or not transcripts of the juvenile hearing shall or may be made by a court reporter.[3] Query: are juveniles

---

*Staff member, COLUMBIA HUMAN RIGHTS LAW REVIEW.

1. Griffin v. Illinois, 351 U.S. 12, 21 (1956) (Frankfurter, J., concurring).

2. Those states are: Colorado, Connecticut, Delaware, Florida, Maine, Massachusetts, Mississippi, Montana, New Jersey, New York, Rhode Island, Virginia, Washington and West Virginia. The territory is the Virgin Islands.

3. It is true that despite statutory silence some juvenile courts (in Manhattan and Brooklyn, for example) do have a stenographer present at adjudicative hearings. This is fine as long as the practice continues presumably at the discretion of the judge. However without specific statutory provision it would seem that a lawyer is subject to the particular traditions of the jurisdiction in which he practices. If a lawyer decides to appeal and no transcript has been made there is no statutory leverage he can exert in a situation that is detrimental to his client. In re Simpson, 199 So. 2d 833 (Miss. 1967), is on point. In that case, the juvenile was represented by counsel in the initial hearing. The lawyer appealed the decision of the juvenile court. Part of his claim was that no transcript had been made and his client did not have an adequate basis for review. In denying his appeal the Mississippi Supreme Court acknowledged the statutory silence of the Mississippi Code on transcripts, but put the burden on counsel to request a transcript in the face of the statute's silence.

The Montana Supreme Court provides an example opposite to the decision in Mississippi. In In re Gonzalez, 139 Mont. 592, 366 P.2d 718 (1961), the Montana Supreme Court reversed and remanded a juvenile commitment order because no stenographic record of the juvenile court hearing was made. The Montana statute provided that appeals from juvenile courts were to be taken in accordance with the state rules of civil procedure. The court found that informal hearings were allowable only in preliminary hearings. However, when a hearing such as the one in this case, was on a formal petition leading to possible commitment, the "procedures for civil trials must be adhered to . . ." and a stenographic record must be made. Present Montana law still does not require that stenographic records of hearings be made.

It is hard to believe that such omissions in state statutes can benefit the juvenile or the system that is supposed to protect him.

getting a fair opportunity to appeal under this vagary in the statutory framework?

The Equal Protection Clause has been used in litigation to attack various aspects of the juvenile statutory system,[4] including some aspects of appellate review.[5] The Supreme Court found in *Griffin v. Illinois*[6] that though appellate review is not required by due process, once a state provides appeals for some, a right to appeal must be extended to all citizens similarly situated. This paper will consider the right to transcripts vis-à-vis due process, and will examine the equal protection ramifications of the statutory silence in fourteen states and the Virgin Islands regarding transcripts of juvenile hearings.

> The informality and flexibility of the juvenile adjudication and the subsequent treatment make the right of appeal perhaps more, and certainly not less, vital to safeguard those subject to the juvenile process from the possible degeneration warned against in *Gault*.[7]

The quotation above is from an opinion in the Third Circuit that discusses the right of the Virgin Islands District Court to selectively review juvenile court cases. The District Court was empowered by statute to deny appeals from juvenile courts while extending an absolute right of appeal in all other civil suits. The Third Circuit Court of Appeals held that though the state has no obligation to offer review to some, it must afford similar opportunity to all in similar situations. On this ground the court held Title 4 section 33 of the Virgin Islands Code an unconstitutional violation of the Equal Protection Clause.[8] A state's right to classify persons by age and impose longer commitments for youths under the Federal Youth Corrections Act than would be allowed for adults tried for similar offenses was upheld as being sufficiently justified by rational state interests against equal protection attacks in *Guidry v. United States*.[9] The interest relied on was *parens patriae*. That much discussed doctrine essentially holds that youth need the state's protection from the often brutalizing effect of the criminal laws.

---

4. In Guidry v. United States, 317 F. Supp. 1110 (E.D. La. 1970), and in In re K.V.N., 116 N.J.S. 580, 283 A.2d 337 (1971), the Equal Protection Clause was used to challenge longer sentences on juveniles imposed by application of the Federal Youth Corrections Act, 28 U.S.C. § 5005 *et seq. See also* In re Wilson, 438 Pa. 425, 264 A.2d 614 (1970). Longer sentencing of juveniles was upheld in these three cases on the grounds that the state had a legitimate interest in trying to rehabilitate those sentenced through the use of superior treatment facilities for extended periods of time.

5. In re Brown, 439 F.2d 47 (3rd Cir. 1971), in which a Virgin Islands appeals statute was declared unconstitutional because it unfairly discriminated against juveniles attempting to appeal decisions of the Juvenile Court.

6. *See* note 1 *supra*. And *see* text accompanying notes 33-34 *infra*.

7. *See* note 5 *supra* at 52.

8. *Id.* at 51, 54.

9. *See* note 4 *supra*.

Longer commitments for youth are justified by a belief that because a young person has a greater capacity to change, he is therefore more susceptible to rehabilitation and so should not be sent away to purely custodial institutions. The theory holds that attempts should be made to rehabilitate a delinquent so that he may re-enter society as a useful person, and rehabilitation takes a long time.

A much debated point is whether or not *parens patriae* is dead as a viable supportive theory for the current juvenile justice system. *In re Gault*,[10] decided by the Supreme Court in 1967, contained now historic language that exposed the extensive failures of *parens patriae*. Mr. Justice Fortas wrote that the Court would look behind the "euphemisms" of the juvenile justice system. As a result of its investigation the Court discovered delinquents stigmatized as criminals and "industrial schools" not much different from adult prisons.[11] On the basis of the underlying reality, the Court saw fit to extend basic due process rights to juveniles, at least for the adjudicative phase of the hearing process.[12]

But as comprehensive as the *Gault* decision was, the Court explicitly did not include the right to transcripts and review in their list of due process rights.[13] Mr. Justice Harlan, concurring in part and dissenting in part, disagreed with this conclusion. He would have included the right to review on his list of due process rights.[14] What is more, the states have endorsed Justice Harlan's view since all of them have some statutory basis of appeal from juvenile court. Nonetheless, the language of the *Gault* majority provides a centerpiece for continuing argument on the importance of transcripts and reviewability of juvenile court decisions.

Succeeding cases utilized the *Gault* decision differently. In the District of Columbia, other procedural rights, specifically those of the Fourth Amendment, were extended to juveniles.[15] *Gault* also provided the springboard for raising the standard of proof in juvenile hearings to "proof beyond a reasonable doubt."[16] In other instances state courts were very careful to limit

---

10. 387 U.S. 1 (1967).

11. *Id.* at 23-24, 27.

12. The rights extended to juveniles by the *Gault* decision were: (a) notice of charges; (b) right to counsel; (c) right to confrontation and cross-examination of witnesses; (d) privilege against self-incrimination. *Id.* at 31-57.

13. *Id.* at 57-59.

14. *Id.* at 72 (Harlan, J., concurring in part and dissenting in part).

15. *E.g.*, Cooley v. Stone, 134 U.S. App. D.C. 317, 414 F.2d 1213 (1969), which said that a sixteen year old taken into custody and detained pending trial, was entitled to a probable cause hearing. This constitutional right was extended in accordance with language in *Gault* to the effect that juveniles were entitled to the protections of the Bill of Rights. *See Gault*, 387 U.S. 1, 61, (Black, J., concurring). *Also see* Brown v. Fauntleroy, 442 F.2d 838 (1971), which extended the holding in Cooley v. Stone, to a juvenile awaiting a hearing in the custody of his mother, even though he was not physically detained.

16. In re Winship, 397 U.S. 358 (1970).

the applicability of the principles of *Gault* to adjudicatory hearings only.[17] These cases reflect a judicial trend toward viewing the adjudicative phase, in which delinquency is determined, as similar to an adult trial. Even *parens patriae* enthusiasts admitted the good sense of *Gault's* insistence that the basic elements of procedural accuracy attend the adjudicative phase of a juvenile disposition. However, in regard to the dispositional phase of the case it was asserted that the informality and flexibility of the traditional juvenile court process must be retained. Disposition in a juvenile case is unlike the sentencing phase of an adult criminal trial. Different factors are considered and many different rehabilitative remedies are available.[18] Hence, wide discretion in the dispositional phase, it was argued, is essential to the best interests of the child as well as the state. The rulings of *Gault* were therefore considered inapplicable to dispositional hearings.[19]

The move to discredit *parens patriae*, sparked by language in the *Gault* opinion, has been vitiated somewhat by language to the contrary in the latest Supreme Court pronouncement on the subject, *McKeiver v. Pennsylvania*.[20] In losing an attempt to extend the right to a jury trial to juveniles, those who favor more constitutional protection for juveniles may have slowed their movement. In *McKeiver*, the Court took the opportunity to reaffirm its confidence in *parens patriae* as good law.[21]

---

17. *E.g.*, Cradle v. Peyton, 208 Va. 243, 156 S.E.2d 874 (1967), and Smith v. State, 444 S.W.2d 941 (Tex. 1969). These cases relied on language in In re Gault that said,

We are not concerned with the procedures or constitutional rights applicable to the prejudicial stages of the juvenile process, nor do we direct our attention to the post adjudicative or dispositional process. 387 U.S. at 13.

18. In disposing of a juvenile's case, social worker and psychiatric reports accumulated over several months of observation of both child and home life will be considered. Most statutes provide that dispositional hearings may be stopped and started by the judge over a period of time. As such, dispositions do not necessarily evolve in one distinct hearing.

Another factor considered is the ability of the parents to pay for different types of institutional care. In one reported instance probation officers recommended the juvenile for commitment in a facility costing $950/month. As the parents were unable to pay, the judge ruled that it was not in the state's best interest to foot the bill and so, despite recommendations to the contrary, the youth was sent to the state industrial school. In re Blakes, 4 Ill. App. 3d 567, 281 N.E.2d 454 (1972).

19. But *see* United States v. Dockery, 447 F.2d 1178, 1194 (D.C. Cir. 1971) (Wright, J., dissenting), which says, " '[t]here is no irrebuttable presumption of accuracy attached to staff reports,' " (citation omitted) and that the adversary process *is* fitting in dispositional hearings. "It is not enough to defeat a due process right simply to characterize the sentencing process as 'nonadversary'." In short, there are some who feel that counsel and the adversary process are just as important in dispositions as they are in adjudications.

20. 403 U.S. 528 (1971). *See* text accompanying note 48 *infra*.

21. [T]he arguments advanced by the juveniles . . . equate the juvenile proceeding—or at least the adjudicative phase of it—with the criminal trial. [They choose] to ignore, it seems to us, every aspect of fairness, of concern, of sympathy and of *paternal attention that the juvenile court system contemplates*. (emphasis added) *Id*. at 550.

Gault and its progeny are due process cases, and, given *McKeiver*, perhaps they have taken due process as far as possible as a means for extending juvenile rights.[22] Whether or not that is true, the recent decision in the Third Circuit, *In re Brown*,[23] illustrates that the Equal Protection Clause can provide another route for extending adult rights to juveniles. Use of the Equal Protection Clause was discussed in 1965 in an article by Addison M. Bowman in *Crime and Delinquency*.[24] Writing before *Gault*, he reviews the state of the law regarding appeals. Bowman concludes that though appeals are not the way to remedy vast deficiencies in the juvenile court system, they are a very valuable check on a system largely unsupervised.[25] He points out, however, that most state juvenile court statutes do not require a transcript of the juvenile hearing. Like Juvenile Court Judge Lindsay Arthur his feeling is that "reviewing a hearing without a transcript is like reviewing a book without reading it."[26]

Bowman argues that equal protection *and* due process can combine to pressure states offering appeal to juveniles to record juvenile court hearings. He feels that insofar as a state does set up an appeal procedure, fairness dictates that it should operate in a uniform manner to provide adequate appeal for all.

> . . . adequacy is the articulation of a minimum standard for all cases, a standard which may not be satisfied without a transcript on appeals.[27]

This kind of argument against discriminatory treatment of juvenile appeals was tested and affirmed in *In re Brown, supra*. The Virgin Islands statute challenged in the case provided an unusual opportunity for applying the equal protection argument. While most juvenile court laws are kept completely separate from adult statutes in state codes, some sections of the Virgin Islands Code dealt simultaneously with adults and juveniles. The law struck down extended an absolute right of appeal to adults while only allowing discretionary appeals to juveniles. The proximity of these two provisions in a single section shed clear light on the discrimination made against juveniles simply because of their age. The opinion analogized the status of

---

22. See Ketcham, *McKeiver v. Pennsylvania: The Last Word on Juvenile Court Adjudications*, 57 CORNELL L. REV. 561 (1972); Note, *McKeiver: a Retreat in Juvenile Justice*, 38 BROOKLYN L. REV. 650 (1972); and Note, *Conflicts of Parens Patriae and Constitutional Concepts of Juvenile Justice*, 6 LIN. L. REV. 65 (1970), for discussions of the impact of the *McKeiver* case.

23. *See* note 5 *supra*.

24. Bowman, *Appeals from Juvenile Courts*, 11 CRIME AND DELINQUENCY 63 (1965).

25. *Id.* at 76-77.

26. Arthur, *Should Children be as Equal as People?* 45 No. DAK. L. REV. 204, 216 (1968).

27. Bowman, *supra* note 24, at 67.

juveniles to that of indigents denied adequate review because they were too poor to purchase a transcript.[28] Applying the reasoning in *Griffin* the court said the Virgin Islands must extend the same right to review to juveniles as it did to adults.[29] Unfortunately, while juveniles are entitled, as a matter of equal protection (in the eyes of at least one court) to appeal rights, not all juvenile appeals are accompanied by transcripts—as are adult appeals. In light of the *Gault* decision, the question of whether "adequate" appeals for juveniles must include transcripts is an open one under a due process test. It is an equally open question whether or not equal protection guarantees transcripts to juveniles even if due process does not.

Whether a law violates the current interpretation of the Equal Protection Clause has been determined by the following test.[30] (1) If the challenged law violates a fundamental right or is based upon certain suspect criteria, the state must show a compelling interest for its enactment.[31] (2) If the challenged law violates a right, but not a fundamental right, the state need only show a rational interest for its law.[32] Query: (1) Is the right that a recording be made of a juvenile delinquency hearing a fundamental right, or is it some lesser right? (2) Are the arguments of cost, undue administrative burden on the juvenile court process and *parens patriae*, sufficiently compelling or rational interests for withholding the right to record hearings from juveniles?

In *Griffin v. Illinois*,[33] the Supreme Court held that due process does not require the state on appeal to provide a verbatim transcript of a trial to an adult, indigent defendant. The state may satisfy the need for a reviewable record with some substitute report of the trial. However, *Griffin* did say that if a state creates machinery for appellate review, it must provide means by which errors complained of "can effectively be brought for review."[34]

In re Gault refused to disturb the holding in *Griffin* and refrained from saying that due process requires a transcript of juvenile hearings. These two cases, then, preclude our asserting that the right to a transcript is a fundamental due process right, even for adults. However, *Griffin* does permit the

28. See note 5 *supra* at 51-52.

29. There was suprisingly little discussion of *parens patriae* in the opinion since it appeared that there was little doubt as to whether *parens patriae* and appellate review could co-exist. The court found

no consideration lying at the core of the concept of a separate system of justice for juveniles which is impaired by an appeal. Far from being harmful, appellate review is a beneficial safeguard for both the juvenile system and the juvenile accused. In re Brown, 439 F.2d at 53.

30. On equal protection generally, *see* Note, *Developments in the Law—Equal Protection*, 82 HARV. L. REV. 1065 (1969).

31. Shapiro v. Thompson, 394 U.S. 618, 634 (1969).

32. Dandridge v. Williams, 397 U.S. 471, 487 (1970).

33. See note 1 *supra*.

34. *Id.* at 24.

assertion that once appellate review is offered there is at least a right to an adequate basis for review for adults. This right, which adults are afforded in the form of transcripts, is denied to juveniles in fourteen state statutes. This proposition is true, of course, unless it can be shown that "adequate" appeals can be had without transcripts. If adequate appeals could be had without transcripts, the fact that adults have them and juveniles do not would not discriminate against juveniles. Under such a formula, juvenile appeals would be "transcriptless" but adequate, and adult appeals would be accompanied by transcripts and adequate.

Two leading cases illustrate that the juveniles' basis for appeal, without a transcript, has sometimes been less than adequate. In *Kent v. Reid*[35] a sixteen year old charged with rape appealed a waiver of jurisdiction by the juvenile court that allowed him to be tried as an adult. He asserted that the statutorily required "full investigation" had not been made. The appellate procedure required the juvenile court to forward a certified copy of the record of the waiver hearing to the Municipal Court of Appeals. The record, consisting of,

> . . . two memoranda and a motion with two supporting affidavits filed in the Juvenile Court by appellant's counsel, the order of waiver of the Juvenile Court stating that full investigation was made, a motion for leave to file two affidavits filed by appellant's counsel in the Municipal Court of Appeals, the order of that court denying that motion and the per curiam opinion and order of the Municipal Court of Appeals . . .[36]

was deemed insufficient for purposes of review. It required the reviewing court to make assumptions as to the basis for the Juvenile Court's decision. *Kent* teaches that review of final orders couched in conclusionary language is not enough. Meaningful review requires the juvenile court to explain the reasoning behind its decision.[37]

Similarly, in *In re Gault* no transcript was made of the hearing at which Gerald Gault confessed to making lewd phone calls. As a result of this deficiency, the appellate court had to reconstruct the delinquency proceeding from testimony taken from the participants. Adult cases from other jurisdictions persuade us that such inadequacies should not be tolerated in

---

35. 114 U.S. App. D.C. 330, 316 F.2d 331 (1963), *vacated and remanded sub nom.* Kent v. United States, 383 U.S. 541 (1966).

36. 114 App. D.C. 330 at 334.

37. The court said

Meaningful review requires that the reviewing court should review. It should not be remitted to assumptions. It must have before it a statement of the reasons motivating the waiver including, of course, a statement of the relevant facts. It may not "assume" that there are adequate reasons nor may it merely assume that "full investigation" has been made. *Id.* at 561.

our juvenile courts. For example, in *Ebersole v. State of Idaho*,[38] parol evidence taken from the participants in an arraignment hearing was required to reconstruct that hearing for the reviewing court. The lack of a transcribed report of the arraignment hearing was held to be such a lack of fundamental fairness and such a deviation from the established rules of procedure as to necessitate the conclusion that appellant had not been offered due process. A 1961 criminal case in Colorado involving a non-indigent adult held that "unless it appears that a defendant has expressly waived the presence of a reporter the county must furnish a reporter in all cases."[39] The court felt that without a transcript appellate review would be inadequate. (It is to be noted that Colorado is one of the states offering appeals to juveniles that does not statutorily provide for recording of juvenile hearings.)

Our argument then is that states which provide a means of recording hearings to adults for purposes of review are discriminating against juveniles by not providing them with the same opportunity. We clearly recognize that due process does not require that transcripts be made. However, once a state does offer appellate review to its citizenry it must "establish machinery to assure fairness and uniformity."[40] *Gault* did recognize the burden placed on appellate machinery by forcing courts to reconstruct hearings from participants' testimony. It seems that it would be relatively simple to remove that burden by recording hearings and put an end to a practice that denies juveniles meaningful appellate review.

Yet, the conclusion remains that the right to a transcript is not a fundamental right. The state need not show a compelling interest, therefore, for denying transcripts to juveniles. However, are states' "rational" justifications for denying juveniles transcripts sufficient? One argument against the creation of transcripts is cost. The argument runs that juvenile courts are often part-time courts. Assignment of a reporter for all juvenile cases would cost too much. In most states juvenile courts are funded by counties; not on a state wide basis.[41] For small counties, it is conceivable that reporter costs would be a hardship. The question then becomes whether this argument is a sufficiently rational basis by which legislatures may deny juveniles a procedure reserved for adults?

Griffin said states have a rational interest in not providing free transcripts to appellants. The Court found that a state need not subsidize appel-

---

38. 91 Idaho 630, 428 P.2d 947 (1967).

39. Herren v. People, 147 Colo. 442, 444, 363 P.2d 1044, 1046 (1961).

40. Bowman, *supra* note 24, at 66.

41. *For example*, the *North Dakota Century Code* § 27-20-05 (1971 Supp.) which says,

(4) the cost of providing suitable quarters for conducting official business, all necessary books, forms, stationary, office supplies and equipment, postage, telephone, travel and other necessary expenses . . . shall be borne by the counties.

late proceedings by financing an inevitable flood of frivolous appeals should free transcripts be offered. Though this paper does not argue for free transcripts, but only for the right to have the hearing recorded so that a transcript may be made, it is recognized that once transcripts are made, the door is open for indigent juveniles to receive free transcripts.[42] Abuse of the system could conceivably lead to significant state expenditures.

A state's "economic" interest for denying rights that are less than fundamental has been upheld in other areas. Specifically, in the welfare field, the *Dandridge v. Williams* Court found that imperfect classifications are permissible in the area of "economic and social welfare."[43] One can argue from these two decisions that cost may be a strong argument for denying juveniles even the right to have their hearings recorded. However, rather than hiring a stenographer to transcribe juvenile court proceedings, an inexpensive solution might be to record the proceedings on a tape machine operated by the court clerk. Transcriptions of the tape would only be made if there was an appeal, otherwise the tape would be erased after the statutory time for making an appeal had elapsed.

The value of an accurate basis for appeals runs both to the juvenile and the state. The former benefits from full review of all that transpired below, the latter benefits from uniform interpretation of its laws made possible by accurate reporting of their application by the juvenile courts. These benefits seem well worth the cost.

Another argument against creation of stenographic records is that the presence of a reporter or tape recorder would place an administrative burden on the court. Relaxed informal discussion between juvenile and judge would be chilled by the necessity of creating a transcript. The court would arguably have to adopt time consuming procedures which would hinder the judge's effectiveness as a personable father figure able to deal flexibly with the problems at hand. However, the dream of a friendly, fatherly judge seriously conversing with an awed youngster has in many cases been reduced to a three minute hearing subject to the pressures of crowded court calendars. The overview of the juvenile justice system painted by the comprehensive Note in the 1965 *Harvard Law Review*[44] was not very encouraging for those in favor of *parens patriae*. Written before the *Gault* decision and cited many times in the opinion, the Note provided support for the Court's contention that *parens patriae* is far from a reality. The poor quality or total lack of

---

42. California is a state that does explicitly reserve a right to transcripts to juveniles, *see Cal. Welfare and Inst'ns Code* § 677 (1971 Supp.), and has extended the commands of *Griffin* to juveniles. J. v. Supreme Court of L.A. County, 4 Cal. 3d 836, 94 Cal. Rptr. 619, 484 P.2d 595, held that an indigent juvenile appellant shall be provided a free copy of the transcript.

43. 397 U.S. at 485.

44. Note, *Juvenile Delinquents: The Police State Courts and Individualized Justice*, 79 HARV. L. REV. 775 (1966) [hereinafter called *Harvard Note*].

facilities to care for delinquents gives judges little actual flexibility in disposing of cases.[45] Such a situation may lead to expedient though inappropriate dispositions.[46]

There is some truth to the point that parts of the hearing process are untranscribable. The dispositional phase, often consisting of many separate meetings, sometimes consisting of telephone conversations between judge and counsel, or judge and heads of rehabilitative centers, are certainly not distinct, easily transcribable events. However as Judge Lindsay Arthur put it, "that which is transcriptive should be transcribed."[47] The transcribable parts of the proceeding would at least include testimony, judge's rulings and the reasons for his rulings. Given the fact that the juvenile justice system is often unable to provide the special type of protection its informal approach was designed to offer, it seems clear that the juvenile should have the protection of a reviewing court.

Ultimately, the state would rest its case for denying transcripts to juveniles on the importance of preserving *parens patriae*. Any argument extending juveniles the right to a transcript must confront barriers thrown up by the Supreme Court's opinion in *McKeiver, supra.* In *McKeiver,* the Court refused to extend the right to jury trials to juveniles. Petitioners argued that they had been tried like adults and sentenced to an adult institution for acts which if committed by adults would have been deemed criminal. They claimed that due process had been violated by denying their timely request for jury trials. The Court found that due process does not require a jury trial if a fair procedure already exists for the purpose of finding facts and determining guilt. The juvenile justice system is designed to perform that function in an informal manner that would be detrimentally disturbed by the introduction of a jury into the adjudicative hearings.

As summarized in *McKeiver,* the *parens patriae* theory includes the following concepts: (1) The pseudocriminal acts of juveniles are not comparable to the malevolent intentional acts of adults; (2) therefore, a finding of delinquency is not equivalent to a judgment of criminal guilt. (3) The juvenile's conduct is not considered the kind of intentional, culpable act

---

45. 1965 statistics showed that 33% of full time juvenile judges had no probation officers or social workers; 83% of all juvenile court judges had no psychiatric staff; and most judges thought that a lack of foster homes in the cities, and detention centers in rural areas, was the number one problem in their field. McKune and Skoler, *Juvenile Court Judges in the U.S., Part I: A National Profile,* 11 CRIME AND DELINQUENCY 121, 127-128 (1965).

46. In re Butterfield, 61 Cal. Rptr. 874, 879 (1967), in which the reviewing court sympathizes with the juvenile court's limitations regarding possible disposition of its cases, but says that crude compromises such as sending an emotionally disturbed girl to a facility lacking a psychiatric staff was an impermissible expedient abusing the court's discretion.

47. Arthur, *supra* note 26, at 217.

that requires punishment; (4) therefore, supervision or confinement is aimed at rehabilitation.[48]

Underlying the *McKeiver* opinion seems to be a feeling by the Court that an adequate procedural balance has been reached in the juvenile courts and that the balance achieved ought not to be tampered with by adding further adversary elements. While the case is decided on due process grounds, language at the conclusion of Mr. Justice Blackmun's opinion discourages future equal protection arguments. Blackmun explicitly rejects petitioners' analogy of juvenile and adult criminal processes, claiming that such an analogy "ignores the fairness, concern, sympathy and paternal attention" of a system for which he still has high hopes.

Judge Orman W. Ketcham of the District of Columbia Superior Court, believes that the *McKeiver* decision is not as formidable a barrier to extending constitutional rights as it seems.[49] Judge Ketcham points out that within the *McKeiver* plurality there is a dispute over some of the basic points made by Justice Blackmun. For example, Justice Harlan, who concurred in the judgment, did so for a different reason. It is his belief that the Sixth Amendment does not require the states to give jury trials to their citizens. However, were it not for this belief he would extend jury trials to juveniles on the premise that juvenile trials "have in practice actually become in many, if not all, respects criminal trials."[50] Justice Brennan observes in his concurrence that the juvenile system has far from realized its promise. The doubts expressed by Justices Harlan and Brennan plus the many concessions made by Justice Blackmun as to the system's failings would seem to weaken the support for the holding.

McKeiver's applicability to juvenile transcripts is also undermined by the special nature of the right sought in *McKeiver*. The refusal of petitioners' request seems to stem in large part from the various philosophies held by members of the Court concerning juries. Juries require convincing. By introducing juries into the system Justice Blackmun feared that hearings would be transformed into full blown adversary proceedings governed by strict rules of evidence carefully manipulated by counsel. The informality of the process would be destroyed. In his concurrence Justice White balked at the introduction of juries because he was not convinced that juries were any better at finding the facts than a well trained judge. Mr. Justice Brennan's view was that although juries are valuable because they bring public scrutiny to bear on the judicial process, if alternative means allowed the accused to appeal to the public, by admitting the press to juvenile hearings for example, there was no need to insist that a jury be present also.

---

48. *See* note 20, *supra* at 551–52 (White, J., concurring).
49. Ketcham, *supra* note 22.
50. *Id.* at 557 (Harlan, J., concurring).

Clearly transcripts would not jeopardize the informality of juvenile proceedings. Neither would transcripts replace the fatherly judge where and when he appears. A recording would simply provide an accurate report of the facts found at the hearing and there is little doubt that an accurate report is preferable to the patchwork description of a hearing like the one reconstructed by the Court in *Gault*.

Parens patriae as a justification for the juvenile justice system has been seriously called into question. Two major documents among a growing number of studies, the 1965 *Harvard Law Review* note, *supra*, and the President's Commission on Law Enforcement and Administration of Justice, *Task Force Report: Juvenile Delinquency and Youth Crime of 1967*, empirically challenge the viability of the present juvenile justice system. In *Gault*, the Supreme Court responded to information collected by those studies and attempted to remedy some of the system's constitutional failings. Though it cannot be said that state and lower federal courts have responded *en masse* to the trend begun in *Gault*, there are at least a few decisions indicating judicial awareness that a youth accused of a serious crime often suffers the same stigmatization and brutalization as an adult, despite the juvenile justice system's attempts to shield him.[51]

Although dictum in all the *McKeiver* opinions conceded the documented failings of the juvenile justice system, the holding reaffirmed the High Court's faith in the *parens patriae* theory. Faith in a system's ideology should not be sufficient to sustain it in the face of documented deficiencies. As long as there is so much doubt about the effectiveness of *parens patriae*, the rational interest under equal protection standards for the states' denial of rights to juveniles on *parens patriae* grounds ought to be questioned.

---

51. For instance in Brown v. Fauntleroy, 442 F.2d 838, 842, n.7 (D.C. Cir. 1971), the D.C. Court of Appeals said this about a youth awaiting delinquency hearings:

[a] juvenile in appellant's situation . . . will nevertheless suffer disadvantages from his newly acquired status. *There is undoubtedly a certain stigma attached to being accused of a crime.* (emphasis added)

Book Review:

11 | When Parents Fail: The Law's Response
to Family Breakdown by Sanford N. Katz

JAMES A. WOLLER *

WHEN PARENTS FAIL: THE LAW'S RESPONSE TO FAMILY BREAKDOWN.
By Sanford N. Katz, Boston: Beacon Press, 1971. 251 Pp. $12.50.

In a wide-ranging, descriptive analysis of the law's intervention into
the parent-child relationship, Sanford N. Katz[1] in WHEN PARENTS FAIL
makes two contributions to the understanding of child welfare law. Professor Katz argues that present child welfare laws: (1) foster discrimination against the poor and (2) allow social welfare agencies and the courts
to impose their middle class values on the parent-child relationship.

The poor, Katz charges, are most often the subjects of public intervention between parent and child (pp. 24 and 91). For example, a 1967
study of parents charged with child neglect found that their median family
income was $75 per week. Thirty percent of the studied group were re-
ceiving some form of public assistance (p. 44 n.5). Katz suggests that this
phenomenon results from the poor family's greater "visibility." Public intervention usually begins when someone reports what he or she perceives
to be child neglect or abuse. Because the lower classes utilize community
resources such as public welfare funds and free medical clinics, their personal affairs, their personal appearances, and those of their children are
subject to public scrutiny by social workers and doctors.[2] Furthermore, a
lower class neighbor is more likely to call the police to quell a family
dispute in an adjoining apartment than a middle class neighbor in the
suburbs who would find meddling in poor taste even if he or she should
hear the dispute (pp. 28-29).

In the foregoing analysis, Professor Katz does not take the position
that the poor are actually more in need of public intervention than other
groups. He instead asserts that the laws more often proscribe behavior
which may be typical of the poor when the laws should apply to parallel
behavior of higher socio-economic groups. In support of this contention

*Staff member, COLUMBIA HUMAN RIGHTS LAW REVIEW.
1. Professor of Law, Boston College.
2. Not only are poor persons subject to scrutiny, but twenty three states require
reporting of child neglect by parties such as doctors and social workers. KATZ,
WHEN PARENTS FAIL: THE LAW'S RESPONSE TO FAMILY BREAKDOWN 45-46, n.13
[hereinafter cited as KATZ].

Katz cites an Illinois statute which makes it a felony for a parent to abandon his or her child even if the parent makes provision for care with a neighbor (pp. 24-25). It is unlikely that a community would brand as a felon the middle class parent who sends his or her offspring away to a boarding school for a long period of time. Arguably, the law makes a valid distinction between dumping a child on a neighbor and spending thousands of dollars on a boarding school even though both parents, rich and poor, may seek the same release from their duty to care for the child. This distinction only reinforces Katz' next argument: child welfare laws are anti-poor laws.

Child welfare statutes give the courts power to sever the parent-child bond when the child's home is "unfit" or when the child's environment is injurious.[3] The circumstances in which an "unfit" home can be found are presumably present in most slum housing. If a child begs or receives alms, he is subject to the custody of the state.[4] When a mother is unmarried and without adequate provisions for the care of her child, the state may elect to place the child in an institution rather than provide the mother with extra money.[5] In each of these statutory schemes the sole determinant of whether a child may be separated from his or her parent may be the mere fact that the parent is poor even though the parent may provide for the child in many meaningful non-economic ways.

Professor Katz not only argues that child welfare statutes discriminate against the poor, but that these statutes give the courts broad discretion to impose what Katz terms "middle class values" on the poor. Katz finds that:

It is the non-specific statute[6] which provides the judge with a vehicle for imposing on others his own preferences for certain child-rearing practices and his own ideas of adult behavior and parental morality (p. 65).

These non-specific statutes provide little guidance for the court in resolving the basic conflict between protecting the integrity of the family and the

3. Thirteen states are cited, KATZ 83 n.12.

4. Here is another example of anti-poor discrimination. Katz might argue that the police will send a middle class hippy home when he or she begs, while the lower class beggar is sent to an institution for essentially identical conduct. KATZ 84 n.17.

5. All fifty states, Washington, D.C., Puerto Rico, Guam and the Virgin Islands participate in the Federal Aid to Families With Dependent Children program, 42 U.S.C. §§ 601 et seq. (1970). Comment, Legal Rights of AFDC Recipients After Rosado v. Wyman and Dandridge v. Williams, 21 AM. U.L. REV. 207 (1971). The states may elect to get the extra money from this program. Furthermore a state may even have funds available to meet emergencies. See SOC. SERV. LAW § 350-j (McKinney 1966). See also KATZ 85 n.24.

6. Five states allow the court to take the child from his or her parents and institutionalize the child when the child's best interests are not being met by the parents, KATZ 84 n.15.

furnishing of a conducive environment outside the family for the proper physical and emotional well-being of the child, since they proscribe certain behavior rather than describe what the child needs. Moreover, there are few appellate decisions upon which the court may rely for an interpretation of the statutes.[7] By default judges must resort to their own values for guidance.

However, in his attack on judicial middle class values, Professor Katz fails to explain which middle class values he finds so offensive, or to define what he means by middle class values. Even more than not defining middle class values, he misuses the term. At page 63, a judge suggests to a youth that he commit suicide. This is reprehensible conduct for the court, but it is hardly middle class values at work. The closest Katz comes to explaining what he means by middle class values is when he indicates that the neglectful parent is not part of the American dream of upward mobility, and the neglectful parent does not share the great American notion of parental indulgence. The reader is simply left to assume that middle class values are evil and are never in the interest of society, the parent or the child.

If Professor Katz were arguing that the child should be able to determine for himself or herself what standards he or she wishes to live by, or if he were arguing that no value judgments should be necessary, then it would not be necessary to know what values Katz finds so offensive. Instead of examining these alternative viewpoints, Katz seeks to substitute his own middle class values for those unstated values he finds so offensive. He assumes that all society accepts his position that sound physical and emotional stability of the child are the highest priorities of parenthood. It is submitted that Katz' reliance on modern theories of child development[8] for solving the problems he finds in the state intervention into the parent-child relationship reflect his own middle class faith in science and theory.

The first step in a meaningful analysis of child welfare law should be an examination of the goals of state intrusion. Professor Katz only hints at those goals. Historically, he says, state intervention was required to provide heirs (p. 114) and to protect the father's property right in his child (p. 4). Today state intervention is increasing (p. 5). Without assessing the current role government seeks to play, Katz is able to argue that legislation is the starting point. Child welfare laws, he states, should be framed to reflect affirmative duties of the parents rather than to proscribe negative conduct. The statutory scheme would require the parent to provide adequate affection, stimulation, and unbroken continuity of care (p. 55). Minnesota and Idaho child neglect statutes are cited as outstanding examples.

---

7. See Note, *Appellate Review For Juveniles: A "Right" To A Transcript*, 4 COLUM. HUMAN RIGHTS L. REV. 485 (1972), where problems of appellate review in juvenile cases are discussed.

8. See KATZ 82 n.3, and 82 n.4.

> They [Minnesota and Idaho] require a judge to measure the strengths and weaknesses of the parent's relationship with the child. The judge must deal with both parents feelings and conduct toward the child. Thus these statutes recognize not merely the child's physical condition but rather the totality of its well-being (p. 62).

It is unclear, even if the cited statutes could *force* a court to weigh certain factors, how requiring a parent to exercise positive duties toward the child would eliminate any of the evils Katz has found. The statutes provide even broader room for discretion on the part of the court. The poor will be no less visible nor more able to meet the material needs of children. Perhaps more middle class parents would be affected by laws which require non-material care, but given the abuse in the system and Katz' own view that the integrity of the family is extremely important, it does not seem advisable to provide for more state intrusion into the parent-child relationship, but more state intrusion is what Professor Katz, in relying on his own faith in more government as an answer, seems to want. An inquiry into the efficacy of state intrusion would be the logical second step toward solving the problems accompanying state intervention.

There is more in Katz' book than his analysis of how a court may decide to break-up a family unit. He also describes how a child is herded through the administrative process before he ever arrives in court, and he laments the precarious position of the foster parent or adoptive parent once the court has decided that a child is to be taken from the family. But here, as in most of the book, Professor Katz' concerns are never clearly focused. The reader is aware that Katz is unhappy about the abuse in the child welfare system. However, the reader is not treated to the in depth analysis which the subject needs.

James Woller